B 32

PHILOSOPHICAL AND FOUNDATIONAL ISSUES IN MEASUREMENT THEORY

edited by

C. Wade Savage
University of Minnesota

Philip Ehrlich
Brown University

LAWRENCE ERLBAUM ASSOCIATES, PUBLISHERS
1992 Hillsdale, New Jersey   Hove and London

Lawrence Erlbaum Associates, Inc., Publishers
365 Broadway
Hillsdale, New Jersey 07642

Library of Congress Cataloging-in-Publication Data
Philosophical and foundational issues in measurement theory / edited by
    C. Wade Savage, Philip Ehrlich.
        p.   cm.
    Includes bibliographical references and index.
    ISBN 0-8058-0726-8
    1. Physical measurements.   I. Savage, C. Wade.   II. Ehrlich,
Philip.
QC39.P45   1991
530.1′6—dc20   91-3356
                                                                      CIP

Printed in the United States of America
10 9 8 7 6 5 4 3 2 1

Contents

About the Contributors

Ernest Adams holds a PhD in philosophy from Stanford University and is currently professor of philosophy at the University of California at Berkeley. He has authored numerous papers on probabilistic aspects of logic, foundations of measurement, foundations of physical geometry and topology, and aspects of psychophysics. He has also written one book, *The Logic of Conditionals: an Application of Probability to Deductive Logic,* and is currently completing another, *Archeological Typology and Practical Reality,* co-authored with his brother, William Y. Adams, professor of anthropology at the University of Kentucky, Lexington.

Wolfgang Balzer is a pupil of K. Schuette and W. Stegmüller. Since 1984 he has been professor of logic and philosophy of science at the University of Munich. He has worked mainly in philosophy of science, and has been an active contributor to the "structuralist" approach in the philosophy of science. He has published books on empirical theories (*Empirische Theorien,* 1982), and on measurement (*Theorie und Messung,* 1985), and is co-author of *An Architectonic for Science* (Dordrecht, 1987, together with C. U. Moulines and J. D. Sneed). In numerous papers he has dealt with the structure of science, theoreticity, incommensurability, invariance, measurement, and reference, among other topics. In addition to many case studies in physics, economics, sociology, genetics, and theory of literature, he has proposed a sociological theory of institutions.

Karel Berka is a member of the Institute for Philosophy and Sociology of the Czechoslovak Academy of Sciences. He is the editor of the journal *Teorie Rozvoje Vedy* and the author of *Measurement* (Reidel, 1983).

John P. Burgess has been a member of the philosophy department at Princeton University since shortly after receiving his doctorate in logic and methodology from the University of California at Berkeley. He has worked in many areas of mathematical and philosophical logic, and more recently in philosophy of mathematics, and is a frequent contributor to anthologies and journals, as well as an editor of the *Journal of Symbolic Logic* and the *Notre Dame Journal of Formal Logic.*

Zoltan Domotor is professor of philosophy and a member of the Cognitive Science Group at the University of Pennsylvania. His research interests are in philosophy of science, applied logic, and foundations of probability. He has written extensively on topics in measurement theory, philosophy of space and time, foundations of quantum mechanics, foundations of probability and decision, and cognitive science. He has recently completed a monograph entitled *Structure and Dynamics of Probabilistic Knowledge.*

Brian Ellis is Foundation Professor of Philosophy at La Trobe University and editor of the *Australian Journal of Philosophy.* He is the author of books on measurement and on the theory of rational belief, and of numerous papers in philosophy of science and other areas of philosophy. Professor Ellis was a visiting professor of philosophy at the Minnesota Center for Philosophy of Science in 1972.

Philip Ehrlich is a member of the philosophy department at Brown University. His research interests are in logic, the philosophy of physics, and the philosophy of mathematics; and his writings have appeared in mathematics, physics, and philosophy journals.

Arnold Koslow is professor of philosophy at the Graduate Center, CUNY, and Brooklyn College. His interests are in the history and philosophy of science, logic, and philosophy of language. He has written on Newton, scientific inference, the concept of mass, and inertia, measurement, and space and time in various journals. He has published an anthology on symmetry and conservation (*The Changeless Order,* Braziller), and his book on the foundations of logic (*A Structuralist Theory of Logic,* Cambridge) is soon to be published. He is currently at work on a book on laws of nature and laws of theories.

Henry E. Kyburg, Jr. is Burbank Professor of Moral and Intellectual Philosophy and also professor of computer science at the University of Rochester. He has had appointments in mathematics (Wesleyan University) as well as in philosophy. He is the author or editor of over a dozen books, and the author or co-author of more than 100 articles in journals whose subject matter ranges across statistics, mathematics, philosophy, and computer science. He is best known as the inventor of "the lottery paradox," discussed in his first book, *Probability and the Logic of Rational Belief.* He is currently active in both philosophy and artificial intelligence as a specialist in the measurement and use of uncertainty. His most recent book is *Science and Reason* (Oxford, 1991).

R. Duncan Luce was educated at Massachusetts Institute of Technology in aeronautical engineering (BS, 1945), and mathematics (PhD, 1950). He switched to mathematical psychology and has held positions at Columbia, Pennsylvania, Harvard (Victor S. Thomas Professor of Psychology, emeritus) and University of California, Irvine (Distinguished Professor of Cognitive Sciences). He is co-author of 7 books, editor or co-editor of 9 volumes, and author of more than 160 papers. His honors include membership in the National Academy of Sciences and a Distinguished Scientific Contributions Award of the American Psychological Association.

Louis Narens is professor of psychology at the University of California, Irvine. He is the author of *Abstract Measurement Theory* (MIT Press, 1985) and a number of papers in measurement theory.

C. Wade Savage received his MA from the University of Iowa and his PhD from Cornell University. He has been a member of the faculty of the University of Minnesota since 1971, where he is a professor in the Department of Philosophy and a member and former director of the Center for Philosophy of Science. He is the author of *The Measure-*

ment of Sensation and editor of several volumes in the series *Minnesota Studies in the Philosophy of Science*.

Patrick Suppes is currently Lucie Stern Professor at Stanford University, where he has been on the faculty since 1950. He is the author of numerous books and articles on the foundations of measurement, probability, and learning theory.

Mario Zanotti began his university education at the University of Turin, and later studied engineering and statistics at Stanford University. While at Stanford, he was a research associate at the Institute of Mathematical Studies in the Social Sciences, with research interests in foundations and applications of probability. He is currently with the Computer Curriculum Corporation.

1 A Brief Introduction to Measurement Theory and to the Essays

C. Wade Savage
University of Minnesota

Philip Ehrlich
Brown University

Until approximately three decades ago, measurement theory was widely assumed to be the avocation of a few physicists, mathematicians, and philosophers of science, and the obsession of a few social scientists who hoped to secure for their fields the authority enjoyed by mathematical physics and chemistry. The recognition of a legitimate, specialized field of inquiry called "measurement theory" is of even more recent origin.

Admittedly theories concerning the nature of quantity date from at least the ancient Greeks, as described in Aristotle's writings on these subjects in the *Categories* and the *Metaphysics* (c. 330 B.C.) and later axiomatized in Euclid's *Elements* (c. 300 B.C.). Furthermore, portions of Euclid's treatise can be regarded as a theory of measurement of spatial extent, in the sense that one line segment, surface, or solid "measures" another by being compared with it. However, this is what we now call *synthetic* geometry. It does not assign numbers in the abstract, arithmetic sense to nonnumerical continua such as lengths, areas, and regions; therefore, it cannot compare magnitudes within such continua by comparing such numbers. Euclidean geometry compares lengths, areas, and regions by comparing physical, nonnumerical *ratios* of these magnitudes and in effect uses such ratios in the place of our arithmetic numbers.

The *analytic* geometry Descartes and Fermat pioneered assumes that numerical measures of length, area, and volume can be assigned to line segments, surfaces, and solids by counting congruent unit objects in a collection that successively approximates the object being measured. It is a theory of measurement in the contemporary sense in which measurement is the assignment of abstract arithmetic numbers to objects. However, it is not a full, explicit theory; it

1

makes the assumption of measurability naively, without attempting to justify it in the manner currently required.

Today, measurement in general is taken to be the assignment of numbers (numerals, say the nominalists) to entities and events to represent their properties and relations. Furthermore, measurement theory is supposed to analyze the concept of a scale of measurement or numerical representation, distinguish various types of scale and describe their uses, and formulate the conditions required for the existence of scales of various types, not just for the case of length and other extensive properties but for measurable properties of all types.

The previous characterization of contemporary measurement theory is heavily influenced by the formalist, representationalist approach to the subject presented in Krantz, Luce, Suppes, and Tversky (1971), hereafter referred to as KLST. As the following essays illustrate, this approach currently dominates the field, serving as a model for most measurement theorists and a target for the rest. To provide an organizing context for the essays and to orient nonspecialist readers, we offer a brief historical survey of contemporary measurement theory.

Contemporary measurement theory can be said to begin with Helmholtz's *Counting and measuring* (1887) and Hölder's *Die Axiome der Quantität und die Lehre vom Mass* (1901), in which axioms for such (extensive) properties as length and mass were formulated. These works, together with influential treatments by Bertrand Russell (1903) and N. R. Campbell (1928, 1957/1920), created what may be called the *conservative conception* of measurement. On this conception counting is defined as placing the members of a collection in one-to-one correspondence with a segment of the natural numbers, and direct (extensive) measurement of a property of an object is then defined as counting concatenations of standard objects that approximately equal the object with respect to the property, where the concatenation has, like addition on numbers, such properties as commutativity, associativity, and so on. What most philosophers knew of formal measurement at the close of the first half of the century was gleaned largely from Campbell (1957/1920) and Cohen and Nagel (1934). Psychologists had, by that time, been exposed to a similar treatment by Bergmann and Spence, (1953/1944).

It appears that, on the conservative definition, length, weight, duration, angle, electric charge, and several other physical properties are directly measurable. However, hardness and temperature seem not to be directly measurable. In addition, such allegedly psychological attributes as hue, pitch, taste, and pain intensity seem even more clearly not to be directly measurable. These latter properties do not seem to possess a natural, empirical operation of concatenation that can be used to define their measure in the manner required by the conservative conception. Of course such properties may still be *indirectly* measurable by measuring a directly measurable, correlated property. Thus, temperature is measured by measuring the length of a column of thermometric fluid in a thermometer. (Henceforth, "measurable" will mean "directly measurable.") Some of the conservative theorists (Nagel, 1931, for example) distinguished extensive and intensive attributes, and they tentatively conceded that some of these other properties might be intensively measurable. Extensive measurement is accomplished by counting concatenations and is supposed to make such statements as "The length of **a** is **n** times greater than the length of **b**" meaningful; intensive measurement does not proceed by counting concatenations and is supposed to make only such statements as "The temperature of **a** is greater than the temperature of **b**" meaningful. However, many conservative theorists did not recognize intensive measurement and claimed that properties without an empirical concatenation are not properly said to be measurable.

Even as the conservative view was being formulated, many psychologists, especially psychophysicists such as Thurstone (1959), were insisting that various psychological properties are measurable; indeed some believed that every property is measurable. In the words of Guilford's (1954/1936) treatise:

> Many psychologists adopt the dictum of Thorndike that "Whatever exists at all exists in some amount" and they also adopt the corollary that whatever exists in some amount can be measured: the quality of handwriting, the appreciation of a sunset, the attitude of an individual toward Communism, or the strength of desire in a hungry rat. (p. 3)

Accordingly, at mid-century, the psychophysicist S. S. Stevens (1946, 1951) formulated what may be called the *liberal conception* of measurement, according to which measurement is defined simply as the assignment of numbers to things and properties according to rule. (For the distinction between the two conceptions of measurement, see Savage, 1970, chapters 4 and 5, where they are called the "narrow" and "broad" views.) Depending on the rule employed, the numerical assignment will constitute a scale of some type. Among conservatives, philosophical questions about measurement often took the form "Is *E* measurable?" where *E* is some property such as hardness, loudness, hue, pain, afterimage area, perceived length, desire, subjective time, welfare, probability, prestige of occupation, value, beauty, and so forth. The liberal theorists argued that this question is fruitless, because everything is held to be capable of measurement of some sort, and substituted for it the question "Of what sort of measurement is *E* capable?". They concluded that the task of measurement theory is to classify and describe the types of measurement.

Stevens (1946, 1951) distinguished four main types of scales of measurement. A *nominal* scale represents only differences among objects (for example, numbers assigned to football players). An *ordinal* scale represents the order of objects with respect to some property (for example, numbers used to rank restaurants). An *interval* scale represents intervals of a property (for example, the Centigrade scale of temperature). A *ratio* scale represents ratios of a property (for example, the inch scale of length). Stevens suggested that scales may also be classified by means of the transformations that leave the scale-form invariant, the "admissible" transformations. If Φ is the original scale, and Φ' is the transformed scale, then the defining transformation for an interval scale is $\Phi' = k\Phi + c$ (for example, Φ' is the Fahrenheit scale of temperature; Φ is the Centigrade scale; k = 1.8; and c = 32); the defining transformation for a ratio scale is $\Phi' = k\Phi$ (for example, Φ' is the centimeter scale of length; Φ is the inch scale; and k = 2.54). On the liberal conception, measurement does not require counting, and it does not require an operation of concatenation on the measured objects. This claim is intuitively obvious for nominal and ordinal scales with a small, finite number of values; for here, numbers can be assigned to the objects one by one, checking each assignment to assure that it represents identity and difference and order. However, Stevens also claimed to have constructed interval and ratio scales of continuous perceptual properties such as perceived loudness, perceived electric shock, and perceived heaviness from the numerical responses of subjects in psychological experiments, without employing any operation of concatenating physical objects, or sensations, or responses.

In the two decades following Stevens' formulation of his conception of measurement, several logical empiricist philosophers of science provided semiformal treatments of the subject—Hempel (1952), Carnap (1966), and Ellis in his *Basic concepts of measurement* (1966). In the operationalist-instrumentalist tradition of Mach, Bridgman, and Stevens, Ellis argued that the function of measurement is not to represent independently existing nonnumerical quantities; indeed quantities (except when identified with an ordering relation) are in effect created by the operations that measure them. Consequently one cannot choose between two additive scales of the same quantity that use different operations of concatenation or even between an additive and a nonadditive scale, on the ground that one better represents length than the other. The only rational ground is that one scale leads to simpler numerical laws of length, area, mass, force, and so forth than the other. In so arguing, Ellis adopted a *conventionalist* view of measurement to some extent. To the extent that he claimed quantities do not exist independently of their measuring operations, his position is *antirealist (operationalist)*. Carnap's writings on measurement express a more strongly conventionalist, operationalist view than those of Ellis. Hempel's work is comparatively neutral on the metaphysical issues involved.

Most of the major contributors to formal measurement theory have been mathematicians and psychologists. For most of the century, psychologists had been concerned with the theory of measuring psychological magnitudes, such as subjective brightness and hue, pain and pleasure, and attitudes and preferences. Most of this work was published in psychological journals and labeled "psychometrics" or "psychological scaling," as if to imply that the issues under discussion concerned only psychological magnitudes. Research of this sort was summarized during the period following Stevens' formulation in Torgerson's *Theory and methods of scaling* (1958). Meanwhile a group of mathematical logicians and mathematical psychologists, building on the results of Cantor, Hölder, Birkhoff, and other mathematicians, began to employ model-theoretic and set-theoretic methods to investigate the conditions and properties of scales of measurement in general, scales from areas as diverse as economics, psychophysics, and physics. This work culminated in 1971 in the landmark *Foundations of measurement, Volume I* by Krantz et al., a book that effectively defines the field known today as formal measurement theory. Volumes II (1989) and III (1990) have recently appeared and will undoubtedly have a comparably profound impact. The subject thus defined is usefully surveyed in Roberts' *Measurement theory* (1979), with special emphasis on applications to decision theory and the social sciences.

Simply described, the approach of KLST is as follows. A nonnumerical (empirical) relational structure is a set of nonnumerical entities E, together with relations (including operations and distinguished elements) $S_1, S_2, \ldots, S_n$ on the set E. A numerical (abstract) relational structure is a set of numerical entities N, together with relations $R_1, R_2, \ldots, R_m$ on the set N. A scale of measurement Φ is a relation-preserving function (i.e., a homomorphism) from a nonnumerical relational structure to a numerical relational structure. The type of the relational structure is defined by the number and degree of the relations in the structure, and the scale type can be defined as the type of the relational structure mapped. Scale type can also be defined in terms of the scale transformations that preserve the mapping. A nominal scale maps an empirical relational structure into $\langle N, = \rangle$, an ordinal scale into $\langle N, > \rangle$, an interval scale into $\langle N, >, - \rangle$, and an additive scale into $\langle N, >, + \rangle$ (or into similar structures with $>$ replaced by $\geq$).

The *first* task of formal measurement theory is to discover the precise conditions required for the existence of scales of various types. More precisely, the task is to discover and prove *representation theorems* asserting the existence of scales of certain types if and (when possible) only if the nonnumerical relational structure in question satisfies certain sets of conditions. For example, let $\langle E, \succsim, \oplus \rangle$ be a nonnumerical structure with $\succsim$ a binary relation on E and $\oplus$ a closed binary operation on E; furthermore, suppose $a \approx b$ is defined as $a \succsim b$ and $b \precsim a$, and $a > b$ is defined as $a \succsim b$ and not $(b \succsim a)$. Given these assumptions, there exists a positive real-valued function $\Phi: E \to R+$, such that, for all $a, b \in E$

(i) $a \succsim b$ if and only if $\Phi(a) \geq \Phi(b)$ and
(ii) $\Phi(a \oplus b) = \Phi(a) + \Phi(b)$

if and only if $\langle E, \succsim, \oplus \rangle$ satisfies the following conditions for all $a, b, c, d \in E$:

1. *(Weak Order)* $\succsim$ is a reflexive, transitive, and connected relation on E.
2. *(Weak Associativity)* $a \oplus (b \oplus c) = (a \oplus b) \oplus c$.
3. *(Monotonicity)* $a \succsim b$ iff $a \oplus c \succsim b \oplus c$ iff $c \oplus a \succsim c \oplus b$.

4. (*Positivity*) $a \oplus b \gtrsim a$.

5. (*Strongly Archimedean*) If $a > b$, then for any $c, d \in E$ there is a positive integer n such that $n(a) \oplus c \gtrsim n(b) \oplus d$ where $n(a)$ is defined inductively as $1(a) \approx a$, $(n + 1)a \approx n(a) \oplus a$.

Nonnumerical relational structures of this kind are known as closed (Archimedean) positive extensive structures, a paradigm example of which is a set of straight, rigid rods where $\oplus$ is the operation of joining rods end-to-end along a straight line and $a \gtrsim b$ means that, when rods a and b are placed side by side with one pair of endpoints coinciding, either the opposite pair of endpoints coincide, or the opposite endpoint of a extends beyond that of b.

Although examples like this have played an important role in the literature on formal measurement theory, they are unrealistic from the standpoint of practical measurement, because the empirical conditions described by the axioms are rarely satisfied. For example, the condition that operation $\oplus$ is closed entails that E is infinite, which in practice rarely, if ever, obtains. Consequently, in recent years, greater emphasis has been placed on conditions for "constructible" scales, scales constructed by operations that under favorable conditions can actually be performed.

The *second* part of the task of formal measurement theory is to discover and precisely characterize the classes of admissible transformations for scales of various types—transformations that produce a new scale Φ' that maps the same relations as the original Φ. One says that a scale type is unique up to a certain subclass of the class of all possible transformations. Thus, additive scales (e.g., the Archimedean extensive structures described previously) are unique up to multiplication by a constant positive real number. Interval scales are unique up to linear transformations, ordinal scales unique up to monotone (order-preserving) transformations, and nominal scales unique up to one-to-one transformations. Accordingly theorems that assert the uniqueness of a scale of a certain type are called *uniqueness theorems,* and the second task of formal measurement theory is to discover and prove such theorems. (Stevens' system of scale classification is controversial and is criticized in Ellis, 1966, chapter 4; Savage, 1970, pp. 166–172; and Krantz et al., 1971, p. 11.)

As described above, the task of formal, representationalist measurement theory is to prove the existence and uniqueness of scales of measurement, where such scales are taken to be homomorphic functions from sets of empirical objects to sets of numbers. This description is undoubtedly overly simple and narrow. It assumes, for example, that scales are functions into number systems and a fortiori that representing structures are necessarily numerical relational structures. However, as the practitioners of formal measurement theory are well aware, the outcomes of measurement may be vectors or other nonnumerical entities. Consequently what we have described above is merely a segment, albeit an important segment, of their program.

In what follows, we briefly describe and comment on the essays. The formalist, representationalist approach dominates measurement theory; therefore, it seems appropriate to begin the volume with essays by some of the leading architects of this approach, following these with essays that attempt to broaden the approach, and these in turn with essays that criticize the approach. Essays with more purely metaphysical or philosophical themes, even if technically articulated, appear at the end.

The Archimedean condition of extensive measurement, which mirrors the familiar Archimedean property of the real number system, is often stated as follows:

5′. For all $a, b \in E$, there is a positive integer n such that, if $a > b$, then $n(b) > \sim a$,

where $n(a)$ is defined inductively as $1(a) \approx a$ and $(n \oplus 1)a \approx n(a) \oplus a$. Historically axiom 5′. was employed to rule out the existence of magnitudes (and differences in magnitudes) that are infinitely small compared with others. It is formulated in terms of a concatenation operation; thus, the axiom clearly fails to apply to structures that do not possess such an operation. Note that axioms 1.–4. and 5′. are not sufficient to guarantee the representation guaranteed by axioms 1.–5.

Luce and Narens (chapter 2 in this volume) seek a generalization of axiom (5′) that will apply to structures that are in some sense Archimedean and yet possess no concatenation operation. They assume that one purpose of an Archimedean axiom is to insure that the structures satisfying it are imbeddable into a classical continuum (i.e., an open Dedekind-complete ordered set with a denumerable order-dense subset). Consequently they attempt to isolate a class of continuously ordered structures that may be reasonably regarded as *intrinsically Archimedean* and to characterize *Archimedean* structures in terms of their ability to be imbedded in intrinsically Archimedean structures in appropriate ways. They are able to report only partial results at the present time, owing to the difficulty in achieving a satisfactory characterization of an intrinsically Archimedean structure. They note that any acceptable generalization of the concept of Archimedeanness must involve higher-order logical concepts, which, according to some theorists, entails that the concept is nonempirical.

A broad conception of representationalist measurement theory seems required to accommodate the essay by Suppes and Zanotti (chapter 3 in this volume). Their subject is the probability (and error) of measurements, for example, the probability of obtaining a given numerical value in measuring the length of a rod with a meterstick. They define a probability in the usual measure-theoretic manner as a function to the closed interval of real numbers [0,1] from a set of subsets (of a set V of basic events or propositions) closed under union, intersection, and complementation, a function that satisfies the classical Kolmogorov axioms.

Such a set of subsets is called a Borel field, or Boolean algebra. The Kolmogorov axioms are, where $Pr(e)$ is the probability of an event (simple or complex): for all e in V (a) $Pr(e) \geq 0$, (b) if e is certain $(e = V)$, then $Pr(e) = 1$, (c) if e_1 and e_2 are incompatible, then $Pr(e_1) + Pr(e_2) = Pr(e_1 \oplus e_2)$. In the usual treatment, the probability of a measurement $\mathbf{r}$ for object $\mathbf{a}$ is approximated by the number of times $\mathbf{r}$ is obtained divided by the total number of measurements of $\mathbf{a}$, and then the mean value and the variance of the measurements are calculated from the distribution of the probabilities of various measurements. The sum of differences between measurements and the mean value is the first moment, which in a normal (symmetrical) distribution is zero. The sum of the squares of these differences is the second moment, or variance, and the square root of the variance is the standard deviation. Instead of proceeding in this familiar manner, the authors define the "qualitative" nth moment of $\mathbf{a}$ without recourse to a (quantitative) probability function and then prove a representation theorem to the effect that their qualitative moments correspond to the quantitative moments of the usual treatment.

The formalist-representationalist approach to measurement has long been criticized on the ground that its narrow focus has neglected important topics in the field (see Adams, 1966, for example). A complaint of this type can be associated with the essay by Adams (chapter 4 in this volume), because his topic is usually neglected by representationalists. It concerns the empirical status of axioms that characterize empirical relational structures and constitute necessary and sufficient conditions for the existence and uniqueness of scales of various sorts. These axiomatized relational structures are called "theories of measurement" by Adams and the representationalists, in conformity with the model-theoretic conception of a scientific theory that has emerged from the approach (see Suppes, 1967). We eschew this usage in favor of "axiomatized structure" or simply "structure" to prevent confusion between a "theory of measurement" in the sense of an axiomatized structure and "measurement theory". Adams' example is the measurement of probability. He distinguishes various classes of axiomatized structures (basic de Finetti structures, n-partitionable structures, Koopman Archimedean structures, etc.), and he describes the inclusion relations between them. He classifies the types of data that can be consistent or inconsistent with these structures and provides the following definitions: (a) T is *empirically as strong* as T' with respect to data of type D, if and only if every set of data of type D that is consistent with T is also consistent with T'; and (b) an axiom *contributes empirical content* to T, if adding it to T yields a T' that is empirically stronger than T. His main theorem describes the relations of empirical strength and empirical equivalence among the various axiomatized structures and shows that axioms may contribute empirical content to a structure with respect to some data and not with respect to others. However, according to Adams, the nonnecessary axioms of equipartitionability and Archimedeanness do not contribute empirical content to certain probabilistically representable structures with respect to data of any sort. These are nonempirical without qualification and, as some have speculated, are employed simply to prove the desired representation theorem on such structures. (Presumably these will not be interpreted realistically, for which see below.) Other nonnecessary axioms, for example, axiom P6' of L. J. Savage's system, do add empirical content with respect to data of a special kind.

Kyburg (chapter 5 in this volume) advances another objection of the "narrowness" type: He complains that representationalists have neglected the problem of errors of measurement, and he proposes a theory of such errors to remedy the neglect. If measurements of three rods, a, b, and c indicate that a is longer than b, b longer than c, and c is longer than a, then one cannot accept all three measurements without contradicting the axiom of transitivity of the longer than relation. Kyburg proposes that here, as elsewhere in theory testing, the experimenter should follow two principles: (a) reject as erroneous the smallest number of data that are inconsistent with the axioms of the theory, and (b) distribute the errors evenly across different kinds of measurement. He suggests that the first principle corresponds to the familiar rule in statistics of minimizing the standard deviation (root mean square difference) in a collection of numerical data. Numerous examples are provided to illustrate the application of the two principles. He notes that, in applying the principles, the theory being tested is used to determine what data may be used to test it. However, he finds no vicious circularity in the process.

A more sweeping narrowness objection is that the representationalist approach studies measurement in isolation from the various empirical theories—physical, biological, psychological, and so forth—in which it functions as a component and consequently misunderstands the process. This objection has been urged by the structuralist measurement theorists—for example, Sneed and his collaborators (Sneed, 1971; Balzer, Moulines, and Sneed, 1987)—and is here presented in the essay by Balzer (chapter 6 in this volume). After comparing the two approaches, he identifies several shortcomings in representationalism. First, it fails to realize that conditions for scales of measurement normally include axioms (laws) of the theory employing the scale and may or may not include axioms of the measured magnitude. For example, the mass of bodies is measured in collisions through the use of the law of mechanics that relates the masses of colliding bodies to their initial and final velocities. Second, representationalism fails to understand that the distinction between fundamental and derived measurement is not absolute but is relative to the theory in which the method is imbedded and that the one type of measurement is not intrinsically better than the other. Which is best will depend on the stage the theory has achieved in its construction. He contends that one achievement of the structuralist program is a correct and formally scrupulous substitute for the unacceptable distinction between theoretical (indirectly measurable) and observational (directly measurable) terms.

If, as the representationalist view assumes, measurement is the representation of empirical relational structures by means of numerical relational structures, then obviously there must be a strong similarity between the represented structure and the representing structure, if measurement is to be possible. Indeed, according to the representationalist, a scale of measurement is defined as a homomorphism from an empirical structure to a numerical structure. It is, therefore, natural to wonder whether the functions served by the numerical representation could not also be served by the nonnumerical counterpart. Simply stated, the function of numerical representations is to make possible the construction of numerical scientific theories that enable us to understand, predict, and control our nonnumerical environments. So the question is whether science without numerical representation is possible. Hartry Field, in his *Science without numbers* (1980), attempted to prove that it is possible where the science is classical mechanics, as (on his interpretation) Hilbert proved it for the science of Euclidean geometry. That is to say, he attempted to prove that synthetic mechanics is possible, as Hilbert proved that synthetic Euclidean geometry is possible.

Burgess (chapter 7 in this volume) argues that, in one sense, Field's thesis is clearly true and that the interesting questions concern its significance. He describes, in full technical detail, a method for replacing analytic (numerical) classical physics with a synthetic (nonnumerical) theory that is supposed to capture the synthetic content of the analytic theory. The synthetic theory is constructed in two stages. First, numbers are coded as triples of collinear points (whose distance ratios uniquely determine the corresponding numbers), and relations on numbers are replaced by relations on point triples. Then a more natural synthetic theory is described by defining relations on point triples in terms of the geometrical relations of betweenness, congruence, equality of ratios of quantity differences, and quantity inequality. Burgess claims that every formula of the analytic theory has a counterpart in the synthetic theory such that the one is provable in its theory if and only if the other is provable in its theory. He concludes with a philosophical comparison of Field's metaphysics and that of W. V. O. Quine. If antinominalism (Platonism) is the view that numbers, functions, and sets exist (or are justifiably held to exist), and nominalism is the view that they do not exist (or are not), then Field is a nominalist and Quine an antinominalist. If realism is the view that a theory is justifiably believed only on the ground that it reflects the world, then Field is a realist and Quine an antirealist. Burgess suggests that Quine's antinominalism flows from his antirealism (which says that belief in numbers is justified by its utility, not by its correspondence to the world) and that Field's nominalism flows from his realism (which says that belief in numbers is unjustified, because it does not causally reflect the world and cannot, because numbers are noncausal). Furthermore, he finds their disagreement too deep to be removed by a technical device that enables us to dispense with numbers in principle, if not in practice.

(Note the ambiguity of "realism." Realism in philosophy of science is usually taken to be the view that the theoretical terms of scientific theories (e.g. "force," "electron," "π") denote real entities and not convenient fictions, and operationalism or instrumentalism is its opposite. Realism in philosophy of mathematics is usually taken to be the view that numbers are real and not fictions or linguistic constructions, and nominalism is its opposite. Realism in measurement theory is usually taken to be the view that numerical relations such as order, difference, addition, multiplication, differentiation, and so forth represent real, nonnumerical empirical relations under appropriate scales of measurement, and conventionalism seems the best choice for its opposite. Realism in epistemology is the view that a theory is justifiably believed only on the ground that it reflects the world (and could be construed as including any or all of the realist positions above); coherentism, subjectivism, and skepticism are its contraries.

Like the synthetic description of the geometric linear continuum found in Euclid, Field's description of the nonnumerical structures with which he would replace numerical structures of geometry and physics revives an ancient question of measurement theory: What is the difference between quality and quantity? between qualitative and quantitative relations? Koslow (chapter 8 in this volume) attempts to answer this question by relativizing the notions of a quantitative or qualitative relation to a partition (set of disjoint subsets) of the domain of the relation. Roughly a relation $R(x_1, \ldots, x_n)$ is defined as *quantitative relative to partition M* only if (a) replacement of a member x_i of the n-tuple $(x_1, \ldots, x_n)$ by a different member of its partition element produces an n-tuple in the relation, and (b) if two n-tuples belonging to R differ in at most the ith component, then those two components belong to the same member of the partition. This definition enables him to show that qualitative (classificatory and comparative) relations and quantitative relations fall into distinct classes and also that many qualitative relations are numerical, and many quantitative relations are nonnumerical. Several criticisms and clarifications ensue. Measurement is typically performed on quantitative empirical structures; therefore, representational theorists of measurement (KLST) are in error when they assert that numerical laws are restatements of qualitative relations. Furthermore, Field's nominalist program should be interpreted as an attempt to show that science without numerical relations, not science without quantitative relations, is possible. The second half of the essay is devoted to a historical study of three quantitative, nonnumerical relations: sameness of ratios as it figures in Euclid's *Elements,* sameness of temperature as it figures in Maxwell's theory of heat, and sameness of quantity of matter (mass) as it figures in Newton's mechanics.

As noted in the previous historical survey, the issues surrounding conventionalism and realism have been especially interesting to philosophers of measurement. They still are. Ellis (chapter 9 in this volume) attempts to rescue what is sound in his quasiconventionalist treatment of measurement (1966) from the holist-realist critique of recent philosophy of science. His earlier view was that any scale of measurement that represents empirical order is acceptable and that choices between acceptable scales are based on conventional, nonempirical criteria, such as simplicity in the resulting numerical laws and invariance of these laws among favored classes of scales (for example, classes of scales that transform under multiplication by a constant). He softens the earlier view by conceding to the holists that there is no useful distinction between conventional and empirical statements, and that criteria such as simplicity and invariance are as important as so-called empirical criteria in selecting theories that can face experience as a whole. Although insisting that spatial and temporal distance are relations and consequently yield to his earlier analysis, he concedes to the realists that quantities such as mass, charge, and spin are properties, and that whether scales of these quantities represent features in addition to linear order is a relevant consideration. He argues that these concessions do not diminish the importance and validity of the conventionalist program of analysis and rational reconstruction of scientific theory and practice, and he recommends its continuation in the theory of measurement and elsewhere.

Berka (chapter 10 in this volume) is completely unsympathetic to conventionalist and antirealist tendencies in measurement theory. He defends what he calls a materialist (or realist) view of measurement, according to which the object of measurement exists independently of and prior to the procedures used to measure it. One main rival to his view is the operationalist view of Bridgman and Stevens, on which measurement is any assignment of numerals according to any operational, empirical rule. His objection to this view is that the grounding operations are not always empirical and that most quantities cannot be defined by a single operation. The other main rival is the formalist view of measurement (KLST), which seeks sets of necessary and sufficient axioms for the existence and uniqueness of scales of measurement. He objects that the relations described by the axioms are not really empirical (or at least are unusable in empirical measurement procedures). He also questions the logical adequacy of the proofs and claims that the proofs are unnecessary, because the theorems proved could simply be assumed as axioms. On his materialist view (but not the others), derived magnitudes cannot become fundamental by a new choice of measuring operation, and units and nonabsolute zeros are not arbitrary but are grounded in empirical reality. He believes his view vitiates many attempts to extend the procedures of physical measurement to magnitudes in the behavioral and social sciences. He concludes with the case study of utility measurement to make the point.

Domotor (chapter 11 in this volume) makes contact with many of the metaphysical and measurement-theoretic questions heretofore considered. He recommends an *interactionist* (realist) approach to measurement in preference to the standard *representationalist* (empiricist, antirealist) approach. He contends that the representationalist approach views measurement as a device to make scientific theories conceptually and calculationally manageable. The goal of measurement theory on this approach is the discovery of axioms for qualitative structures that make it possible to derive a Ramsey sentence—the representation theorem—which entails that theoretical terms are eliminable in principle. The interactionist, on the other hand, views measurement as a real, causal interaction between a physical system and a measuring instrument, an interaction that can be characterized mathematically as an inner product on spaces of intensive and extensive quantities generated by rings of measurable magnitudes. Domotor illustrates this idea with a representation of a qualitative, comparative probability structure by means of a quantitative, Kolmogorov probability structure. He proposes that, by treating measurement structures as a mathematical *category,* one can define a *projection map* from quantitative to qualitative structures, in addition to the usual *injective map* (representation) in the reverse direction. The discovery of such projections is, on his approach, as important to measurement as the discovery of injections; he believes it will reduce the confusing proliferation of representation theorems and unify the field of measurement.

REFERENCES

Adams, E. W. (1966). On the nature and purpose of measurement. *Synthese, 16,* 125–169.

Aristotle (c. 330 B.C.). *The basic works of Aristotle.* New York: Random House, 1941.

Balzer, W., Moulines, C. Ulises, & Sneed, J. D. (1987). *An architectonic for science: The structuralist program.* Dordrecht & Boston: Kluwer.

Bergmann, G., & Spence, K. W. (1953/1944). The logic of psychophysical measurement. In H. Feigl & M. Brodbeck (Eds.), *Readings in the philosophy of science* (pp. 103–119). New York: Appleton-Century-Crofts. Reprinted from *Psychological Review, 51,* 1944 1–24.

Campbell, N. R. (1957). *Foundations of science.* New York: Dover. Reprinted as *Physics: The elements,* 1920. Cambridge: Cambridge University Press, 1920.

Campbell, N. R. (1928). *An account of the principles of measurement and calculation.* London: Longmans, Green.

Carnap, R. (1966). *Philosophical foundations of physics.* New York: Basic Books.

Cohen, M. R. & Nagel, E. (1934). *An introduction to logic and scientific method.* New York: Harcourt, Brace.

Ellis, B. (1966). *Basic concepts of measurement.* Cambridge: Cambridge University Press.

Euclid (c. 300 B.C.). *The elements*: Translated by T. L. Heath, *The thirteen books of Euclid's elements* (2nd ed., Vols. I–III). New York: Dover, 1956.

Field, H. (1980). *Science without numbers.* Princeton: Princeton University Press.

Guilford, J. P. (1954). *Psychometric methods* (rev. ed.). New York: McGraw-Hill. First edition 1936.

von Helmholtz, H. (1887). Zählen und Messen: erkenntnis-theoretisch. In *Philosophische Aufsätze Eduard Zeller gewidmet,* Leipzig. English translation by C. L. Bryan, *Counting and measuring,* Princeton: van Nostrand, 1930.

Hempel, C. G. (1952). *Fundamentals of concept formation in empirical science.* International Encyclopedia for Unified Science (Vol. II, No. 7). Chicago: University of Chicago Press.

Hölder, O. (1901). Die Axiome der Quantität und die Lehre vom Mass. *Berichte über die Verhandlungen der Königlich der sächsischen Gesellschaft der Wissenschaften, Mathematisch-physische Klasse,* Leipzig, *53,* 1–64.

Krantz, D., Luce, R. D., Suppes, P., & Tversky, A. (1971). *Foundations of measurement: Volume I. Additive and polynomial representations.* New York & London: Academic Press. Suppes, et. al., vol. II, Luce et. al., 1989, vol. III, 1990.

Nagel, E. (1931). Measurement. *Erkenntnis, 2*, 313–333.

Quine, W. V. O. (1961). *From a logical point of view* (2nd ed.). Cambridge, MA: Harvard University Press.

Roberts, F. S. (1979). *Measurement theory: With applications to decisionmaking, utility, and the social sciences.* Reading, MA: Addison-Wesley.

Russell, B. (1903). *Principles of mathematics.* New York: Norton.

Savage, C. W. (1970). *The measurement of sensation.* Berkeley & Los Angeles: University of California Press.

Sneed, J. D. (1971). *The logical structure of mathematical physics.* Dordrecht/Boston/London: Reidel.

Stevens, S. S. (1946). On the theory of scales of measurement. *Science, 103,* 677–680.

Stevens, S. S. (1951). Mathematics, measurement, and psychophysics. In S. S. Stevens (Ed.), *Handbook of experimental psychology* (pp. 1–49). New York: Wiley.

Suppes, P. (1967). What is a scientific theory? In S. Morgenbesser (Ed.), *Philosophy of science today* (pp. 55–67). New York & London: Basic Books.

Thurstone, L. L. (1959). *The measurement of values.* Chicago: University of Chicago Press.

Torgerson, W. S. (1958). *Theory and methods of scaling.* New York: Wiley.

2 Intrinsic Archimedeanness and the Continuum

R. Duncan Luce
Harvard University and University of California at Irvine

Louis Narens
University of California at Irvine

1. INTRODUCTION

1.1 Background

The Archimedean axiom has its roots in ancient mathematics, where it was used to banish from consideration both infinitely large and infinitesimally small quantities. This was essentially the only rigorous means available to eliminate such quantities until very late in the nineteenth century when G. Cantor gave a fully rigorous description of the continuum in terms of an ordering relation. In a great many contexts, Cantor's method provides a different means for eliminating the infinitely large and small. Although the two approaches are quite different, they are interrelated in subtle ways. Part of this chapter focuses on such relationships.

Both the Archimedean and Cantorian approaches to the continuum use second-order logical concepts in their formulations. As will follow from results presented subsequently, some sort of higher-order logical concept is necessary in any description of the continuum. Thus, in particular, any part of science that uses the continuum necessarily assumes higher-order concepts.

Many who work in the foundations of science believe higher-order concepts to be inherently nonempirical and, thus, believe that scientific concepts based on a continuum include some nonempirical component. A similar situation exists for those scientific concepts that foundationally have bases in situations less rich than the continuum but nevertheless require imbeddability into structures based on the continuum. Usually an Archimedean axiom is used to effect the imbedding. Therefore, it is not surprising that each coherent, effective program for science to emerge has incorporated a theory of measurement based on some higher-order concept.

15

In practice, the Cantor axioms have not been widely used in measurement theory because of the nonconstructive nature of the axiom postulating the existence of a countable, order-dense subset (see below). Preference has been accorded the more constructive Archimedean approach, when it is available.

Historically, to assure that all magnitudes and differences of magnitudes are commensurable, the concept of Archimedeanness has been defined in terms of an operation, usually assumed to be associative. Its justification in these contexts has consisted in trying to make intuitively clear that, in terms of recursively generated applications of the operation as a method of determining size, no element is infinitely large with respect to another and that no two elements are infinitesimally close together. In this chapter, we seek to extend the concept of Archimedeanness—of commensurability—to general structures that may have no operation among its defining relations (*primitives*). In such situations, we see no way to keep Archimedeanness from becoming a much more abstract notion and correspondingly a much more difficult one to justify as correct.

Our approach is to formulate, in a very general fashion, what Archimedeanness should accomplish and then show that this imposes severe restrictions that are satisfied by only one concept (up to logical equivalence). In this approach, the resulting concept of Archimedeanness will be justified by theorems; intuition will play a role only at the beginning stages in stating what should be accomplished. Many of the theorems are difficult to prove and require concepts of abstract algebra, particularly those of group theory. No proofs will be presented in this paper, but references are provided to the original publications. Most of them can also be found in Luce, Krantz, Suppes, and Tversky (1990).

Our basic goal is to find the correct general concept and to justify it as such. Unfortunately our theory of Archimedeanness is not yet completely worked out; there are important gaps, which will be indicated throughout the chapter often as conjectures, tantalizing ideas, or unresolved technical questions.

1.2   The Research Agenda

Cantor (1895) gave the following simple and elegant characterization of the continuum: $C = \langle X, \succeq \rangle$ is said to be a *continuum*,[1] if and only if the following three conditions are met:

1. C is a totally ordered set without endpoints.
2. C is Dedekind complete (i.e., each nonempty bounded subset of X has a least upper bound in X).
3. There is a denumerable subset Y of X that is order dense in X (i.e., for each x, y in X, there exists z in Y such that $x > z > y$).

---

[1]Throughout this chapter, we consider only continuua without endpoints. The results easily generalize to situations with either one or two endpoints.

Cantor proved that each continuum is isomorphic to the ordered positive real numbers, which we designate as $\langle Re^+, \geq \rangle$.

Historically one of the principal uses made of Archimedean axioms was to establish the isomorphic imbedding of structures into ones based on a continuum. We take this to be a principal characteristic of Archimedeanness. The basic idea is as follows.

There are certain structures that shall be taken to be intrinsically Archimedean—we discuss what this might mean shortly. Such structures will take the following general form: $\langle X, \gtrsim, R_1, \ldots, R_i, \ldots \rangle$, where the R_i may be elements of X, relations on X, relations of relations of X, and so on, and $\langle X, \gtrsim \rangle$ is a continuum, and certain other conditions are satisfied that will be stated later. None of the R_i need be an operation or partial operation. A structure $\mathscr{S} = \langle S, \gtrsim, S_1, \ldots, S_i, \ldots \rangle$ is said to be *Archimedean* if and only if there is an intrinsically Archimedean structure $\mathscr{X}$ and an isomorphism ϕ from $\mathscr{S}$ into $\mathscr{X}$ such that $\phi(S)$ is a dense subset of an open interval of $\mathscr{X}$. This definition consciously omits cases where the ordering on S may be discrete or have gaps in it. There are obviously discrete structures that are Archimedean (e.g., $\langle I^+, \geq, + \rangle$, where I^+ is the positive integers), and the approach presented in this chapter can be extended to such cases.

Given the general framework of distinguishing intrinsically Archimedean and Archimedean structures, the plan of the research is obvious: Provide a precise definition of intrinsically Archimedean, argue that it is the correct one, and then describe conditions that allow other structures to be appropriately imbedded into intrinsically Archimedean ones. Unfortunately this seems to be a difficult plan to carry out, and, as was mentioned, only partial results can be reported at this time. Mainly they concern attempts to capture the concept of intrinsic Archimedeanness. In fact, this chapter could well be entitled "Seeking the intrinsically Archimedean."

2.   POSITIVE CONCATENATION STRUCTURES

2.1   Archimedeanness in Standard Sequences

Archimedeanness has been traditionally defined in terms of operations, for which the following algebraic concepts are useful.

Let $\mathscr{X} = \langle X, \gtrsim, \bigcirc \rangle$ be such that X is a nonempty set, $\gtrsim$ is a binary relation on X, and $\bigcirc$ is a binary (closed) operation on X. Then $\mathscr{X}$ is said to be a *concatenation structure*[2] if and only if the following four conditions are met:

---

[2]The general concept of a concatenation structure in the literature (e.g., Narens & Luce, 1976; Luce & Narens, 1985) assumes $\bigcirc$ is a partial, not a closed, operation and does not assume density. We are mainly concerned here with homogeneous structures, which are necessarily closed, and with the continuum, which is dense; thus, it is convenient to use the more restrictive definition.

1. X has at least two elements.
2. $\succsim$ is a total ordering.
3. $\langle X, \succsim \rangle$ is dense.
4. $\bigcirc$ is (strictly) monotonic in each variable (i.e., for all x, y, z in X, $x \succsim y \leftrightarrow x \bigcirc z \succsim y \bigcirc z \leftrightarrow z \bigcirc x \succsim z \bigcirc y$).

The operation $\bigcirc$ is said to be

Positive if and only if $x \bigcirc y > x$ and $x \bigcirc y > y$ for all x, y in X.

Associative if and only if $x \bigcirc (y \bigcirc z) = (x \bigcirc y) \bigcirc z$ for all x, y, z in X.

Commutative if and only if $x \bigcirc y = y \bigcirc x$ for all x, y in X.

Idempotent if and only if $x \bigcirc x = x$ for all x in X.

Further, $\mathscr{X}$ is said to be *Archimedean in standard sequences,* often written *ss–* Archimedean, if and only if for each x and y in X, there exists a positive integer n such that $nx > y$, where the *standard sequence* $\{kx\}$ is defined inductively as follows: $1x = x$, and for $k > 1$, $kx = [(k - 1)x] \bigcirc x$.

Note that, for positive structures, standard sequences are increasing, and so *ss*–Archimedeanness can be used to say there are no infinitely large elements. However, for idempotent structures, *ss*–Archimedeanness is false, because $kx = x$ for all positive integers k. Other forms of the Archimedean axiom will be given later that apply to both positive and nonpositive structures.

2.2   A Problematic Example

Example 2 below will show that *ss*–Archimedeanness is problematic even for positive operations, but first we present a nonproblematic example.

EXAMPLE 1. Let $\mathscr{E}_1 = \langle Re^+, \succsim, + \rangle$. $\mathscr{E}_1$ is defined on a continuum and is positive, associative, and commutative. $\mathscr{E}_1$ is an archetypical example of an Archimedean structure, and if any structure is going to be described as intrinsically Archimedean, then $\mathscr{E}_1$ certainly will. It is interesting to ask if there are any other intrinsic Archimedean structures, not isomorphic to $\mathscr{E}_1$, that are positive, associative, and commutative. The following example is very instructive.

EXAMPLE 2. Let β denote some object that is not a real number, and let R denote the set of nonnegative real numbers. Let $(x_o, \ldots, x_i, \ldots)$ denote the infinite sequence whose ith term is x_i. Let B be the set of all sequences each of whose terms, except for one, is the element β; the exceptional one is an element of R. The notation $\vec{a}_i = (\beta, \ldots, a_i, \beta, \ldots)$ indicates both that the element of R is in the ith term of the sequence $\vec{a}_i$ and that that term has the numerical value a_i. Let $A = B - \{0, \beta, \beta, \ldots\}$. Suppose $\vec{a}_i$, $\vec{b}_j$, and $\vec{c}_k$ are arbitrary elements of A. Define $\succsim$ and $\bigcirc$ as follows:

$$\vec{a}_i \succsim \vec{b}_j \text{ iff either } i = j \text{ and } a_i \geq b_j \text{ or } i > j,$$

and

$$\vec{a}_i \bigcirc \vec{b}_j = \vec{c}_k \text{ iff } i + j = k \text{ and } a_i + b_j = c_k.$$

Let $\mathscr{E}_2 = \langle A, \succsim, \bigcirc \rangle$. Then $\mathscr{E}_2$ is a concatenation structure; $\langle A, \succsim \rangle$ is a continuum; and $\mathscr{E}_2$ is positive, associative, commutative, and ss–Archimedean. It is easy to show that $\mathscr{E}_2$ is not isomorphically imbeddable in $\langle Re^+, \geq, + \rangle$. Although $\mathscr{E}_2$ satisfies ss–Archimdeanness, do we really want to call it Archimedean? Clearly, because of ss–Archimdeanness, it does not have one element infinitely larger than another (in terms of $\bigcirc$). However, the elements of the sets

$$A_i = \{\vec{a}_i \mid \vec{a}_i \in A \text{ and } a_i \in R\}$$

look like they are infinitesimally close to one another.

2.3   Archimedeanness in Standard Differences

However, how are we going to define what it means for $\vec{a}_i$ and $\vec{b}_i$ to be infinitesimally close in a context like Example 2? Given generic elements a and b, the usual way is to find an element c that represents their difference, (e.g., if $a > b$, then $a = b \bigcirc c$) and show that some element of A is infinitely large with respect to c. However, for elements of A_i, no such c can be found, so this strategy is not immediately applicable. Another approach is to try to use an alternative axiom that Roberts and Luce (1968) proposed for extensive measurement structures for which solvability was not a postulated condition. It is this: A structure is said to be *Archimedean in standard differences*, written sd–Archimedean, if and only if, for all x, y, u, v in A, if $x > y$, then there exists a positive integer n such that

$$nx \bigcirc u \succsim ny \bigcirc v.$$

This axiom was motivated in Krantz, Luce, Suppes, and Tversky (1971, p. 74) as follows (with the notation changed to ours):

> It should be noted that [the sd–Archimedean axiom] is, in fact, the ordinary Archimedean property for differences. For, if we define $(x, y) \succsim (u, v)$ to mean $x \bigcirc u \succsim y \bigcirc v$, then [the sd–Archimedean axiom] simply says that if (x, y) is positive (i.e., $x > y$) then for some positive integer n,
> $$n(x, y) = (nx, ny) \succsim (u, v).$$

The problem with their motivation is in justifying the last equation. The inequality $(nx, ny) \succsim (u, v)$ does seem to capture adequately the idea that the difference between n copies of x and n copies of y is greater than or equal to the difference between u and v. However, this in itself is not sufficient to say that the difference between x and y is not infinitely close. To do that, one needs the equation $n(x, y) = (nx, ny)$ which identifies n copies of the difference between x and y with the difference between n copies of x and n copies of y. However, this latter equation is not justified; it is simply taken as a definition of what n copies of the difference means.

Let us look at this problem in another way. Suppose $x > y\bigcirc z$. Then it is reasonable to say that the "difference between x and y is greater than z." Using this concept of difference, we can formulate the idea of x and y not being infinitely close by requiring that, for each element w, a positive integer n can always be found for which n copies of z exceeds w. This approach, which relies entirely on being able to find a z such that $x > y\bigcirc z$, fails when no such z exists, as is the case for elements from A_i.

An obvious strategy is to attempt to extend (i.e., imbed) the structure $\mathscr{E}_2$ to (in) a structure $\mathscr{E}_2' = \langle A', \succsim', \bigcirc' \rangle$ that allows one to find a z such that $x > y\bigcirc'z$ whenever $x > y$. When x and y belong to A_i, this z will belong to $A' - A$ and will be infinitesimally small with respect to elements of A (i.e., if w is in A, then $w > nz$, for all positive integers n). As an example, let $A' = A \cup Re^+$. Extend $\succsim$ to $\succsim$ ' by requiring all elements of A to be $>'$ all elements of Re^+, and by requiring $\succsim$ ' restricted to Re^+ to be the usual ordering $\geq$ on Re^+. Extend $\bigcirc$ to $\bigcirc'$ as follows: For all r and s in Re^+; and all $\vec{a}_i$ and $\vec{b}_j$ in A,

$$r\bigcirc's = r + s,$$

and

$$r\bigcirc'\vec{a}_i = \vec{a}_i\bigcirc'r = \vec{b}_j \text{ iff } i = j \text{ and } a_i + r = b_j.$$

Then Re^+ are the infinitesimals, and, for all x and y in A', if $x >' y$, then, for some z in A', $x >' y\bigcirc'z$. $\mathscr{E}_2'$ is a concatenation structure that is positive, associative, commutative, but it is not ss–Archimedean. If we let (x, y) stand for the difference between x and y, then, when $x = y\bigcirc'z$, $z = (x, y)$, and, thus,

$$nz = n(x, y),$$

and by using commutativity and associativity, it follows that

$$nx = n(y\bigcirc'z) = ny\bigcirc'nz,$$

and, thus,

$$nz = (nx, ny).$$

However, does the previous argument really justify assuming the sd–Archimedean axiom? After all, one might just as well find a way of assigning infinitesimals to appropriate differences in an extended structure that is not associative and not commutative so that the previous argument will not go through. The sd–axiom might be easier to justify by observing that, in $\mathscr{E}_2$, functions of the form $\gamma_n(x) = nx$ preserve the relations $\succsim$ and $\bigcirc$, that is for all x, y in A,

$$x \succsim y \text{ iff } \gamma_n(x) \succsim \gamma_n(y),$$

and

$$\gamma_n(x\bigcirc y) = \gamma_n(x)\bigcirc\gamma_n(y).$$

Perhaps we should require, as is often done in considerations of meaningfulness, that structure-preserving maps extend to structure-preserving maps in the extension (see Chapter 22 of Luce et al., 1990). If we do so in the case of extensions of $\mathscr{E}_2$ that introduce infinitesimal differences, one retains $n(x, y) = (nx, ny)$ as before. This latter approach also applies to situations where the original operation $\bigcirc$ need be neither associative nor commutative. It needs only to satisfy $\gamma_n(x\bigcirc y) = \gamma_n(x)\bigcirc\gamma_n(y)$, a condition that often obtains, as we shall see.

2.4 Associative Structures on the Continuum

The following theorem can be shown:

> **THEOREM 2.1.** *Let $\mathscr{X} = \langle X, \succeq, \bigcirc \rangle$ be a concatenation structure, $\langle X, \succeq \rangle$ be a continuum, and $\mathscr{X}$ be positive and associative. Then the following five statements are equivalent:*
>
> 1. *$\mathscr{X}$ is isomorphic to $\langle Re^+, \geq, + \rangle$.*
> 2. *$\mathscr{X}$ satisfies the sd–Archimedean axiom.*
> 3. *$\mathscr{X}$ satisfies the ss–Archimedean axiom and right restricted solvability (i.e., for all x, y in X, if $x > y$, then, for some z in X, $x > y\bigcirc z$).*
> 4. *$\mathscr{X}$ is right solvable in the sense that, for all x, y in X, if $x > y$, then, for some z in X, $x = y\bigcirc z$.*
> 5. *$\mathscr{X}$ is homogeneous in the sense that for each x and y in $\mathscr{X}$, an automorphism[3] β of $\mathscr{X}$ exists such that $\beta(x) = y$.*

This theorem and the previous discussion somewhat justify the following assertion: *All intrinsically Archimedean concatenation structures that are positive and associative are isomorphic to $\langle Re^+, \geq, + \rangle$ (and are, therefore, also commutative).*

The subtle interplay between the concepts of ss–Archimedeanness, right-restricted solvability, right solvability, homogeneity, and Dedekind completeness, such as is described in Theorem 2.1 for the special case of a positive and associative operation, will be explored more generally throughout this chapter. Homogeneity will play an especially key role in our investigations.

It is nearly trivial to see that statement 1 implies each of the others. Proofs of the converses were, we believe, first given in the following sources: Statement 2 in Roberts and Luce (1968; see Theorem 3.1 in Krantz et al., 1971); statement 3 in Krantz et al. (1971, Theorem 3.3); statement 4 is a variant on a result for ordered groups due to Loonstra (1946; see Fuchs, 1963, p. 47; it also follows from Theorem 2.1 of Luce and Narens, 1985, which shows, in a far more general

---

[3]An *automorphism* of a structure $\mathscr{X}$ is an isomorphism from $\mathscr{X}$ onto itself.

setting, that statement 4 implies *ss*–Archimedeanness); statement 5 is an un-published result of Michael Cohen (1986; among other things, it shows that, in certain instances, homogeneity implies right-restricted solvability).

2.5   Additional Problematic Examples

There are certain inherent difficulties in trying to classify more general structures as being Archimedean, as the following two examples make clear:

> **EXAMPLES 3 and 4.** Let $\oplus$ be the following operation on Re^+:
> $$x \oplus y = (x + y)/(1 + xy), \text{ if } x \text{ and } y < 1;$$
> $$x \oplus y = x + y, \text{ otherwise.}$$

(Note that $\oplus$, when restricted to the positive reals < 1, is the relativistic "addition" formula for velocities *less than* the velocity of light—1 in this representation.) Let

$$\mathscr{E}_3 = \langle Re^+, \geq, \oplus \rangle.$$

It is easy to verify that $\oplus$ is positive, commutative, and right restrictively solvable. It is not, however, *ss*–Archimedean, because *n* copies of ½ is < 1 for all positive integers n. Let

$$\mathscr{E}_4 = \langle Re^+, \geq, \oplus, + \rangle.$$

$\mathscr{E}_3$ and $\mathscr{E}_4$ are very closely related: $\mathscr{E}_4$ is definable from the primitives $\oplus$ and $\geq$ of $\mathscr{E}_3$ as follows:[4]

$$x + y = z \text{ iff } \exists \, w \, \forall \, u \, \forall \, v[(u < w \ \& \ v < w \to u \oplus v < w), \text{ and}$$
$$(z \oplus w) \oplus w = (x \oplus w) \oplus (y \oplus w)].$$

The structures $\mathscr{E}_3$ and $\mathscr{E}_4$ describe the same situation, $\mathscr{E}_4$ in a little more redundant way. Thus, if one is to be Archimedean or nonArchimedean, then the other should be the same. Observe, however, that, in terms of $\oplus$, $\mathscr{E}_4$ appears not to be Archimedean, whereas in terms of $+$, it does appear to be Archimedean. At this point, it is best not to call it either but to investigate further what the consequences might be in making such distinctions in general.

2.6   Archimedeanness in Difference Sequence

The simplest (and oldest) example of a qualitative concatenation structure is the classical model for additive physical quantities, called *extensive,* which was

---

[4]In this definition, w is forced to have the value 1, which acts like the velocity of light in the relativistic "addition" formula; however, by the way $\oplus$ was defined, it follows that, for all $x < 1$, $x \oplus 1 \neq 1$ rather than $= 1$, which would follow from the relativistic formula. Furthermore, because 1 is not among the primitives of $\mathscr{E}_3$, we cannot explicitly mention it in the definition.

described in Theorem 2.1. There the concept of ss–Archimedeanness is a direct analogue of the definition used in the real number system. Note that, because the structure is associative and commutative, it does not really matter how we compose n copies of x, because, for example, $((x\bigcirc x)\bigcirc x)\bigcirc x$, $(x\bigcirc x)\bigcirc(x\bigcirc x)$, and $x\bigcirc(x\bigcirc(x\bigcirc x))$ are all equivalent.

When it comes to working with general, nonassociative concatenation structures, which are the ones of interest when any form of averaging is involved or when the variables have a factorial structure, as is often true in the behavioral and social sciences, there are at least two possible sources of trouble in defining Archimedeanness.

The first is that, in the positive case which is the natural generalization of extensive structures, there are an indefinite number of distinct ways of defining an infinite standard sequence, and none seems outstandingly better than the others. The one commonly selected is the inductive definition given earlier, and, in one case of major interest (positive, right restrictely solvable, and homogeneous), the choice is immaterial, because it implies the same property for all definitions of standard sequences.[5] However, we have no proof that this is so in a completely general positive concatenation structure. This is an important open problem.

The following example, due to Margaret Cozzens (personal communication), shows that the definition of a standard sequence definitely matters in some nonidempotent concatenation structures.

EXAMPLE 5. Let $\mathscr{E}_5 = \langle Re^+, \geq, \oplus\rangle$, where, for x, y, z in Re^+, $x \oplus y = z$ iff $x + \frac{1}{2}y = z$.

By induction, it is not difficult to show that $nx = x(n + 1)/2$, but for x_n defined by $x_1 = x$ and $x_n = x \oplus x_{n-1}$, then, by induction, $x_n = x(2^n - 1)/2^{n-1} \leq 2x$. Thus, it is Archimedean in nx but not in x_n.

The other trouble arises when we turn to the class of idempotent structures, typified by averaging, that are necessarily nonassociative but also are not positive. For such structures, standard sequences according to any definition of repeated combinations of an element with itself are all trivial, and so, in particular, the definitions of ss– and sd–Archimedeanness are useless. An alternative adopted for such cases is to say that $\{x_n\}$ is a *difference sequence* iff there exist u, v in X with $v > u$ such that, for each n, $x_n\bigcirc u = x_{n-1}\bigcirc v$. Then the structure is said to be *Archimedean in difference sequences*, abbreviated ds–*Archimedean*, if and only if each bounded difference sequence is finite.

---

[5]The proof of this follows from the methods of proof used in Lemmas 2.4.8 and 2.4.9 of Narens (1985) or from similar theorems of Cohen and Narens (1979), which show how to translate Archimedean-like conditions of the structure to its automorphism group and vice versa.

Note that this third concept of Archimedeanness is defined for all concatenation structures, including positive ones. Thus, one would like to know, for various general classes of positive structures, the implication relationships among the three Archimedean axioms. Observe that the standard sequence definition really has bite only if the operation is quite generally defined, whereas the difference sequence definition has bite only if the structure is *solvable* in the sense that, given x, $y \in x$ with $x < y$, there exist z, z' in X such that $x \bigcirc z = z' \bigcirc x = y$.

2.7   Relations Among Three Concepts of Archimedeanness

Two additional definitions are needed to formulate what is known about the relations among the three kinds of Archimedean axioms thus far considered: $\mathscr{X} = \langle X, \succsim, \bigcirc \rangle$ is said to be *uniformly, restrictedly right solvable* if and only if, for each x, y, r, s in X with $x < y$ and $r < s$, there exists z in X such that for all u in X for which $r \precsim u \precsim s$, $(u \bigcirc x) \bigcirc z \precsim u \bigcirc y$. The n–copy operator nx (n a positive integer) is said to be *operation preserving* if and only if, for all x, y in X, $n(x \bigcirc y) = nx \bigcirc ny$.

THEOREM 2.2 (Luce, 1987, Theorem 3.3) *Suppose $\mathscr{X}$ is a positive concatenation structure.*

   (i). *If $\mathscr{X}$ is uniformly, restrictedly right solvable, then ss–Archimedeanness implies ds–Archimedeanness.*

   (ii). *If $\mathscr{X}$ is right solvable, then ds–Archimedeanness implies ss–Archimedeanness.*

   (iii). *Suppose $\mathscr{X}$ is restrictedly right solvable and the n–copy operators are operation preserving for each positive integer n. Then the following is true:*

   (a) *ss–Archimedeanness implies sd–Archimedeanness;*
       and

   (b) *if $\mathscr{X}$ is order dense, then sd–Archimedeanness implies ss–Archimedeanness.*

It is worth noting that $\mathscr{E}_2$ (Example 2) is *ss*–Archimedean but not *ds*–Archimedean.

The next result establishes that, on the continuum, solvability is sufficient to get *ss*– and *ds*–Archimedeanness.

THEOREM 2.3 (Luce & Narens, 1985, Theorem 2.1) *Suppose $\mathscr{X}$ is a Dedekind complete concatenation structure. If $\mathscr{X}$ is positive and right solvable, then $\mathscr{X}$ is ss–Archimedean. If $\mathscr{X}$ is (right and left) solvable, then $\mathscr{X}$ is ds–Archimedean.*

3. CLASSIFICATION OF AUTOMORPHISM GROUPS

3.1 Automorphism Groups of PCSs

One of the more striking discoveries about concatenation structures that are positive, ss–Archimedean, and restrictedly right solvable—the so-called PCSs—is that the Archimedeanness of the structure devolves to the important algebraic structure called the automorphism group, where an *automorphism* is an isomorphism of a structure with itself. (Physicists call automorphisms "symmetries" of the structure.) Under function composition, the set of all automorphisms forms a mathematical group (closed and associative operation, an identity, and inverses). Moreover, a partial order can be imposed on the group in terms of the asymptotic behavior of the automorphisms as follows: if α and β are automorphisms, then $\alpha \succeq' \beta$ if and only if there exists some x in X such that, for all $y > x$, $\alpha(y) \succeq \beta(y)$. The relation $\succeq'$ is called the *asymptotic ordering* of the automorphism group. For PCSs, one can in fact show that $\succeq'$ is connected and much more:

THEOREM 3.1 (Cohen & Narens, 1979, Theorem 2.3) *If $\mathscr{X}$ is a PCS, then its automorphism group together with its asymptotic ordering is an Archimedean ordered group.*

Thus, by Hölder's (1901) theorem, the automorphism group is isomorphic to a subgroup of the additive reals, and, therefore, it has a very simple structure, including being commutative. This comes as somewhat of a surprise, because PCSs are moderately weak structures when compared to the ordered structures generally encountered in algebra. Of course the most irregular of them have no automorphisms aside from the identity. In addition, some, for example,

$$x \bigcirc y = x + y + (xy)^2,$$

which from many points of view are highly regular, also have no nontrivial automorphisms.

One can view a great deal of the recent work in measurement theory as exhibiting two major thrusts. The one that we are reporting on here attempts to gain a deeper understanding of the conditions for which some version of Theorem 3.1 holds for general relational structures other than PCSs. Although much is now known about this, there are still major gaps to be filled in. For example, we still cannot say anything general about the automorphism groups of arbitrary idempotent structures. Only by imposing additional restrictions do we get results of interest (see Sections 3.2, 4.1, and 4.6), both for concatenation structures and for much more general ones.

The other approach is based on the fact that a good deal is known about the possible automorphism groups for structures defined on the continuum (see

Theorem 6.4). The strategy followed is to accept some fairly weak structural assumptions (e.g., those of a concatenation structure) and then attempt to characterize the resulting kinds of structures in terms of the possible kinds of automorphism groups. Such a strategy is effective because the automorphism groups are highly constrained, as is formulated in Theorem 6.4. This approach has been carried out to some extent for concatenation (see Theorem 4.3) and conjoint structures (Luce & Narens, 1985).

3.2   Dilations, Translations, Homogeneity, and Uniqueness

$\mathscr{X} = \langle X, \succsim, S_j \rangle_{j \in J}$ is said to be an *ordered relational structure* if X is a set, $\succsim$ is a weak ordering of X (that is, a transitive and connected relation on X), J is a set of integers, and, for each $j \in J$, S_j is a relation on X of finite order. As was noted above, an automorphism of $\mathscr{X}$ is any isomorphism of the structure with itself.

The most important classifications of automorphisms of a continuum so far discovered are of three main types. The first is the distinction between *dilations,* which are automorphisms with at least one fixed point (i.e., an element a in X such that $\alpha(a) = a$), and the *translations,* which are those with no fixed point. It is convenient to treat the identity map as both a dilation and a degenerate translation. In terms of the familiar (nonnegative) affine transformations of the real numbers, the dilations are of the form $\alpha(x) = rx + s$, where r is positive and $\neq 1$, or $r = 1$, and $s = 0$, and the translations are of the form $\alpha(x) = x + s$. The major distinction between the two types of transformations is that, in terms of the asymptotic ordering, the translations are all infinitesimal relative to each dilation with $r > 1$. Furthermore, in terms of the asymptotic order and function composition, the translations with $s > 0$ form a solvable ss–Archimedean extensive structure (or, put in algebraic terms, the entire set of translations form an *Archimedean ordered group*). In the case of PCSs, all automorphisms are translations.

The second distinction has to do with the scope of the action of the automorphism group or, put another way, with the extent to which symmetries exist. A subset $\mathscr{H}$ of automorphisms is said to be *M–point homogeneous* if and only if for each pair of similarly strictly ordered M–tuples of elements, there is an automorphism that maps the one M–tuple into the other. If the entire automorphism group is M–point homogeneous, then the structure itself is said to be M–point homogeneous. A structure that is M–point homogeneous for some $M \geq 1$ is called *homogeneous*. In terms of the nonnegative affine transformations as the automorphism group of some structure, the translations are 1–point homogeneous, and the group itself is 2–point homogeneous.

The third distinction has to do with the level of redundancy in the automorphism group. A subset $\mathscr{H}$ of automorphisms is said to be *N–point unique* if and only if whenever two automorphisms agree at N or more distinct points, then they agree everywhere. A structure is said to be *unique* if its automorphism group is N–point unique for some finite N. In terms of the nonnegative affine group, the translations are 1–point unique and the entire group is 2–point unique.

If the largest degree of homogeneity of a structure is M and the least degree of uniqueness is N, then the automorphism group is said to be of *scale type* (M, N). Thus, a homogeneous PCS, which can be shown to be isomorphic to a real PCS with all translations as its automorphism group (Cohen and Narens, 1979), is of scale type $(1, 1)$. Any structure with the entire nonnegative affine group as its automorphism group is of scale type $(2, 2)$.

A major question is to understand fully the types of measurement structures that can arise in the sense of classifying the possible automorphism groups and then developing a description of classes of structures having those groups. This has been completed for all homogeneous and unique structures on the positive real numbers (Theorem 6.4) and is partially done for more general structures in which the translations form, as they do in the case just mentioned, a group that is both $(1, 1)$ and Archimedean ordered. We first look into these questions for concatenation structures and then move on to more general ones.

4. HOMOGENEOUS, UNIQUE CONCATENATION STRUCTURES

4.1 Two General Results

Our first result classifies both the structures and scale types that are possible for homogeneous and unique concatenation structures.

> **THEOREM 4.1** (Luce & Narens, 1985, Theorem 2.2) *Suppose $\mathcal{X}$ is a homogeneous concatenation structure. Then $\mathcal{X}$ is either idempotent, weakly positive (for all x, $x \bigcirc x > x$), or weakly negative (for all x, $x \bigcirc x < x$). If $\mathcal{X}$ is also unique, then either $N = 1$ or both $N = 2$ and $\mathcal{X}$ is idempotent.*

We see, therefore, that, for homogeneous and unique concatenation structures, the possible scale types are just $(1, 1)$, $(1, 2)$, and $(2, 2)$. At this level of generality, aside from the PCS case (Theorem 3.1), we know very little about the structure of the automorphism group. In particular, we would like to know when the translations form an Archimedean ordered group. One reason for interest in this question is the following:

> **THEOREM 4.2** (Luce, 1987, Theorem 3.5) *Suppose $\mathcal{X}$ is a concatenation structure for which the set of translations forms a homogeneous, Archimedean-ordered group. Then the structure is ds–Archimedean and, if it is positive, it is also ss–Archimedean.*

As we shall see in Section 6, under these conditions, any ordered relational structure has a numerical representation of a particular type.

Before turning to such structures, some comment needs to be made about what it means to assume the translations form an ordered group. The group property can easily be shown to be equivalent to assuming the translations are 1–point unique (Luce, 1986, Theorem 2.1). The assumption that the asymptotic order is a total order is tantamount to assuming that the translations do not *cross* in the sense that there are x and y such that $\gamma(x) > x$ and $\gamma(y) < y$. (In the order-dense, Dedekind complete case, such crossing is impossible because it implies the automorphism has a fixed point.)

4.2   Unit Concatenation Structures

In the case of a homogeneous, unique concatenation structure on the positive reals—the Dedekind complete case—the operation has a particularly simple form:

THEOREM 4.3 (Cohen & Narens, 1979; Luce & Narens, 1985, Theorems 3.9, 3.12, and 3.13) *Suppose $\mathfrak{R} = \langle Re^+, \geq, \bigcirc \rangle$ is a concatenation structure that is homogeneous and unique. Then there is a function f from Re^+ onto Re^+ that is strictly increasing, $f(x)/x$ is strictly decreasing, and the operation $\odot$ defined by $x \odot y = yf(x/y)$ is such that $\mathfrak{R}$ is isomorphic to $\langle Re^+, \geq, \odot \rangle$.*

Cohen and Narens (1979) called this kind of representation a *unit* (concatenation) *structure*. (They dealt only with the positive case; however, their methods and concepts extend to the general case, and this is expressed in Theorem 4.3.) The translations are simply multiplication by positive constants, and so they form an Archimedean-ordered group and Theorem 4.2 applies. It is easy to verify that the n–copy operators are of the form $nx = xf^{n-1}(1)$, and, thus, each is an automorphism. In particular, $n(x\bigcirc y) = nx\bigcirc ny$. Section 6 will generalize the concept of unit structures to general ordered relational structures.

For this class of structures, the following is true:

THEOREM 4.4 (Luce, 1987, Corollary to Theorem 3.3) *Suppose $\mathfrak{X}$ is a positive (homogeneous) unit concatenation structure. Then, in addition to being ds– and ss–Archimedean, it is sd–Archimedean.*

5.   INTRINSIC ARCHIMEDEANNESS:
A POSSIBLE DEFINITION

Examples 3 and 4, and even more pathological ones that can be easily devised, quickly lead one to the following conclusion: *In an intrinsically Archimedean structure, every reasonable positive operation that is definable from the primitives should be sd–Archimedean.* Of course, for this assertion to be effective, "reasonable" and "definable" need to be given precise definitions—which will be done shortly.

First, we consider what we might mean by reasonable. As Example 2 shows, ss–Archimedeanness and positivity by themselves are not effective in eliminating infinitesimally close elements in a concatenation structure. Therefore, some additional or stronger conditions are needed. Theorem 2.3 suggests that right-restricted solvability might suffice. However, it is, in general, too strong a condition because there are structures with positive operations that are clearly Archimedean and are not right restrictedly solvable. As a case in point, consider the following:

EXAMPLE 6. $\mathscr{E}_6 = \langle Re^+, \geq, \oplus' \rangle$, where, for all x, y, z in Re^+, $x \oplus' y = z$ if and only if $2x + 2y = z$. In this structure, $1.5 > 1$, but $1 \oplus' w > 1.5$ for all w in Re^+.

The condition we shall focus upon in this chapter for capturing intrinsic Archimedeanness is homogeneity. At present, we do not have an adequate theory of intrinsic Archimedeanness for nonhomogeneous cases. For homogeneous structures with positive operations $\bigcirc$ on the continuum, we know, by the remarks following Theorem 4.3, that the equation $n(x\bigcirc y) = nx\bigcirc ny$ is valid for all elements x and y of the domain and all positive integers n. Furthermore, because of this and the earlier discussion of the sd–Archimedean axioms, we feel somewhat confident about invoking the sd–Archimedean axiom as a necessary condition for intrinsic Archimedeanness in homogeneous situations with positive operations. (Observe that $\mathscr{E}_6$ above is homogeneous and sd–Archimedean.) With these considerations in mind, we will, for homogeneous structures, adopt sd–Archimedeanness of definable positive operations as a critical characteristic of intrinsic Archimedeanness. However, it should be noted that, in some circumstances, this requirement is empty because there may be no positive operation definable from the primitive relations that make up the structure.

Second, we consider what we might mean by definable. Although there is no agreed upon general definition of what it means for a relation—in particular, an operation—to be definable in terms of given relations, for a number of specific concepts, it can be shown that the defined relation must be invariant under the automorphisms of the given structure, and it is widely agreed that any general definition should exhibit this property. Of course there may be invariant relations that are not definable, e.g., the relation may only exist through the Axiom of Choice. We make the invariance condition explicit.

Let $\mathscr{X}$ and $\mathscr{C}$ be structures that have a common domain D. Then $\mathscr{C}$ is said to be *invariant under the automorphisms of* $\mathscr{X}$ if and only if, for each automorphism β of $\mathscr{X}$, each n–ary primitive relation R of C and each $a_1, \ldots, a_n$ in D, the following is satisfied:

$$R(a_1, \ldots, a_n) \text{ iff } R[\beta(a_1), \ldots, \beta(a_n)].$$

If the primitives of $\mathscr{C}$ are defined from the primitives of $\mathscr{X}$ through first-order, second-order, or any higher-order logic, then it can be proved that $\mathscr{C}$ is invariant under the automorphisms of $\mathscr{X}$. (For a detailed description of the relationships between definability concepts and invariance, see Narens, 1988.) Thus, the structures with domain D that are "definable" from $\mathscr{X}$ are a subset of those that are invariant under the automorphisms of $\mathscr{X}$. Further, because of this inclusion, invariance under automorphisms is a good generalization of first-order, second-order, and so forth definablity.

A structure $\mathscr{X} = \langle X, \gtrsim, R_1, \ldots \rangle$ is said to be *intrinsically z–Archimedean*, where $z = ss, sd,$ or $ds,$ if and only if the following hold:

1. $\langle X, \gtrsim \rangle$ is a continuum.
2. There exists a (positive) operation on X that is z–Archimedean and invariant under the automorphisms of $\mathscr{X}$.
3. Any other (positive) operation on X that is invariant under the automorphisms of $\mathscr{X}$ is also z–Archimedean.

The following striking theorem can be shown.

THEOREM 5.1 *Suppose* $\mathscr{X} = \langle X, \gtrsim, R_1, \ldots \rangle$, *the automorphisms of $\mathscr{X}$ form a homogeneous, Archimedean-ordered group, and* $\langle X, \gtrsim \rangle$ *is a continuum. Then $\mathscr{X}$ is intrinsically* ss-, sd-, *and* ds-*Archimedean.*

Theorem 5.1 is an immediate consequence of Theorems 4.2, 4.3, and 4.4.

Although Theorem 5.1 covers some important cases, others are not covered. First, there are weakly positive structures that fail to be positive, so they are not covered. Some, such as Example 5, are decidedly ambiguous as to ss–Archimedeanness. Second, there are homogeneous idempotent structures for which no positive concatenation structure is automorphism invariant because they are of scale type (1, 2) or (2, 2). Some of these structures are remarkably Archimedean, as, for example, $\langle Re, \geq, \bigcirc \rangle$, where $x \bigcirc y = \frac{1}{2}(x + y)$. For these, we can at best expect to arrive at ds–Archimedeanness. Toward that end, the next section investigates the consequences of a relational structure having a homogeneous, Archimedean ordered group of translations.

6.   HOMOGENEOUS, ORDERED RELATIONAL STRUCTURES

The main result of this section characterizes, in terms of a particularly nice kind of numerical representation, those general, ordered relational structures whose translations form a homogeneous, Archimedean ordered group. As we saw in Theorem 4.2, these conditions on the translations of a concatenation structure imply ds–Archimedeanness and, as will be seen shortly, lead to a numerical representation (which is one of the major reasons for invoking Archimedeanness); therefore, it is possible that, for homogeneous structures, the property of the translations forming an Archimedean ordered group is a suitable generalization of Archimedean operations. An ultimate decision on this awaits a deeper understanding of Archimedeanness at the structural level when no operation is present as a primitive, which is partially clarified in Theorem 6.5.

6.1 Real Unit Structures

To formulate the main result of the section, we need to give a generalization of the concept of a real unit structure, introduced for PCSs by Cohen and Narens (1979) and later generalized to all concatenation structures on Re^+ by Luce and Narens (1985) (see Theorem 4.3 of Section 4.2). We continue to use the same term in the general case.

Suppose $\mathfrak{R} = \langle R, \geq, R_j \rangle_{j \in J}$, where $R \subseteq Re^+$, is a numerical relational structure. $\mathfrak{R}$ is said to be a *real unit structure* if and only if there exists $T \subseteq Re^+$ such that the following conditions are met:

1. T is a group under multiplication.
2. T maps R into R.
3. T restricted to R is the set of translations of $\mathfrak{R}$.

THEOREM 6.1 [Luce, 1987, Theorem 5.1.(i) and (ii)] *Suppose $\mathfrak{X}$ is an ordered relational structure. Then $\mathfrak{X}$ is isomorphic to a real unit structure with a homogeneous group of translations if and only if the translations of $\mathfrak{X}$ together with the asymptotic ordering form a homogeneous, Archimedean-ordered group.*

COROLLARY. *If, in addition, $\mathfrak{X}$ is order dense, then the automorphism group of its unit representation is a subgroup of the nonnegative affine group restricted to R.*

As we saw in Theorem 4.3, real unit concatenation structures have a particularly nice form.

A further equivalence to the translations forming a homogeneous, Archimedean ordered group, one that is of great relevance to dimensional analysis, is given in Section 6.4.

6.2 Dedekind Complete, Ordered, Relational Structures

As we pointed out in the introduction, Archimedeanness captures the commensurability but not the completeness (as far as limits of bounded sequences go) of the real numbers. That is embodied in the idea of Dedekind completeness (or equivalently the existence of least upper bounds within the domain). In this section, we explore that property as a source of structure and how it interrelates with homogeneity and uniqueness.

> **THEOREM 6.2** (Luce, 1987, Theorem 4.1) *Suppose* $\mathfrak{R} = \langle R, \geq, R_j \rangle_{j \in J}$ *is a real unit structure. Then the following are true:*
>
> (i). *$\mathfrak{R}$ can be densely imbedded in a Dedekind complete unit structure $\mathfrak{R}^*$, where this imbedding is the identity.*
>
> (ii). *Each automorphism of $\mathfrak{R}$ extends to an automorphism of $\mathfrak{R}^*$.*
>
> (iii). *If the group T of translations of $\mathfrak{R}$ is homogeneous, then the domain of $\mathfrak{R}^*$ is Re^+, and the group T^* of translations of $\mathfrak{R}^*$ is homogeneous.*

The next result gives a condition in the Dedekind complete case that leads to the translations being Archimedean.

> **THEOREM 6.3** (Luce, 1986, Theorem 2.4; Luce, 1987, Theorem 2.1) *Suppose $\mathfrak{X}$ is a Dedekind complete, ordered relational structure. If the translations form a group (i.e., are 1-point unique) and are uncrossed, then they form an Archimedean ordered group. A sufficient condition for them to be uncrossed is that $\mathfrak{X}$ also be order dense.*

If homogeneity is also satisfied, then we know by Theorem 6.1 that the structure is isomorphic to a homogeneous unit structure.

Our last result on Dedekind complete structures considers what happens when we add the further condition that the structure is unique. We do not know very much about the uniqueness of general real unit structures, but in the homogeneous case, we have strong results. (Note that the following theorem states that the translations form a group, which is surprisingly hard to show.)

> **THEOREM 6.4** (Alper, 1987, Theorem 3.10) *Suppose $\mathfrak{X}$ is a relational structure that is Dedekind complete, order-dense, homogeneous, and unique. Then the translations form a homogeneous, Archimedean ordered group, and $\mathfrak{X}$ is isomorphic to a real unit structure that has a subgroup of the nonnegative affine transformations as its automorphism group. Thus, the structure is 1- or 2-point unique.*

This important result is the culmination of work begun by Narens (1981a, 1981b) for the (M, M) scale types and extended by Alper (1985) to the $(M, M + 1)$ case. What it shows is that homogeneous and unique structures that can be mapped onto the reals are of just three scale types—(1, 1) or ratio scale, (2, 2) or interval scale, and the in-between (1, 2) case. An example of the later is the group of discrete interval scales of the form $x \rightarrow k^n x + s$, where $k > 0$ is fixed and n ranges over the integers.

It is clear, especially in view of Theorem 6.1, that we should try to gain a better understanding of the uniqueness of homogeneous, real unit structures whose domains are not Re^+.

6.3   Intrinsic *ds*–Archimedeanness

We may use the previous results, in particular Theorems 4.3, the corollary to Theorem 6.1, and Theorem 6.4, to get the following, quite general characterization of intrinsic *ds*–Archimedeanness.

> **THEOREM 6.5** *Suppose* $\mathfrak{X} = \langle X, \succeq, R_j \rangle_{j \in J}$ *is a relational structure that is homogeneous and finitely unique, and suppose* $\langle X, \succeq \rangle$ *is a continuum. Then* $\mathfrak{X}$ *is intrinsically ds–Archimedean.*

It is important to note that, for the property of *ds*–Archimedeanness to be nontrivial, it is necessary that an unbounded *ds*–sequence exist, and, for that to be so, some form of solvability must be satisfied. This means that Theorems 6.5 and 5.1, although apparently parallel, have somewhat different significance, because, in the positive case, both *ss*– and *ds*–sequences always exist.

It should also be pointed out that we do not have any generalization of Theorem 6.5 to, for example, structures that are not homogeneous but whose translations continue to form an Archimedean ordered group or to structures not on a continuum. Presumably some of these should continue to be considered to be Archimedean in some sense.

6.4   Distribution of Unit Structures in Conjoint Ones

Suppose $\mathscr{C} = \langle X \times P, \succeq \rangle$, where $\succeq$ is a weak ordering (i.e., transitive and connected) of $X \times P$. $\mathscr{C}$ is said to be a *conjoint structure* if and only if $\succeq$ exhibits monotonicity in each of the two factors (this is often called "independence") and, therefore, in an obvious way, induces weak orderings $\succeq_X$ on X and $\succeq_P$ on P. A sequence $\{x_i\}$ from X is said to be *standard* if and only if there are p, q in P that are not equivalent under $\sim_p$ such that, for x_i and x_{i+1} in the sequence, $(x_{i+1}, p) \sim (x_i, q)$. $\mathscr{C}$ is said to be *Archimedean* if and only if each bounded standard sequence is finite. There are a number of notions of solvability for conjoint structures, the simplest and strongest being that, given any three of x, y in X and p, q in P, the fourth exists that solves the equivalence $(x, p) \sim (y, q)$. This form is called *unrestricted solvability* (Luce and Tukey, 1964).

There have been two lines of work connecting conjoint structures with other structures. One, which we do not go into here, involves recoding the information embodied in the conjoint structure as an operation on one of its components. In the Archimedean case, these operations are very closely connected to PCSs, and the whole problem of representing conjoint structures numerically is readily reduced to that of PCSs.

The other line of work has been a series of gradually more general results of the following character: Suppose that one of the factors, say X, of an Archimedean conjoint structure has on it a homogeneous structure with a homomorphism ϕ onto a real unit structure. Suppose, further, that this structure is suitably interconnected with the conjoint one according to a concept of distribution. Then the conjoint one is necessarily an "additive conjoint structure" with a multiplicative representation of the form $\phi\psi$. This was first shown to hold when that structure on X is extensive and distribution is defined for operations (Narens, 1976; Narens & Luce, 1976); it was next extended to PCSs (Narens, 1981a; Luce & Cohen, 1983) and then further clarified for general closed concatenation structures (Luce & Narens, 1985) and ultimately put in the form given below for homogeneous real unit structures (Luce, 1987). The interest in the result is mainly embodied in the second result of this section that shows how the structure of physical units can be extended to incorporate these unit structures.

To state the results, we first formulate, in a very general fashion, the notion of a structure on one component being compatible with the conjoint structure. Two n–tuples of X, $(x_1, \ldots, x_n)$ and $(y_1, \ldots, y_n)$, are said to be *similar* in $\mathscr{C}$ if and only if there exist p, q in P such that, for each $i = 1, \ldots, n$, $(x_i, p) \sim (y_i, q)$. (For example, any n–term subsequence of successive terms of a standard sequence and the subsequence obtained by shifting the indices up by one are similar.) Note that similarity is not transitive. Let S be a relation of order n on X. S is said to *distribute* in $\mathscr{C}$ if and only if, for each similar pair of n–tuples, when one is in S, then so is the other. An ordered relational structure $\mathscr{X} = \langle X, \succsim_X, S_j \rangle_{j \in J}$ is said to distribute in $\mathscr{C}$ if and only if, for each j in J, S_j distributes in $\mathscr{C}$. (Note it is easy to show that $\succsim_X$ always distributes in $\mathscr{C}$.)

THEOREM 6.6 [Luce, 1987, Theorem 5.1.(ii) and (iii)] *Suppose $\mathscr{X}$ is a densely ordered relational structure and its set of translations, $\mathscr{T}$, forms a group. Then $\mathscr{T}$ is a homogeneous, Archimedean ordered group if and only if there exists an Archimedean, solvable, conjoint structure C and a relational structure $\mathscr{X}'$ on X such that $\mathscr{X}$ and $\mathscr{X}'$ are isomorphic and $\mathscr{X}'$ distributes in C. In this case, C satisfies the Thomsen condition[6] leading to a multiplicative representation.*

Note that the condition of $\mathscr{T}$ being a homogeneous, Archimedean ordered group is identical to that of Theorem 6.1, and, therefore, it says that a homogeneous, real unit structure is distributive in some multiplicative conjoint structure. Thus, the two results bring together three important ideas—real unit structures, distribution in a conjoint structure, and Archimedean ordered translations—that are not obviously linked, and it shows that, in the homogeneous case, they are equivalent ideas.

Perhaps the most important aspect of this is that it makes clear the circum-

---

[6] If $(x, r) \sim (u, q)$ and $(u, p) \sim (y, r)$, then $(x, p) \sim (y, q)$.

stances under which nonadditive, numerical scales can be introduced into the dimensional structure of physics. To this end, we have the following result.

THEOREM 6.7 (Luce, 1987, Theorem 5.2). *Suppose* $\mathcal{C} = \langle X \times P, \gtrsim \rangle$ *is a conjoint structure that is solvable and Archimedean. Suppose, further, that* $\mathcal{X} = \langle X, \gtrsim_X, S_j \rangle_{j \in J}$ *is a relational structure whose translations form an Archimedean ordered group.*

(i). *If* $\mathcal{X}$ *is distributive in* $\mathcal{C}$, *then* $\mathcal{X}$ *is 1–point homogeneous and* $\mathcal{C}$ *satisfies the Thomsen condition.*

(ii). *If, in addition,* $\mathcal{X}$ *is Dedekind complete and order dense, then, under some mapping* ϕ *from X onto* Re^+, $\mathcal{X}$ *has a homogeneous unit representation and there exists a mapping* ψ *from P into* Re^+ *such that* $\phi\psi$ *is a representation of* $\mathcal{C}$.

(iii). *If, further, there is a Dedekind complete relational structure on P that distributes in an analogous way in* $\mathcal{C}$ *and there exists a homogeneous unit representation* ψ, *then there exists a real constant* ρ *such that* $\phi\psi^\rho$ *is a representation of* $\mathcal{C}$.

This yields the familiar representation of units of measurement as products of powers of other units that underlies the method of dimensional analysis (see Krantz, Luce, Suppes, & Tversky, 1971, chapter 10; Luce, 1978).

7. NON-ARCHIMEDEAN STRUCTURES

We will now discuss very briefly some of the metamathematical results that apply to the axiomatization of Archimedean structures. The first, and perhaps the most profound, is that Archimedeanness can never be expressed or even implied through first-order sentences. The proof is a very straightforward consequence of the Löwenheim–Skolem Theorem[7] of mathematical logic and does not depend in any interesting way on the particular concept of Archimedeanness used.

Let $\mathcal{X} = \langle X, \gtrsim, R_1, \ldots, R_n \rangle$ be an ordered relational structure. To make matters interesting, we assume X is infinite. Let $\mathcal{L} = \mathcal{L}(\gtrsim, R_1, \ldots, R_n)$ be a first-order language that describes $\mathcal{X}$. Then, by the Upward Löwenheim–Skolem Theorem, it follows that there exists a class $\mathcal{M}$ of models of $\mathcal{L}$ of arbitrarily high cardinality that have exactly the same true statements in $\mathcal{L}$ as $\mathcal{X}$. Because $\mathcal{X}$ is totally ordered and a "total ordering" is expressible in $\mathcal{L}$, it follows that each model in $\mathcal{M}$ that has cardinality greater than the reals cannot be imbedded in a structure based on the reals, and, therefore, cannot be imbedded in any structure based on a continuum. Thus, in particular, they cannot be imbedded in any intrinsic Archimedean structure. Imbeddability into an intrinsic Archimedean structure is taken as an essential condition of Archimedeanness; therefore, it

---

[7]Exact statement and proof of the Löweheim–Skolem Theorem can be found in Narens (1985), Skala (1975), and Robinson (1963).

follows that those elements of $\mathcal{M}$ with domains of high cardinalities cannot be Archimedean. Furthermore, it is easy to show that there exists arbitrarily large $\mathcal{X}'$ $= \langle X', \gtrsim', R_1', \ldots, R_n' \rangle$ in $\mathcal{M}$ (i.e., those that are "not cofinal with ω") such that, for each strictly increasing, positive operation $\bigcirc$ on X' and each x in X', there exists y in X' such that, for all positive integers n, $y >' nx$. (Note that it is not assumed that $\bigcirc$ is monotonic or invariant under automorphisms of $\mathcal{X}'$.)

The previous results show that no reasonable concept of Archimedeanness can be captured in a first-order way. Thus, those who hold that empirical concepts can always be formulated in a first-order language must accept Archimedeanness as being necessarily nonempirical.

The assumption of Archimedeanness, however, often has empirical consequences. The class $\mathcal{C}$ of positive, associative, restrictedly solvable concatenation structures is a good example of this. This class is axiomatizable through a first-order language. Some of the structures in $\mathcal{C}$ are Archimedean and represent widely used, important empirical situations; others are non-Archimedean. The following can be shown: (a) for structures in $\mathcal{C}$, ss–Archimedeanness implies commutativity, and (b) there are structures in $\mathcal{C}$ that are not commutative. Note that it follows from (a) and (b) that, for elements of $\mathcal{C}$, noncommutativity—a first-order and often an empirically verifiable condition—implies non-Archimedeanness. However, it can also be shown (using the Robinson model completeness test) that the subclass $\mathcal{D}$ of elements of $\mathcal{C}$ that are divisible—that is, first-order statements of the form $\forall x \, \exists \, y(ny = x)$ are true for all positive integers n—commutative and solvable have the same first-order consequences in the presence of the assumption of Archimedeanness as they would without it. In fact, it can be shown that the theory $\mathcal{D}$ is complete in the sense that a first-order sentence is true about one of its elements if and only if it is true about all of its elements.

The upshot of these results can be summarized as follows. If we take first-order expressibility as a necessary characteristic of empirical, then we have the following: (a) Archimedeanness (in an infinite setting) is never an empirical consequence; (b) non-Archimedeanness is sometimes an empirical consequence; (c) in some empirical situations, the assumption of Archimedeanness adds new empirical consequences; and (d) in some empirical situations, the assumption of Archimedeanness adds no new empirical consequences. Clearly statement (d) characterizes a highly desirable state of affairs. We do not know, however, how generally it applies to situations that one is likely to encounter in science.

8.   CONCLUSIONS

The issue addressed in this paper is what Archimedeanness might mean for ordered structures that may not include operations. The solution proposed first involves defining the intrinsically Archimedean structures. These we take to have continua as domains. Structures that are densely imbeddable in them are considered to be the Archimedean ones, or, in other words, a structure is said to be Archimedean if and only if it has a Dedekind completion that is an intrinsic Archimedean structure. Therefore, the issue is what the latter means.

Intrinsically Archimedean structures we take to be ones to which we can adjoin operations that have two essential features: (a) They have enough structure themselves to be viewed as Archimedean (e.g., they are monotonic and satisfy some strong form of Archimedeanness); and (b) they are invariant under the automorphisms of the given structure. The justification for (b) rests on the observation that all operations definable in terms of the primitives of the structure are invariant under the automorphisms of the structure, so such invariance can be viewed as a generalization of definability.

For homogeneous structures on the continuum, we argue that the class of unit structures are suitable for testing the Archimedeanness of the given structure. In the positive case, these structures can be shown to satisfy all three versions of Archimedeanness that have been proposed for positive structures: in standard sequences, in standard differences, and in difference sequences. In the idempotent case, we do not have equally satisfactory results, partly because our current concepts of Archimedeanness for this case are nontrivial only if a solvability condition is satisfied.

With these unit structures as our criterion, it can then be shown that a homogeneous ordered structure on a continuum is Archimedean if and only if its translations (i.e., automorphisms with no fixed point plus the identity) form an Archimedean ordered group (where the group ordering is naturally induced from the ordering of the structure). This kind of structure has been shown to have nice numerical representations and to be exactly the class of structures that can be incorporated into the structure of dimensions that arose in classical physics.

Although we have succeeded in pinning down a general and sensible concept of Archimedeanness for those structures that can be extended to a homogeneous structure on a continuum, we do not at this time know much at all about the Archimedeanness of structures that cannot be so extended.

ACKNOWLEDGMENTS

This work has been supported by National Science Foundation Grant IST–8602765 to Harvard University.

REFERENCES

Alper, T. M. (1985). A note on real measurement structures of scale type (m, m + 1), *Journal of Mathematical Psychology, 29,* 73–81.

Alper, T. M. (1987). A classification of all order-preserving homeomorphism groups of the reals that satisfy finite uniqueness. *Journal of Mathematical Psychology, 31*, 135–154.

Cantor, G. (1985). Beiträge zur Begründung der Transfiniten Mengenlehre. (Contribution to the foundations of the theory of transfinite quantities.) *Mathematische Annalen, 46*, 481–512.

Cohen, M. (1986). Unpublished research.

Cohen, M., & Narens, L. (1979). Fundamental unit structures: a theory of ratio scalability. *Journal of Mathematical Psychology, 20*, 193–232.

Fuchs, L. (1963). *Partially ordered algebraic systems.* Reading, MA: Addison-Wesley.

Hölder, O. (1901). Die Axiome der Quantität und die Lehre vom Mass. (The axioms of quantity and the theory of mass.) *Berichte über die Verhandlungen der Königlich Sächsischen Gesellschaft der Wissenschaften zu Leipzig, Mathematische-Physiche Klass, 53*, 1–64.

Krantz, D. H., Luce, R. D., Suppes, P., & Tversky, A. (1971). *Foundations of Measurement* (Vol. 1). New York: Academic Press.

Loonstra, F. (1946). Ordered Groups. *Proceedings Koninklijke Nederlandse Akademie van Wetenschappen, 49*, 41–46.

Luce, R. D. (1978). Dimensionally invariant numerical laws correspond to meaningful qualitative relations. *Philosophy of Science, 45*, 1–16.

Luce, R. D. (1986). Uniqueness and homogeneity of ordered relational structures. *Journal of Mathematical Psychology. 30*, 391–415.

Luce, R. D. (1987). Measurement structures with Archimedean ordered translation groups. *Order, 4*, 165–189.

Luce, R. D., & Cohen, M. (1983). Factorizable automorphisms in solvable conjoint structures I. *Journal of Pure and Applied Algebra, 27*, 225–261.

Luce, R. D., Krantz, D. H., Suppes, P., and Tversky, A. (1990). *Foundations of Measurement, Vol. 3*, New York: Academic Press.

Luce, R. D., & Narens, L. (1985). Classification of concatenation measurement structures according to scale type. *Journal of Mathematical Psychology, 29*, 1–72.

Luce, R. D., & Tukey, J. W. (1964). Simultaneous conjoint measurement: a new type of fundamental measurement. *Journal of Mathematical Psychology, 1*, 1–27.

Narens, L. (1976). Utility–uncertainty tradeoff structures. *Journal of Mathematical Psychology, 13*, 296–322.

Narens, L. (1981a). A general theory of ratio scalability with remarks about the measurement-theoretic concept of meaningfulness. *Theory and Decision, 13*, 1–70.

Narens, L. (1981b). On the scales of measurement. *Journal of Mathematical Psychology, 24*, 249–275.

Narens, L. (1985). *Abstract measurement theory.* Cambridge, MA: MIT Press.

Narens, L. (1988). Meaningfulness and the Erlanger Program of Felix Klein. *Mathematiques, Informatique et Sciences Humaines, 101*, 61–72.

Narens, L., & Luce, R. D. (1976). The algebra of measurement. *Journal of Pure and Applied Algebra, 8*, 197–233.

Roberts, F. S., & Luce, R. D. (1968). Axiomatic thermodynamics and extensive measurement. *Synthese, 18*, 311–326.

Robinson, A. (1963). *Introduction to model theory and to the metamathematics of algebra.* Amsterdam: North Holland.

Skala, H. J. (1975). *Non-Archimedean utility theory.* Dordrecht: Reidel.

3

Qualitative Axioms for Random-Variable Representation of Extensive Quantities

Patrick Suppes
Mario Zanotti
Stanford University

In the standard theory of fundamental extensive measurement, qualitative axioms are formulated that lead to a numerical assignment unique up to a positive similarity transformation. The central idea of the theory of *random* quantities is to replace the numerical assignment by a random-variable assignment. This means that each object is assigned a random variable. In the case of extensive quantities, the expectation of the random variable replaces the usual numerical assignment, and the distribution of the random variable reflects the variability of the property in question, which could be intrinsic to the object or due to errors of observation. In any case, the existence of distributions with positive variances is almost universal in the actual practice of measurement in most domains of science.

It is a widespread complaint about the foundations of measurement that too little has been written that combines the qualitative structural analysis of measurement procedures and the analysis of variability in a quantity measured or errors in the procedures used. In view of the extraordinarily large number of papers that have been written about the foundations of the theory of error, which go back to the eighteenth century with fundamental work already by Simpson, Lagrange, and Laplace, followed by the important contributions of Gauss, it is surprising that the two kinds of analysis have not received a more intensive consideration. Part of the reason is the fact that, in all of this long history, the literature on the theory of errors has been intrinsically quantitative in character. Specific distributional results have usually been the objective of the analysis, and the assumptions leading to such results have been formulated in quantitative probabilistic terms. This quantitative framework is also assumed in the important series of papers by Falmagne and his collaborators on random-variable representations for interval, conjoint, and extensive measurement (see Falmagne, 1976, 1978, 1979, 1980, 1985; Falmagne & Iverson, 1979; Iverson & Falmagne, 1985).

In light of this long history, we would certainly not want to claim that the various results presented in this chapter solve all the natural kinds of questions that have been in the air for some time. We do believe that we have taken a significant step toward combining in one analysis the qualitative structures characteristic of the foundations of measurement and the probabilistic structures characteristic of the theory of error or the theory of variability.

The approach to the distribution of the representing random variables of an object consists of developing, in the usual style of the theory of measurement, qualitative axioms concerning the *moments* of the distribution, which are represented as expectations of powers of the representing numerical random variable. The first natural question is whether or not there can be a well-defined qualitative procedure for measuring the moments. This is discussed in the first section. Section 2 presents the qualitative primitive concepts and Section 3 the axiom system. The representation theorem and its proof are given in Section 4.

1. VARIABILITY AS MEASURED BY MOMENTS

The approach to the distribution of the representing random variable of an object consists of developing, in the usual style of the theory of measurement, qualitative axioms concerning the *moments* of the distribution, which are represented as expectations of powers of the representing numerical random variable. The classic problem of moments in the theory of probability enters in an essential way in the developments to follow. We lay out in an explicit way the qualitative assumptions about moments that are made.

Before giving the formal developments, we address the measurement of moments from a qualitative standpoint. We outline here one approach without any claim that it is the only way to conceive of the problem. In fact, we believe that the pluralism of approaches to measuring probability is matched by that for measuring moments, for reasons that are obvious given the close connection between the two.

The one approach we outline here corresponds to the limiting relative-frequency characterization of probability, which we formulate here somewhat informally. Let s be an infinite sequence of independent trials with the outcome on each trial being heads or tails. Let $H(i)$ be the number of heads on the first i trials of s. Then, relative to s,

$$P(\text{heads}) = \lim_{i \to \infty} H(i)/i,$$

with the provision that the limit exists and that the sequence s satisfies certain conditions of randomness that need not be analyzed here. In practice, of course, only a finite initial segment of any such sequence is realized as a statistical sample. However, ordinarily in the case of probability, the empirical procedure encompasses several steps. In the approach given here, the first step is to use the limiting relative-frequency characterization. The second step is to produce and analyze a finite sample with appropriate statistical methods.

Our approach to empirical measurement of qualitative moments covers the first step but not the second of giving detailed statistical methods. Thus, let a_0 be an object of small mass of which we have many accurate replicas—so we are assuming here that the variability in a_0 and its replicas, $a_0^{(j)}$, $j = 1,2,\ldots$ are neglible. Then we use replicas of a_0 to qualitatively weigh an object a. On each trial, we force an equivalence, as is customary in classical physics. Thus, on each trial i, we have

$$a \sim \{a_0^{(1)}, a_0^{(2)}, \ldots, a_0^{(m_i)}\}.$$

The set shown on the right we symbolize as $m_i a_0$. Then, as in the case of probability, we characterize a^n, the nth qualitative raw moment of a, by

$$a^n \sim \lim_{j \to \infty} \frac{1}{j} \sum_{i=1}^{j} m_i^n a_0,$$

but, in practice, we use a finite number of trials and use the estimate $\hat{a}^n$:

$$\hat{a}^n \sim \frac{1}{j} \sum_{i=1}^{j} m_i^n a_0,$$

and so also only estimate a finite number of moments. It is not to the point here to spell out the statistical procedures for estimating a^n. Our objective is only to outline how one can approach empirical determination of the qualitative raw moments.

There is one important observation to deal with. The observed data, summarized in the integers $m_1, m_2, \ldots, m_j$, on which the computation of the moments is based, also constitute a histogram of the distribution. Why not estimate the distribution directly? When a distribution of a particular form is postulated, there need be no conflict in the two methods, and the histogram can be of further use in testing goodness of fit.

The reason for working with the raw moments is theoretical rather than empirical or statistical. Various distributions can be qualitatively characterized in terms of their raw moments in a relatively simple way, as the examples in the Corollary to the Representation Theorem show. Furthermore, general qualitative conditions on the moments are given in the Representation Theorem. Alternative qualitative approaches to characterizing distributions undoubtedly exist and as they are developed may well supersede the one used here.

We now turn to the formal developments. In proving the representation theorem for random extensive quantities in this section, we apply a well-known theorem of Hausdorff (1923) on the one-dimensional moment problem for a finite interval.

HAUSDORFF'S THEOREM. *Let* μ_0, μ_1, μ_2, ... *be a sequence of real numbers. Then a necessary and sufficient condition that there exist a unique probability distribution F on* [0, 1] *such that* μ_n *is the* n*th raw moment of the distribution F, that is to say,*

$$\mu_n = \int_0^1 t^n dF, \qquad n = 0,1,2,\ldots , \qquad (1)$$

is that $\mu_0 = 1$ *and all the following inequalities hold*:

$$\mu_\nu - \binom{k}{1}\mu_{\nu+1} + \binom{k}{2}\mu_{\nu+2} + \ldots + (-1)^k\mu_{\nu+k} \geq 0 \text{ for } k,\nu = 0,1,2,\ldots . \quad (2)$$

A standard terminology is that a sequence of numbers μ_n, $n = 0, 1, 2, \ldots$ is *completely monotonic* iff Inequalities (2) are satisfied, in more compact binomial notation $\mu^\nu(1 - \mu)^k \geq 0$, for k, $\nu = 0, 2, \ldots$ (for detailed analysis of many related results on the problem of moments, see Shohat & Tamarkin, 1943).

It is important to note that we do not need an additional separate specification of the domain of definition of the probability distribution in Hausdorff's theorem. The necessary and sufficient conditions expressed in the Inequalities (2) guarantee that all the moments lie in the interval [0, 1], and so this may be taken to be the domain of the probability distribution without further assumption.

2.   QUALITATIVE PRIMITIVES FOR MOMENTS

The idea, then, is to provide a qualitative axiomatization of the moments for which a qualitative analogue of Inequalities (2) obtains and then to show that the qualitative moments have a numerical representation that permits one to invoke Hausdorff's theorem. Thus, the qualitative structure begins first with a set G of objects. These are the physical objects or entities to which we expect ultimately to associate random variables. More precisely, we expect to represent the selected extensive attribute of each object by a random variable. However, in order to get at the random variables, we must generate from G a set of entities that we can think of as corresponding to the raw moments and mixed moments of the objects in G. To do that, we must suppose that there is an operation ◆ of combining so that we can generate elements $a^n = a^{n-1} ◆ a$, which, from a qualitative point of view, will be thought of as corresponding to the raw moments of a. It is appropriate to think of this operation as an operation of multiplication, but it corresponds to multiplication of random variables, not to multiplication of real numbers. We shall assume as axioms that the operation is associative and commutative, but that it should not be assumed to be distributive with respect to disjoint union (which corresponds to numerical addition) can be seen from the following random-variable counterexample, given in Gruzewska (1954). Let X_1, X_2, X_3 be three random variables, where

$$X_1 = X_2 = \begin{cases} 0 \\ 1 \end{cases} \text{ with } P_1(X_2 = 0) = P_1(X_1 = 1) = \frac{1}{2},$$

$$X_3 = 1 \text{ with } P_3(X_3 = 1) = 1.$$

Then

$$X_2 + X_3 = \begin{cases} 1 \text{ with } P(X_2 + X_3 = 1) = \dfrac{1}{2} \\[2mm] 2 \text{ with } P(X_2 + X_3 = 2) = \dfrac{1}{2} \end{cases}$$

$$L_1 = X_1(X_2 + X_3) = \begin{cases} 0 \text{ with } P(L_1 = 0) = \dfrac{1}{2} \\[2mm] 1 \text{ with } P(L_1 = 1) = \dfrac{1}{2}\cdot\dfrac{1}{2} = \dfrac{1}{4} \\[2mm] 2 \text{ with } P(L_1 = 2) = \dfrac{1}{2}\cdot\dfrac{1}{2} = \dfrac{1}{4} \end{cases}$$

and

$$X_1X_2 = \begin{cases} 0 \text{ with } P(X_1X_2 = 0) = \dfrac{3}{4} \\[4mm] 1 \text{ with } P(X_1X_2 = 1) = \dfrac{1}{4} \end{cases}$$

$$X_1X_3 = \begin{cases} 0 \text{ with } P(X_1X_3 = 0) = \dfrac{1}{2} \\[4mm] 1 \text{ with } P(X_1X_3 = 1) = \dfrac{1}{2} \end{cases}$$

and

$$L_2 = X_1X_2 + X_1X_3 = \begin{cases} 0 \text{ with } P(L_2 = 0) = \dfrac{3}{8} \\[2mm] 1 \text{ with } P(L_2 = 1) = \dfrac{3}{8} + \dfrac{1}{8} = \dfrac{4}{8} = \dfrac{1}{2} \\[2mm] 2 \text{ with } P(L_2 = 2) = \dfrac{1}{8} \end{cases}$$

(The computations make clear the assumptions of independence made.) As can be seen, L_1 and L_2 have different distributions, although

$$E(X_1(X_2 + X_3)) = E(X_1X_2 + X_1X_3).$$

We turn now to the explicit definition of a semigroup that contains the associative and commutative axioms of multiplication.

DEFINITION 1. *Let A be a nonempty set, G a nonempty set, · a binary operation on A and 1 an element of G. Then $\mathfrak{A} = (A, G, ·, 1)$ is a* commutative semigroup with identity *1* generated by *G iff the following axioms are satisfied for every a, b, and c in G.*

1. *If $a \in G$, then $a \in A$.*
2. *If $s,t \in A$, then $(s·t) \in A$.*
3. *Any member of A can be generated by a finite number of applications of Axioms 1–3 from elements of G.*
4. *$a · (b · c) = (a · b) · c$.*
5. *$a · b = b · a$.*
6. *$1 · a = a$.*

Note that, because of the associativity axiom, we omit parentheses from here on. Note, further, that, on the basis of Axiom 3, we think of elements of A as finite strings of elements of G. Intuitively the elements of A are qualitative mixed moments. Furthermore, because the product operation · is associative and commutative, we can always write the mixed moments in a standard form involving powers of the generators. For example, $a·a·a·c·a·b·c = a^4·b·c^2$. This expression is interpreted as the qualitative mixed moment consisting of the fourth raw moment of a times the first one of b times the second one of c. We denote this semigroup by A.

Our last primitive is a qualitative ordering of moments. As usual, we will denote it by $\succeq$. The first question concerns the domain of this relation. For purposes of extensive measurement, it is useful to assume that the domain is all finite subsets from the elements of the semigroup A. We may state this as a formal definition:

DEFINITION 2. *Let A be a nonempty set and $\succeq$ a binary relation on $\mathscr{F}$, the family of all finite subsets of A. Then $\mathfrak{A} = (A, \mathscr{F}, \succeq)$ is a* weak extensive structure *iff the following axioms are satisfied for every B, C, and D in $\mathscr{F}$:*

1. *The relation $\succeq$ is a weak ordering of $\mathscr{F}$.*
2. *If $B \cap D = C \cap D = \varnothing$, then $B \succeq C$ iff $B \cup D \succeq C \cup D$.*
3. *If $B \neq \varnothing$, then $B > \varnothing$.*

Superficially the structure just defined looks like a familiar structure of qualitative probability, but in fact it is not. The reason is that because A is an infinite set, we cannot assume $\mathscr{F}$ is closed under complementation, because that would violate the assumption that the subsets in $\mathscr{F}$ are finite.

An important conceptual point is that we do require the ordering in magnitude of different raw moments. One standard empirical interpretation of what it means to say that the second raw moment, a^2, is less than the first, a^1, was outlined previously. A formal point, appropriate to make at this stage, is to contrast the uniqueness result we anticipate for the representation theorem with the usual uniqueness up to a similarity (i.e., multiplication by a positive constant) for extensive measurement. We have, in the present setup, not only the extensive operation but also the semigroup multiplication for forming moments; therefore, the uniqueness result is absolute (i.e., uniqueness in the sense of the identity function). Given this strict uniqueness, the magnitude comparison of a^m and a^n for any natural numbers m and n is not a theoretical problem. It is of course apparent that any procedure for measurement of moments, fundamental or derived, will need to satisfy such strict uniqueness requirements in order to apply Hausdorff's or other related theorems in the theory of moments.

Within $\mathscr{F}$, we may define what it means to have n disjoint copies of $B \in \mathscr{F}$:

$$1B = B$$
$$(n + 1)B \sim nB \cup B',$$

where $nB \cap B' = \varnothing$, and $B' \sim B$ and $\sim$ is the equivalence relation defined in terms of the basic ordering $\succsim$ on $\mathscr{F}$. Axiom 3 will simply be the assumption that such a B' always exists, and so nB is defined for each n. It is essential to note that this standard extensive or additive recursive definition is quite distinct from the one for moments a^n given earlier.

3.   AXIOM SYSTEM FOR QUALITATIVE MOMENTS

Our goal is to provide axioms on the qualitative raw moments such that we can prove that object a can be represented by a random variable $\mathbf{X}_a$, and the nth raw moment a^n is represented by the nth power of $\mathbf{X}_a$ (i.e., by $\mathbf{X}_a^n$).

For convenience, we shall assume the structures we are dealing with are bounded in two senses. First, the set G of objects will have a largest element 1, which intuitively means that the expectation of the random variables associated with the elements of a will not exceed that of 1. Moreover, we will normalize things so that the expectation associated with $\mathbf{X}_1$ is 1. This normalization shows up in the axiomatization as 1 acting as the identity element of the semigroup. Second, because of the condition arising from the Hausdorff theorem, this choice means that all of the raw moments are decreasing in powers of n (i.e., if $m \leq n$, then $a^n \precsim a^m$). Obviously the theory can be developed so that the masses are greater than 1, and the moments become larger with increasing n. This is the natural theory when the probability distribution is defined on the positive real line. As might be expected, the conditions are simpler for the existence of a probability distribution on a finite interval, and this is also realistic from a methodological standpoint. The exponential notation for qualitative moments a^n

is intuitively clear, but it is desirable to have the following formal recursive definition:

$$a^0 = 1,$$
$$a^n = a^{n-1} \cdot a,$$

in order to have a clear interpretation of a^0.

Before giving the axiom system, we must discuss more fully the issue of what will constitute a qualitative analogue of Hausdorff's condition, Inequality (2).

We have only an operation corresponding to addition and not to subtraction in the qualitative system; thus, for k, an even number, we rewrite this inequality solely in terms of addition as follows:

$$\mu_\nu + \tbinom{k}{2}\mu_{\nu+2} + \cdots + \mu_{\nu+k} \geq \tbinom{k}{1}\mu_{\nu+1} + \cdots + k\mu_{\nu+(k-1)}, \tag{3}$$

and a corresponding inequality for the case in which k is odd. In the qualitative system, the analogue to Inequality (3) must be written in terms of union of sets as follows for k even:

$$a^\nu \cup \tbinom{k}{2}a^{\nu+2} \cup \cdots \cup a^{\nu+k} \gtrsim \tbinom{k}{1}a^{\nu+1} \cup \cdots \cup ka^{\nu+(k-1)}. \tag{4}$$

When k is odd,

$$a^\nu \cup \tbinom{k}{2}a^{\nu+2} \cup \cdots \cup ka^{\nu+(k-1)} \gtrsim \tbinom{k}{1}a^{\nu+1} \cup \cdots \cup a^{\nu+k}. \tag{5}$$

There are several remarks to be made about this pair of inequalities. First of all, we can infer that, for $a < 1$, as opposed to $a \sim 1$, the moments are a strictly decreasing sequence (i.e., $a^\nu > a^{\nu+1}$). Second, the meaning of such terms as $\tbinom{k}{2}a^{\nu+2}$ was recursively defined earlier, with the recursion justified by Axiom 3 below. It is then easy to see that the unions indicated in Inequalities (2) and (5) are of disjoint sets. On the basis of the earlier terminology, we can then introduce the following definition. A qualitative sequence $a^0, a^1, a^2, a^3, \ldots$ is *quali-tatively completely monotonic* iff Inequalities (4) and (5) are satisfied.

DEFINITION 3. *A structure* $\mathfrak{A} = (A, \mathfrak{F}, G, \gtrsim, \cdot, 1)$ *is a* random extensive structure with independent objects—*the elements of* G—*iff the following axioms are satisfied for a in* G, *s and t in* A, *k, m, m', n, and n' natural numbers and* B *and* C *in* $\mathfrak{F}$:

1. *The structure* $(A, \mathfrak{F}, \gtrsim)$ *is a weak extensive structure.*
2. *The structure* $(A, G, \cdot, 1)$ *is a commutative semigroup with identity 1 generated by* G.
3. *There is a* C' *in* $\mathfrak{F}$ *such that* $C' \sim C$, *and* $C' \cap B = \varnothing$;
4. *Archimedean. If* $B > C$, *then, for any* D *in* $\mathfrak{F}$, *there is an* n *such that*
   $$nB \gtrsim nC \cup D.$$
5. *Independence. Let mixed moments s and t have no common objects:*
   a. *If* $m1 \gtrsim ns$, *and* $m'1 \gtrsim n't$, *then* $mm'1 \gtrsim nn'(s \cdot t)$.
   b. *If* $m1 \lesssim ns$, *and* $m'1 \lesssim n't$, *then* $mm'1 \lesssim nn'(s \cdot t)$.

6. *The sequence a^0, a^1, a^2, . . . of qualitative raw moments is qualitatively completely monotonic.*

The content of Axiom 1 is familiar. What is new here is, first of all, Axiom 2, in which the commutative semigroup, as mentioned earlier, is used to represent the mixed moments of a collection of objects. Axiom 3 is needed in order to make the recursive definition of $(n + 1)B$ well defined as given earlier. The special form of the Archimedean axiom is the one needed when there is no solvability axiom, as discussed in Section 3.2.1 of Krantz, Luce, Suppes, and Tversky (1971). The dual form of Axiom 5 is just what is needed to prove the independence of the moments of different objects, which means that the mixed moments factor in terms of expectation. Note that it is symmetric in $\gtrsim$ and $\lesssim$. The notation used in Axiom 5 involves both disjoint unions, as in *m1*, and the product notation for mixed moments, as in $(s \cdot t)$. Axiom 6 formulates the qualitative analogue of Hausdorff's necessary and sufficient condition as discussed above.

4. REPRESENTATION THEOREM AND PROOF

REPRESENTATION THEOREM. *Let $\mathfrak{A} = (A, \mathscr{F}, G, \gtrsim, \cdot, 1)$ be a random extensive structure with independent objects. Then there exists a family $\{X_B, B \in \mathscr{F}\}$ of real-valued random variables such that:*

  (i). *every object a in G is represented by a random variable X_a whose distribution is on $[0, 1]$ and is uniquely determined by its moments,*

 (ii). *the random variables $\{X_a, a \in G\}$ are independent,*

(iii). *for a and b in G, with probability one,*

$$X_{a \cdot b} = X_a \cdot X_b,$$

 (iv). $E(X_B) \geq E(X_C)$, *iff* $B \gtrsim C$,

  (v). *if* $B \cap C = \varnothing$, *then* $X_{B \cup C} = X_B + X_C$,

 (vi). *if* $B \neq 0$, *then* $E(X_B) > 0$,

(vii). $E(X_1^n) = 1$ *for every* n.

Moreover, any function ϕ from Re to Re such that $\{\phi(X_B), B \in \mathscr{F}\}$ satisfies (i)–(vii) is the identity function.

PROOF. First, we have, by familiar arguments from Axioms 1, 3, and 4, the existence of a numerical assignment ϕ. For any B in $\mathscr{F}$, we define the set S of numbers:

$$S_B = \{\frac{m}{n} : m1 \geq nB\}. \tag{6}$$

It is easy to show that S is nonempty and has a greatest lower bound, which we use to define ϕ:

$$\phi(B) = g.\ell.b.S_B.$$

It is then straightforward to show that, for B and C in $\mathcal{F}$,

$\phi(B) \gtrsim \phi(C)$ iff $B \gtrsim C$;
if $B \cap C = \varnothing$, then $\phi(B \cup C) = \phi(B) + \phi(C)$;
if $B \neq \varnothing$, then $\phi(B) > 0$.

Second, it follows from Axiom 2 that

$$1^n = 1, \tag{8}$$

whence

$$\phi(1) = 1. \tag{9}$$

From Axiom 6, we infer that, for any object a in G, the numerical sequence

$$1, \phi(a), \phi(a^2), \phi(a^3), \ldots$$

satisfies Inequalities (2) and, hence, determines a unique probability distribution for a, which we represent by the random variable $\mathbf{X}_a$. Furthermore, the expectation function E is defined by $E(\mathbf{X}_a^n) = \phi(a^n)$. The independence of mixed moments s and t that have no common object is derived from Axiom 5 by the following argument that uses the sets S_B defined in (6) and their symmetric analogue sets T_B defined below. From 5a, we have at once, if

$$\frac{m}{n} \in S_s \text{ and } \frac{m'}{n'} \in S_t,$$

then

$$\frac{mm'}{nn'} \in S_{st},$$

whence

$$\phi(s)\phi(t) \geq \phi(st). \tag{10}$$

Correspondingly, in order to use Axiom 5b, we define

$$T_B = \{\frac{m}{n} : m1 \leqslant nB\}.$$

Each set T_B is obviously nonempty and has a least upper bound. We need to show that

$$\ell.u.b. \ T_B = g.\ell.b. \ S_B = \phi(B).$$

Suppose, by way of contradiction, that

$$\ell.u.b. \ T_B < g.\ell.b. \ S_B.$$

(That the weak inequality $\leq$ must hold is evident.)
Then there must exist integers m and n such that

$$\ell.u.b. \ T_B < \frac{m}{n} < g.\ell.b. \ S_B.$$

Thus, we have, from the left-hand inequality,

$$m1 > nB,$$

and from the right-hand one,

$$m1 < nB,$$

which together contradict the weak order properties of $\succsim$. However, from the definition of T_B, we may then also infer

$$\phi(s)\phi(t) \geq \phi(st),$$

which, together with (8), establishes that

$$\phi(s)\phi(t) = \phi(st).$$

The previous argument establishes (i). We next want to show that, with probability one,

$$\mathbf{X}_{a \cdot b} = \mathbf{X}_a \cdot \mathbf{X}_b.$$

We do this by showing the two random variables have identical nth moments for all n. If $a \neq b$, we have independence of $\mathbf{X}_a$ and $\mathbf{X}_b$ by the argument given previously:

$$E(\mathbf{X}_{a \cdot b}^n) = \phi(a^n \cdot b^n) = \phi(a^n)\phi(b^n) = E(\mathbf{X}_a^n)E(\mathbf{X}_b^n).$$
$$= E(\mathbf{X}_a^n \cdot \mathbf{X}_b^n) = E((\mathbf{X}_a \cdot \mathbf{X}_b)^n),$$

which also establishes (ii) by obvious extension.
If $a = b$, we have the following:

$$E(\mathbf{X}_{a \cdot a}^n) = \phi((a \cdot a)^n) = \phi(a^n \cdot a^n) = \phi(a^{2n})$$
$$= E(\mathbf{X}_a^{2n}) = E(\mathbf{X}_a^n \cdot \mathbf{X}_a^n) = E((\mathbf{X}_a \cdot \mathbf{X}_a)^n),$$

which completes the proof of (iii).
For the empty set, because $\phi(\varnothing) = 0$,

$$\mathbf{X}_\varnothing = 0,$$

and for B, a nonempty set in $\mathscr{F}$, define

$$X_B = \sum_{s \in B} X_s. \tag{11}$$

Each $s \in B$ is a multinomial moment; thus, $\mathbf{X}_B$ is a polynomial in the random variables $\mathbf{X}_a$, with a in some string $s \in B$. Such a random variable is clearly a Borel function, and so its distribution is well defined in terms of the joint product distribution of the independent random variables $\mathbf{X}_a$. Parts (iv)–(vi) of the theorem then follow at once from (7) and (11), and (vii) from (8) and (9).

Finally the uniqueness of the representation follows from the fact that $\phi(\varnothing) = 0$ and $\phi(I) = 1$. $\diamondsuit$

If we specialize the axioms of Definition 3 to qualitative assertions about distributions of a particular form, we can replace Axiom 6 on the complete monotonicity of the sequence of qualitative moments of an object by much simpler conditions. In fact, we know of no simpler qualitative way of characterizing distributions of a given form than by such qualitative axioms on the moments. The following corollary concerns such a characterization of the uniform, binomial, and beta distributions of [0, 1], where the beta distribution is restricted to integer-valued parameters α and β.

COROLLARY TO REPRESENTATION THEOREM. *Let* $\mathfrak{A} = (A, \mathcal{F}, G, \succeq,$ $\cdot, 1)$ *be a structure satisfying Axioms 1–5 of Definition 3, and, for any a in G, assume* $a \precsim 1$.

    I. *If the moments of an object a for* $n \geq 1$ *satisfy*
$$(n + 1)a^n \sim 2a,$$
      then $\mathbf{X}_a$ *is uniformly distributed on* [0, 1].

    II. *If the moments of an object a for* $n \geq 1$ *satisfy*
$$a^n \sim a,$$
      then $\mathbf{X}_a$ *has a Bernoulli distribution on* [0, 1].

    III. *If the moments of an object a for* $n \geq 1$ *satisfy*
$$(\alpha + \beta + n)a^{n+1} \sim (\alpha + n)a^n,$$
      where α *and* β *are positive integers, then* $\mathbf{X}_a$ *has a beta distribution on* [0, 1].

PROOF. We only give the proof for the Bernoulli distribution in any detail. First, we use the hypothesis $a^n \sim a$ to verify Inequalities (4) and (5). For k even,

$$(1 + (\tfrac{k}{2}) + \ldots + 1)a \succeq ((\tfrac{k}{1}) + \ldots + k)a$$

certainly holds, and similarly for k odd,

$$(1 + (\tfrac{k}{2}) + \ldots + k)a \succeq ((\tfrac{k}{1}) + \ldots + 1)a,$$

which shows that Axiom 6 of Definition 3 is satisfied, and so the unique numerical function ϕ of the Representation Theorem exists, with

$$\phi(a) = \phi(a^n) = p$$

for p, some real number such that $0 < p \leq 1$, and the distribution is uniquely determined by the moments. The moment-generating function for the Bernoulli distribution with parameter p is, for $-\infty < t < \infty$,

$$\psi(t) = pe^t,$$

and so the nth derivative of ψ with respect to t is equal to p at $t = 0$, which completes the proof.

In the case of the beta distribution, we just show how the recursion is derived. Verification of Inequalities (4) and (5) is routine but tedious. The moment-generating function of the beta distribution is not easy to work with, but by direct integration, we have as follows:

$$E(X^n) = \frac{(\alpha + \beta - 1)!}{(\alpha - 1)!(\beta - 1)!} \int_0^1 x^{n+\alpha-1}(1 - x)^{\beta-1}dx$$

$$= \frac{(\alpha + \beta - 1)!(\alpha + n - 1)!}{(\alpha + \beta + n - 1)!(\alpha - 1)!}$$

Using this last expression, it is easy to derive that

$$(\alpha + \beta + n)E(X^{n+1}) = (\alpha + n)E(X^n).$$

Finally the uniform distribution on $[0, 1]$ is a special case of the beta distribution, namely when $\alpha = \beta = 1$. $\diamondsuit$

Note that a Bernoulli distribution of X_a implies that all the probability weight is attached to the end points of the interval, so that, if p is the parameter of the distribution, as in standard notation, then

$$E(X_a) = (1 - p) \cdot 0 + p \cdot 1 = p.$$

We remark informally that some other standard distributions with different domains may also be characterized qualitatively in terms of moments. For example, the normal distribution on $(-\infty, \infty)$ with mean equal to zero and variance equal to one is characterized as follows:

$$a^0 \sim 1,$$
$$a^1 \sim \varnothing,$$
$$a^2 \sim 1,$$
$$a^{2(n+1)} \sim (2n + 1)a^{2n} \qquad \text{for } n \geq 1.$$

ACKNOWLEDGMENTS

We are indebted to Duncan Luce for helpful comments on earlier drafts of this chapter. The basic idea of a qualitative theory of moments was presented by the first author some years ago for the special case of the uniform distribution at the

1980 meeting in Madison, Wisconsin of the Society for Mathematical Psychology.

REFERENCES

Falmagne, J.-C. (1976). Random conjoint measurement and loudness summation. *Psychological Review, 83*, 65–79.

Falmagne, J.-C. (1978). A representation theorem for finite random scale systems. *Journal of Mathematical Psychology, 18*, 52–72.

Falmagne, J.-C. (1979). On a class of probabilistic conjoint measurement models: Some diagnostics properties. *Journal of Mathematical Psychology, 19*, 73–88.

Falmagne, J.-C. (1980). A probabilistic theory of extensive measurement. *Philosophy of Science, 47*, 277–296.

Falmagne, J.-C. (1985). *Elements of psychophysical theory.* New York: Oxford University Press.

Falmagne, J.-C., & Iverson, G. (1979). Conjoint Weber laws and additivity. *Journal of Mathematical Psychology, 20*, 164–183.

Gruzewska, H. M. (1954). L'Arithmétique des variables aléatoires (The arithmetic of random variables). *Cahiers Rhodaniens, 6*, 9–56.

Hausdorff, F. (1923). Momentprobleme für ein endliches Intervall (Moment problem for a finite interval). *Mathematische Zeitschrift, 16*, 220–248.

Iverson, G., & Falmagne, J.-C. (1985). Statistical issues in measurement. *Mathematical Social Sciences, 10*, 131–153.

Krantz, D. H., Luce, R. D., Suppes, P., & Tversky, A. (1971). *Foundations of measurement* (Vol. I). New York: Academic Press.

Shohat, J. A., & Tamarkin, J. D. (1943). *The problem of moments.* New York: American Mathematical Society.

4 On the Empirical Status of Measurement Axioms: The Case of Subjective Probability

Ernest W. Adams
University of California, Berkeley

This chapter contributes to the study of the empirical status of axioms in theories of fundamental measurement, following the lines of a previous study (Adams, Fagot, & Robinson, 1970) (see also Pfanzagl, 1968; Adams, 1974; and Manders, 1977). Here we will focus on theories of subjective probability representation, specifically considering variations on theories discussed in Krantz, Luce, Suppes, and Tversky (1971), section 5.2; Fine (1973), section IIB; Narens (1985) section 2.8e; and Roberts (1979), section 8.5, which in turn are variations and refinements on theories due to de Finetti (1937); Koopman (1940); and Savage (1954), section 3.2. To get an idea of our problems and approach, let us go quickly over the methodological and model-theoretic background.

The axioms in axiom systems for subjective probability fall into the following two categories: those that are *necessary conditions* for the existence of subjective probability representations ("necessary conditions of representability," Manders, 1979) and those that are not logically necessary but that have to be added to obtain sufficient conditions or that serve other theoretical purposes. Most of the necessary conditions included in well known axiom systems have the form of purely universal laws, such as that the subjective probability ordering should be transitive.[1] These laws are "empirically transparent," not only because they can

---

[1]These are universal laws on systems with *operations,* where the closure assumptions are not themselves purely universal. This complication will not concern us. Of course not all necessary conditions of representability need be purely universal. Certain versions of Archimedean conditions are necessary, and Manders (1979) considered very interesting classes of elementary "nontrivially necessary" conditions of representability, which are not of purely universal form. Intuitively these nontrivially necessary elementary axioms have the effect of "excluding infinitesimals," but they deserve careful study both from the mathematical and the empirical point of view.

be directly tested for logical consistency with observational data, but because they can be inductively confirmed, either as exactly true or as "true in most instances" (cf. Adams, 1974; however, see section on Other Data, in this chapter, for an important qualification of this). The nonnecessary conditions that enter into the axiom systems we are concerned with are never purely universal, and they seldom have such a transparently empirical character. Savage's nonnecessary axiom P6′ (Savage, 1954, p. 38) is typical. It says that if an event B is subjectively less probable than another event C, then it is possible to partition the event space into a finite number of "mini-events" in such a way that the union of B with any one of these is still subjectively less probable than C. It is easily seen that any finite amount of data whatever on subjective probability orderings must be logically consistent with this law taken by itself. Moreover, although Savage gave a persuasive a posteriori justification of P6′, to be commented on in section 4.2, it is not a form that is subject to standard experimental confirmation, and it is not clear what a particular instance of it would be.[2] Given this, one may be led to think that P6′ and similar laws stand in no need of empirical justification, because they have no empirical content. Like continuity and Archimedean assumptions, they seem to be *technical* conditions that are sufficiently justified by "theoretical reasons of state" (i.e., they are needed to attain a theoretical objective such as that of proving a representation theorem).[3] Nevertheless the appearance of empirical contentlessness is deceiving, as the following elementary model-theoretic considerations show.

Let us picture the space of subjective probability "systems" as filling the rectangle shown in Fig. 4.1, subregions of which correspond to systems that satisfy particular conditions. The most important special class is the class P of all systems satisfying the *probabilistic representability hypothesis* (i.e., that there exist subjective probability representations for these systems, which is shown as the smallest rectangle in the figure and is in turn divided into subregions P1 and P2. Now fix on a particular system of axioms for subjective probability representations. A subset of its axioms will be purely universal laws that are necessary conditions for representability, and the class of systems satisfying these laws can be depicted as filling the large rectangle U. This is shown containing P as a subregion, because all representable systems must satisfy these axioms. We will suppose that the remaining axioms of the system are not all necessary conditions for representability, but together with the universal axioms, they are sufficient. The class of systems satisfying these axioms is represented as filling circle N ("nonnecessary conditions"), which does not contain P, because these condi-

---

[2]It is worth noting that, although informal justifications have been offered, for instance for P6′ (see section; Justification of Nonnecessary Axioms), systematic experimental studies of these sorts of axiom systems (cf. Davidson, Siegel, & Suppes, 1957) have only studied the purely universal laws these systems involve.

[3]For instance, Luce and Galanter (1963, p. 259) said, concerning two axioms in a theory of Pfanzagl (1959): "Axioms 1 and 3 are largely technical and need not be discussed."

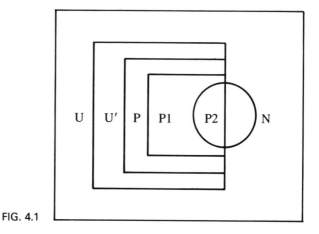

FIG. 4.1

tions are not necessary, but whose intersection with U is inside P, because the totality of the universal and the nonnecessary conditions is sufficient for representability. One other region, U', depicts the class of systems satisfying not only the universal laws of the particular axiom system in question but those satisfying all possible universal laws that are necessary conditions of representability.

Let us note the following among the various model-theoretic relationships depicted by Fig. 4.1. First, U' is shown as a proper subregion of U. This means that the purely universal laws of our axiom system do not by themselves logically entail all necessary conditions of representability. In fact, it follows from a fundamental theorem of Scott and Suppes (1958) that no finite set of purely universal axioms can logically entail all such conditions, and, therefore, unless our axiom system is infinite, U' must be a proper subset of U.[4]

The second point is that P is shown as a proper subregion of U', which means that not even the infinite totality of purely universal necessary conditions for representability is *sufficient* for this. This is an obvious consequence of the Skolem–Lowenheim Theorem (Lowenheim, 1915), given that the necessary conditions we are considering are first-order, and, therefore, they must have models of too high a cardinality to be representable by real-valued probabilities. The same argument shows that the nonuniversal laws defining region N must include at least one axiom that is not first-order, like condition P6'.

The third point is that, whereas the intersection of U and N is a subregion of P, it is a *proper* subregion of it, which simply means that the totality of the

---

[4]Scott (1965) did indeed present an infinite set of universal laws that are necessary conditions of representability and that entail all such conditions (see also the related axioms in Adams, 1965). Here we consider just finite axiom systems, in part because it is not clear how one might inductively confirm an infinite totality of independent laws. However, it is an interesting question whether the class of necessary conditions of representability, *including* the nontrivially necessary axioms studied by Manders (footnote 1), is finitely axiomatizable. Footnote 8 comments further on Scott's methods.

axioms are sufficient for representability but not necessary. However, it is methodologically important that, for many of the axiom systems that have been put forward, it can be shown that all representable systems not satisfying *the axioms* are *subsystems* of ones that do (i.e., all systems in P_1 can be 'extended to' ones in P_2. If this is so, then it follows that, although the axioms are *logically* stronger than the representability hypothesis, nevertheless any observational data *consistent* with the representability hypothesis must also be consistent with the axioms. This point will be returned to in section 4.1, but for now let us note that, although it could be seen as reinforcing the "mere technicality" thesis, the nonnecessary axioms stand in need of empirical justification, because they do in fact have substantive content.

Finally, and most importantly for present purposes, because the totality of the axioms are sufficient for representability, as shown by the fact that the intersection of U and N is inside region P, they must also entail the totality of necessary conditions for representability, because P is itself a subregion of U'. Hence, given that U' is a proper subregion of U, the totality of the axioms must logically entail some purely universal laws that are not entailed by U alone. This in turn implies that there can be observational data that would be consistent with the purely universal laws defining U but that would be inconsistent with the universal laws *plus* the nonnecessary conditions defining N.[5] In other words, although it may be that, taken by themselves, the nonnecessary axioms have no empirical content, because they are logically consistent with any data whatever, nevertheless they can have "contributory empirical content" in the context of a larger axiom system, because there may be data consistent with the system with the axioms deleted but not with the entire system. Even if such axioms are not directly testable by observation, they cannot be justified solely on the grounds of technical convenience.

The axiomatizer's dilemma is that, in order to attain the objective of proving a representation theorem, it is necessary to include nonnecessary axioms that have contributory empirical content and hence, that require justification by more than "reasons of state," although they may have no independent empirical content. In the remarks that conclude this paper, we will essay a few inconclusive speculations on how such axioms may be justified, but our main objective is more modest. It is simply to *identify* the axioms requiring such justification. The point is that, although we know a priori that certain nonnecessary axioms must have contributory empirical content, most axiom systems include more than one nonnecessary axiom, and we may wish to know which of these requires special attention.

---

[5]Note that it is a special property of universal laws that, *if and only if* they are logically independent of other elementary axioms will it be the case that they will have contributory empirical content when added to these other axioms. This can be viewed as a kind of "generalized independent testability property."

In fact, our study is somewhat more fine-grained. It can happen that certain axioms are empirically contentless, even in a contributory sense, relative to certain kinds of data but not to data of other kinds. Thus, in the case of subjective probability, there are at least three kinds of atomic formulas that might be considered as data. The most obvious "empirical facts" are data about the subjective probability ordering, such as that one event is subjectively less proba-ble than another. However, the language of subjective probability includes at least two other sorts of atomic formulas: those expressing the fact that one event is a "subevent" of another, and those expressing the fact that two events are *the same*. Perhaps we are inclined to regard these as expressing "purely logical facts" that play no role in an empirical evaluation of a theory, but, as with the appearance of mere technicality, we will see that this too can be misleading. Furthermore, even when the appearance is correct, it may be useful to prove this, which may also help to explain why we should regard subjective probability relations as more empirical than the logical relations of subeventhood and of identity.

Now we are ready to turn to details, beginning with the specification of certain theories of subjective probability, of certain kinds of empirical data, and of what it is for such data to be consistent with one of these theories. Following that, we will state our main theorems on empirical equivalences and inequivalences be-tween theories of subjective probability defined in terms of their consistency with data of certain kinds, which will allow us to identify the nonnecessary axioms in them that have contributory empirical content. A concluding section will make some speculative remarks about several methodological issues, including the justification of these axioms. Because of the fact that similar theorems are proved in Adams, Fagot, and Robinson (1970), we will include only one sample proof, which will give some idea of the essential mathematical methods employed and also of limitations that seem to bar the way to extensions to more complex theories. Also it should be stressed that the present study makes no pretense to exhaustiveness in its survey of theories of subjective probability. Certain repre-sentative ones are considered, but our objective is to illustrate themes and meth-ods and not to apply them to all cases.

BASIC DEFINITIONS

The axiom systems to be considered apply to *ordered boolean algebras* (OBA), which will themselves be defined in stages. A *boolean algebra of sets* (BAS) is an ordered septuple $BAS(K) = \langle K, \cap, \cup, -, \varnothing, V, \subseteq \rangle$ in which K is a set of subsets of some fixed nonempty set V, which is closed under intersection, union, and complementation with respect to V; $\cap$, $\cup$, and $-$ are the intersection, union, and complementation operations; $\varnothing$ is the empty set; and $\subseteq$ is the subset relation restricted to K. Obviously $BAS(K)$ is uniquely determined by K. Two boolean algebras of sets that will be of special importance in what follows are the systems $U = \mathrm{BAS}([0, 1])$ and $U- = \mathrm{BAS}((0, 1])$. In the first of these, K is the set of all finite (possibly empty) unions of subintervals of the closed unit interval $[0, 1]$, and, in the second, K is the set of finite unions of left-open, right-closed subintervals of $(0, 1]$.

A *boolean algebra of events*, or more briefly a *boolean algebra*, (BA) is any septuple $\mathscr{E} = \langle K, \cap, \cup, -, \varnothing, V, \subseteq \rangle$, which is homomorphic to a boolean algebra of sets. Stones's Representation Theorem (Stone, 1936) shows that BAs can also be characterized by first-order axioms, but the present characterization is simpler for our purposes.

A *probability function* for an arbitrary BA, $\mathscr{E} = \langle K, \cap, \cup, -, \varnothing, \vee, \subseteq \rangle$ is a real-valued function p mapping K into $[0, 1]$ and satisfying the standard Kolmogorov (1956) axioms: for all x and y in K, (a) if $x \subseteq y$, then $p(x) \le p(y)$; (b) $p(V) = 1$; and (c) if $x \cap y \subseteq \varnothing$ (i.e., if x and y are *disjoint*), then $p(x \cup y) = p(x) + p(y)$. Such a function is *regular*, if $p(x) = 0$ only for $x \subseteq 0$. Note that the two functions p_U and p_{U-}, which map the subintervals of $[0, 1]$ and $(0, 1]$ into their *lengths*, are probability functions for U and $U-$ respectively, and, furthermore, p_{U-} is regular.

An *ordered boolean algebra* (OBA) is a system $\langle \mathscr{E}, \precsim \rangle$ in which $\mathscr{E}$ is a BA, and $\precsim$ is a weak ordering of its domain. Specifically, if K is the domain of $\mathscr{E}$, then, for all x, y, and z in K, the following occurs: (a) either $x \precsim y$, or $y \precsim x$; and (b) if $x \precsim y$, and $y \precsim z$, then $x \precsim z$. A (set-theoretical) *theory* of OBAs is simply a set of these structures, and we will regard an individual OBA as a degenerate theory that is the singleton set that contains that OBA. These are the theories with whose empirical equivalences we are concerned, which will in turn shed light on the empirical status of the axioms characterizing them. Empirical equivalence will be defined after we have stated further axioms and related conditions that characterize theories of particular interest.

When the equivalence,

(P) $\qquad\qquad x \precsim y$ if and only if $p(x) \le p(y)$

holds for all x and y in K, we will say that $\precsim$ is *generated by p* and that p *represents* $\precsim$.[6] Obviously any probability function p for $\mathscr{E}$ generates a unique ordering $\precsim_p$ of K, and $\langle \mathscr{E}, \precsim_p \rangle$ is the corresponding OBA. Furthermore, for most OBAs, $\langle \mathscr{E}, \precsim \rangle$, there is at most one probability function that represents the weak

---

[6]The representation defined here is not the only sort that has been considered in the literature. In particular, Savage (1954, p. 34) defined an *almost agreeing* probability function to be one in which only the "only if" direction of the biconditional holds—this could be viewed as an application to subjective probability of Holman's (1973) approach—whereas an *agreeing* probability function is one satisfying the biconditional in both directions. The technical advantage of the unidirectional formulation is that it does not require the Archimedean condition. The distinction between agreeing and almost agreeing probability functions is closely connected to that between regular and "general" probability representations.

ordering $\precsim$. Two important OBAs are the systems, OBA(U) and OBA($U-$), whose orderings are represented by the length measures on U and $U-$ respectively.

When the probabilities $p(x)$ and $p(y)$ that attach to elements in the domains of BAs are subjective, the corresponding ordering relations $x \precsim_p y$ are of particular importance, because they are commonly assumed to furnish the observational *data* from which the subjective probabilities are inferred. In consequence, theories of subjective probability measurement are generally stated in terms of these orderings. Definition 1 formulates conditions on these orderings, which figure in well known theories of this kind. Note that Savage's axiom P6' is not included among the conditions listed, which reflects the fact that this is a condition for what Savage (1954, p. 34) calls an "almost agreeing" representation. This is more general than an "agreeing" representation, which is what we here call simply a "representation." This is commented on a greater length later.

DEFINITION 1. Let $\mathscr{C} = \langle K, \cap, \cup, -, \varnothing, \vee, \subseteq \rangle$ be a BA, and let $\precsim$ be a weak ordering of K.

1.1. $\langle \mathscr{C}, \precsim \rangle$ is a *Basic de Finetti Structure*, if for all x, y, and z in K: (i) if $x \subseteq y$, then $x \precsim y$; (ii) if x and z are disjoint, and y and z are disjoint, then $x \cup z \precsim y \cup z$, if and only if $x \precsim y$; and (iii) not $V \precsim \varnothing$.

1.2. $\langle \mathscr{C}, \precsim \rangle$ is *regular* if $x \precsim \varnothing$ implies $x \subseteq \varnothing$ for all x in K.

1.3. Members $x_1, \ldots, x_n$ of K form an *equal n-partition* of an element x of K if all are disjoint, $x_1 \sim \ldots \sim x_n$ (where $\sim$ is the equivalence relation generated by $\precsim$) and $x \sim x_1 \cup \ldots \cup x_n$; x is *equal n-partitionable* if it has an equal n-partition and $\langle \mathscr{C}, \precsim \rangle$ is *uniformly equal n-partitionable*, if every x in K is equal n-partitionable.

1.4. $\langle \mathscr{C}, \precsim \rangle$ is *Koopman Archimedean* if, for all $x < y$ in K (i.e., for all x and y such that not $y \precsim x$): for some n, there exists an equal n-partition $V_1, \ldots, V_n$ of V and some $m \leq n$ such that $x \precsim V_1 \cup \ldots \cup V_m \precsim y$.

1.5. $\langle \mathscr{C}, \precsim \rangle$ is *probabilistically representable* if there exists a probability function for $\mathscr{C}$ that represents $\precsim$.

The three conditions defining Basic de Finetti Structures are direct consequences of axioms originally due to de Finetti (1937) (cf. also Roberts, 1979, p. 387). These are either postulated, or they are direct consequences of postulates in all of the well known direct axiomatizations of subjective probability independent of preference. Moreover, these are all necessary conditions for the probabilistic representability of an OBA.

Sufficient conditions for probabilistic representability have been exhaustively studied (cf. Krantz et al., 1970, chapter 5, and Roberts, 1979, section 8.5). These can be obtained by adding certain nonnecessary axioms to those for Basic de Finetti Structures. One such set of conditions adds the requirements that the universe V should be equal n-partitionable for arbitrarily large n and that it should satisfy the Koopman Archimedean condition (actually the second of these entails the first, but we want to keep the assumptions distinct in order to consider which adds empirical content to the theory). Luce and Suppes (1969) formulated another set of sufficient conditions by adding to the Basic de Finetti Axioms the requirement that the system should be uniformly equal 2-partitionable, together with a modified Archimedean axiom that can be replaced by the Koopman Archimedean condition. If the regularity requirement is added to either of the previous sets of sufficient conditions, we obtain sufficient conditions for representability by regular probability functions. Our concern is with the empirical status of the nonnecessary axioms such as those noted above, which have to be added to obtain sufficient conditions for probability representability.

Next we define various theories of OBAs, whose empirical equivalences relative to different kinds of data will be investigated.

DEFINITION 2. Theories of OBAs.

2.1. F is the theory of all Basic de Finetti Structures.

2.2. For $n = 1, 2, \ldots, E_n$ is the theory of all Basic de Finetti Structures that are uniformly equal n-partitionable.

2.3. V is the theory of all Basic de Finetti Structures whose universe elements are equal n-partitionable for arbitrarily large n.

2.4. For $n = 1, 2, \ldots, E_nA$ is the theory of all OBAs in E_n that satisfy the Koopman Archimedean condition, and VA is the theory of all OBAs in V that satisfy this condition.

2.5. For $n = 1, 2, \ldots, E_nR$ and E_nAR are the theories of all regular OBAs in E_n and E_nA respectively, and VR and VAR are the theories of all regular OBAs in V and VA respectively.

2.6. P and RP are respectively the theories of all OBAs that are probabilistically representable and of all OBAs that are representable by regular probability functions.

Given facts already noted (that all Basic de Finetti Structures that satisfy the Koopman Archimedean condition that are either equal 2-partitionable or whose universe elements are equal n-partitionable for arbitrarily large n are probabilistically representable), it follows immediately that $E_2A \subset P$, and $VA \subset P$, whereas $E_2AR \subset RP$, and $VAR \subset RP$. Trivially also OBA$(U) \subset P$, and OBA$(U-) \subset RP$. Obviously none of these subset relations can be reversed, because the conditions defining the theories E_2A, VA, and OBA(U) are sufficient but not necessary for probabilistic representability, whereas E_2AR, VAR, and OBA$(U-)$ are sufficient but not necessary for regular probabilistic representability. However, it does not follow that the nonnecessary conditions for probabilistic representability add empirical content to the theories involving them, because it is conceivable that finite data consistent with the weaker theories would also be consistent with these same theories augmented by these nonnecessary conditions. Let us now describe 'elementary' data; the section on

Other Data will comment on the possibility of adding certain less elementary formulas to the data.

An (elementary) *datum* will be a relational formula of one of the following six forms:

1. $t_1 = t_2$.
2. $t_1 \neq t_2$.
3. $t_1 \subseteq t_2$.
4. $t_1 \not\subseteq t_2$.
5. $t_1 \precsim t_2$.
6. $t_1 \not\precsim t_2$.

Note that t_1 and t_2 are *boolean terms*. These terms are formed from the constant symbols V, and $\varnothing$, and variables 'x', 'y', etc., combined by the binary operation symbols '$\cap$' and '$\cup$', and the unary operation symbol "$-$." All data formed from these terms are atomic formulas or their negations, and we will call the atomic formulas *positive data* and call their negations *negative data*. Formulas of types (1) and (2) will be called *identity data;* those of types (3) or (4) will be called *inclusion data;* and ones of types (5) or (6) will be called *ordinal data*. Intuition suggests that ordinal data are the most empirically significant, however, because theories of subjective probability involve both identities and inclusions, we must consider data involving these relations to be *prima facie* relevant to tests of these theories. Results following will help to explain why identity in particular plays a special role in considerations of empirical adequacy.

The idea of a datum or set of data D being *consistent* with an OBA $\langle \mathscr{E}, \precsim \rangle$ is defined in terms of a *valuation f* of the terms involved in the data *in* the domain K of the OBA. This is defined recursively, starting with variables 'x', 'y', . . . , whose values $f('x'), f('y'), \ldots$ are members of K, and the constants 'V' and '$\varnothing$', whose values are given by $f(V) = V$ (the universe element of K) and $f('\varnothing')$ $= \varnothing$. Given these valuations, $f(t_1 \cap t_2)$ is defined as $f(t_1) \cap f(t_2), f(t_1 \cup t_2) =$ $f(t_1) \cup f(t_2)$, and $f(-t) = -f(t)$. Given a valuation f of the terms in D in K, a particular datum of form (1) *holds* in $\langle \mathscr{E}, \precsim \rangle$ if $f(t_1) = f(t_2)$; one of form (2) holds if $f(t_1) \neq f(t_2)$, and holding is defined analogously for data of forms (3)–(6). A set D of data is *consistent* with $\langle \mathscr{E}, \precsim \rangle$ if there exists a boolean valuation of the terms in it such that all data in D hold in $\langle \mathscr{E}, \precsim \rangle$.

Now we can define the consistency of data with *theories* of OBAs, which in turn permits us to define certain kinds of empirical equivalences between these theories.

DEFINITION 3. Let D be a finite set of data, and let T and T' be two theories of OBAs.

3.1. D is *consistent with* T if there is an OBA in T with which D is consistent.

3.2. *T* is *empirically at least as strong as T'* with respect to data of a given kind if any finite set of data of that kind that is consistent with *T* is also consistent with *T'*.

3.3. *T* and *T'* are *empirically equivalent* with respect to data of a given kind if each is empirically at least as strong as the other with respect to that kind of data.

If adding an axiom to the conditions defining a theory *T* yields a theory *T'* that is empirically stronger than *T* with respect to a given kind of data (positive or negative ordinal, inclusion, etc.), then that axiom has contributory empirical content in the context of the axioms defining *T'* relative to the given kind of data, whereas, if *T* and *T'* are empirically equivalent with respect to such data, the axiom can be treated as merely technical in its context, at least insofar as concerns empirical tests involving that sort of data. Now we are ready to inquire into the conditions that do add contributory content to the contexts in which they appear and those that do not.

EMPIRICAL EQUIVALENCES

Before giving technical results, we will state a result that justifies disregarding identity data in analyzing equivalences among theories of a wide variety, including all of those considered here.

THEOREM 1. Let *T* be a theory of OBAs that is closed under homomorphic images and their inverses; let $D = E- \cup E+ \cup D'$ be a set of data partitioned into subsets of negative identity data $E-$, positive identity data $E+$, and inclusion and ordinal data D'; and let $I(E+)$ be the set of positive inclusion data $t_1 \subseteq t_2$ for which either $t_1 = t_2$ or $t_2 = t_1$ is in $E+$. Then *D* is consistent with *T* if and only if $E- \cup E+$ is logically consistent, and $I(E+) \cup D'$ is consistent with *T*.

Theorem 1, whose proof is omitted, because it is similar to that of Theorem 2 of Adams, Fagot, and Robinson (1970, p. 400), tells us that, in considering the consistency of data (including positive and negative identities with a theory of OBAs that is closed under homomorphisms, which includes all of the theories that concern us), we only need to consider the purely logical question of whether the identity data by themselves are consistent (which they should be a priori), and the consistency of the nonidentity data (inclusion and ordinal) with the theory, provided the inclusion data are augmented to include all inclusions $t_1 \subseteq t_2$ and $t_2 \subseteq t_1$ that are derived from identities $t_1 = t_2$ in the data. A test of a theory of OBAs in terms of its consistency with data, therefore, divides into a purely logical part, having to do with the logical consistency of positive and negative identities in the data, and an empirical part having to do with the theory's consistency with ordinal and inclusion data. Therefore, because we are concerned with empirical questions, we may disregard identities, henceforth, and focus exclusively on data just involving inclusions and ordinal relations.

Theorem 2 states our main results on empirical equivalences. As previously stated, only the proof of Part 2.1 will be sketched.

THEOREM 2. Empirical equivalences.

2.1. The following theories are empirically equivalent with respect to ordinal data: P, RP, $OBA(U)$, $OBA(U-)$, VA, VAR, and E_n, E_nA, E_nR, E_nAR, for $n = 2$, $3, \ldots$.

2.2. The following theories are empirically equivalent with respect to ordinal and inclusion data: P, U, VA, E_n, and E_nA, for $n = 2, 3, \ldots$.

2.3. The following theories are empirically equivalent to respect to ordinal and inclusion data: RP, $OBA(U-)$, VAR, and E_nR and E_nAR, for $n = 2, 3, \ldots$.

2.4. P is empirically stronger than E_1 and V with respect to ordinal data.

2.5. RP is empirically stronger than P with respect to ordinal and inclusion data.

Proof of 2.1

It will be shown that, for any finite set D of ordinal data, if D is consistent with $OBA(U-)$, it is consistent with the other theories listed, and, if it is consistent with the other theories listed, then it is consistent with $OBA(U-)$. It follows from that that $OBA(U-)$ is equivalent to these other theories with respect to ordinal data.

Suppose first that D is consistent with $OBA(U-)$. Trivially $OBA(U-)$ belongs to all of the theories listed except $OBA(U)$, hence, D must be consistent with all of these theories except possibly $OBA(U)$. That D is also consistent with $OBA(U)$ follows from the fact that $OBA(U)$ is an extension of $OBA(U-)$, and, therefore, any data consistent with $OBA(U-)$ is also consistent with $OBA(U)$.

Now we will show in turn that, if D is consistent with VA, with $OBA(U)$, with P, and with E_n, for $n > 1$, it must be consistent with $OBA(U-)$. If this can be shown, it will follow that, if D is consistent with the other theories listed, it is consistent with $OBA(U-)$, because each of these is stronger than at least one of VA, $OBA(U)$, P, or E_n, for $n > 1$.

That ordinal data D consistent with VA must also be consistent with P and, therefore, with $OBA(U-)$ follows from the theorem that all Basic de Finetti structures whose universes are equal n–partitionable for arbitrarily large n and that satisfy the Koopman Archimedean axiom are probabilistically representable; hence, VA is logically stronger than P, and all data consistent with the former must be consistent with the latter.

Next suppose that D is consistent with $OBA(U)$. Given this, there must be a valuation, $f(t)$, of the terms t in D in the closed unit interval $[0, 1]$ that is the domain of $OBA(U)$ such that all data in D hold in $OBA(U)$ under f. $f(t)$ generates a "reduced mapping," $f'(t)$, of the terms in D in the domain $(0, 1]$ of $OBA(U-)$ in the following way. $f(t)$ is a finite union $I_1 \cup \ldots \cup I_n$ of closed, open, and half-closed subintervals of $[0, 1]$. Given any I_i, let the corresponding subinterval

I_i' of $(0, 1]$ be the right-closure of the interior of I_i, and let $f'(t)$ be the union $I_1' \cup \ldots \cup I_n'$. Ordinal data D can be interpreted as length inequalities, and the lengths of the intervals I_i equal those of the corresponding intervals I_i'; thus, it follows immediately that if data D hold in OBA(U) under f, then they will also hold in OBA($U-$) under f'; hence, D must also be consistent with OBA($U-$).

To prove that data D consistent with P or with any E_n, for $n > 1$, must be consistent with OBA($U-$), it will be useful to construct equivalent "boolean vector forms" of the terms involved in D. We may suppose that these terms are formed from n variables $v_1, \ldots, v_n$ and that intersections of these and their complements form "boolean atoms" $a_j = \pm v_1 \ldots \pm v_n, j = 1, \ldots, 2^n$, where $\pm v_i$ is either v_i or $-v_i$ for $i = 1, \ldots, n$. Each term t is formally equivalent to a union of these atoms and can in turn be written in equivalent boolean vectorial form as follows:

$$t \sim t(a_1)a_1 + \ldots + t(a_k)a_k, \tag{1}$$

where "$+$" is disjoint union; $t(a_i)$ is the universe V or the empty set $\varnothing$, according as a_i formally entails t or not; and $t(a_i)a_i = t(a_i) \cap a_i$. We will say that an atom a_j "occurs" in this vectorial form, if $t(a_j) = V$ or equivalently that a_j formally entails t. In effect, (1) says that t is equivalent to the union of the atoms that occur in it.

Now suppose that D is consistent with P. We will show that, if D is consistent with P, it must be consistent with OBA(U) and, therefore, with OBA($U-$), as we have just seen. Given the consistency of D with P, there is an OBA $\langle \mathcal{E}, \preceq \rangle$ with probability representation p and valuation f of the terms in D into the domain K of $\mathcal{E}$ such that all of the formulas in D hold in $\langle \mathcal{E}, \preceq \rangle$. Given that f maps the variables v_i into K, it must also map the atoms a_j into K, and, furthermore, because p is a probability function, the numbers $p(f(a_1)), \ldots, p(f(a_k))$ form a probability distribution. This generates a mapping $\phi(t)$ of the terms t in D into the domain, $[0, 1]$ of OBA(U) as follows.

First, let $s_\varnothing = \varnothing$; set $s_j = p(f(a_1)) + \ldots + p(f(a_j))$; and let $\phi(a_j) = [s_{j-1}, s_j]$, for $j = 1, \ldots, k$. The intervals $\phi(a_j)$ partition the unit interval $[0, 1]$, except for overlaps at their end points. Now rewrite each term t in D in the equivalent boolean vector form given by (1), and define

$$\phi(t) = t(a_1)\phi(a_1) \cup \ldots \cup t(a_k)\phi(a_k),$$

where $t(a_j)$ is now the unit interval or the empty interval, according as a_j formally entails t or not. Given the mapping $\phi(t)$ defined in this way, it is routine to verify that all formulas in D must hold in OBA(U) under $\phi(t)$. Therefore, they are consistent with OBA(U) and also with OBA($U-$).

To prove that ordinal data set D consistent with any E_i for $i > 2$ must be consistent with OBA($U-$), suppose that D is the union of negative ordinal data $D- = \{r_i < s_i : i = 1, \ldots, p\}$ (where "$r < s$" abbreviates "$s \nleq r$") and positive ordinal data $D+ = \{t_i \preceq u_i; i = 1, \ldots, q\}$, but this union is *inconsistent* with

OBA($U-$). Rewriting the terms in D in boolean vectorial form, the data themselves get rewritten as follows:

$$r_i(a_1)a_1 + \ldots + r_i(a_k)a_k < s_i(a_1)a_1 + \ldots + s_i(a_k)a_k, \ i = 1, \ldots, p$$
$$(D_i^-)$$

for $i = 1, \ldots, p$, and

$$t_i(a_1)a_1 + \ldots + t_i(a_k)a_k \lesssim u_i(a_1)a_1 + \ldots + u_i(a_k)a_k, \ i = 1, \ldots, q,$$
$$(D_i^+)$$

for $i = 1, \ldots, q$. These data can be reinterpreted as numerical inequalities, with "a_1", $\ldots$, "a_k" now being interpreted as real variables; with $r_i(a_k)$ reinterpreted as 1 or 0, according as a_j formally entails r_i or not; with "$+$" reinterpreted as the numerical addition, and the relations "$<$" and "$\leq$" being reinterpreted as the numerical inequality signs. It is easily seen that, if the original data are inconsistent with P, then the reinterpreted data must be mathematically inconsistent. More exactly, if D is inconsistent with P, then the numerical inequalities have no solutions for which the reinterpreted values a_j form a probability distribution.

Necessary and sufficient conditions for the solvability of linear inequalities, such as those above by probability distributions are given in Adams, Fagot, and Robinson (1970, pp. 390–391), following from standard theorems on solutions to systems of linear inequalities, and these in turn imply the following. If there does not exist a solution in probability distributions to the reinterpreted inequalities, then one of two things must be the case. Case (1): the set $D-$ is nonempty (i.e., $p > 0$), and there exist nonnegative integers b_i, $i = 1, \ldots, p$, at least one of which is positive, and nonnegative integers c_i, $i = 1, \ldots, q$ such that

$$\sum_{i=1}^{p} b_i r_i(a_j) + \sum_{i=1}^{q} c_i t_i(a_j) \geq \sum_{i=1}^{p} b_i s_i(a_j) + \sum_{i=1}^{q} c_i u_i(a_j) \qquad (2)$$

for all $j = 1, \ldots, k$. Case (2): the set $D-$ is empty, and all of the inequalities (2) hold strictly (i.e., with "$\geq$" replaced by "$>$"). We will show that, in Case (1), the original inequalities must be inconsistent with E_n for any $n > 1$, whereas the similar but simpler proof of inconsistency in Case (2) will not be given.

Suppose that a new list D' of data items is written, with each item D_i^- now being repeated in the list b_i times, and each item D_i^+ now repeated c_i times. There would be at least one strict inequality in the list, because at least one b_i is greater than 0. Given inequality (2), it would follow that each boolean atom a_j would occur on the left side of inequalities in the new list at least as often as it did on the right side, and at least one of these inequalities would be strict. Now, if each a_j occurred at most once on the left side of an inequality in the new list and at most once on the right, it would follow from the axioms for Basic de Finetti

Structures (Definition 1.1) that these inequalities could be "added" to yield the following strict inequality:

$$\sum_{j=1}^{k} \left(\sum_{i=1}^{p} b_i r_i(a_j) + \sum_{i=1}^{q} c_i t_i(a_j) \right) a_j < \sum_{j=1}^{k} \left(\sum_{i=1}^{p} b_i s_i(a_j) + \sum_{i=1}^{q} c_i u_i(a_j) \right) a_j \quad (3)$$

However, this would be a single strict inequality in which each atom occuring on the right also occured on the left, which would be trivially inconsistent with the axioms for Basic de Finetti structures.

To get around the difficulty caused by the fact that the atoms a_j may occur several times on either side of the inequalities in the new list D', we use the possibility of equally partitioning them that is guaranteed in structures in E_n for $n > 1$. Clearly, for any structure in E_n, each a_j must have equal m–partitions $a_{j1}, \ldots, a_{jm}$ for all powers m of n. Fixing on a particular power m, it also follows from the axioms of Basic de Finetti Structures that ordinal data in the new list must hold, if each a_j is replaced by an arbitrary "submultiple" a_{jh} in an equal m–partition of a_j, and, furthermore, if m is high enough, these submultiples can be so chosen that each one occurs at most once on the left side of an inequality in the new list and at most once on the right. Moreover, these can still be so chosen that any one occuring on the right also occurs on the left. Given this, the inequalities can once again be "added" to yield a strict inequality of form (3) in which each atom occuring on the right also occurs on the left, which is inconsistent with the Basic de Finetti Structure axioms.

This concludes the proof.

CONCLUDING REMARKS

Results on Empirical Equivalences

Here we will draw attention to a few implications of the results stated in Theorem 2. Note first the way in which theories that are equivalent with respect to ordinal data alone (Theorem 2.1) partition into "regular" theories (condition R, Theorem 2.3) and "nonregular" ones (Theorem 2.2), when inclusion data are added. In virtue of Theorem 2.5, these two groups are not equivalent to one another with respect to ordinal and inclusion data. That the two groups are not equivalent with respect to both kinds of data shows that regularity conditions have contributory empirical content in their contexts when both kinds of data are considered but not when ordinal data alone are. Among other things, this shows that, contrary to what might be thought a priori, inclusion data can be regarded as empirical in the testing of at least some subjective probability theories.

Second, note the light that our results throw on the status of the Koopman Archimedean axiom (condition A). It has no contributory empirical content in the context of theory E_nA for $n > 1$, the theory of Basic de Finetti Structures that are universally equal n–partitionable and that satisfy the Koopman Archimedean Axiom (Theorem 1.1), but it does in the context of VA, the theory of Basic de Finetti Structures whose universe elements are equal n–partitionable for arbitrarily large n (Theorems 2.1 and 2.4) and satisfy the Archimedean condition. This is interesting for the following reason. In a sense, VA is a theory of measurement of the subjective probabilities of events in which the universe and its equipartitions form a system of *standards,* like standard weights, with which all other events are compared to determine their probabilities, and in this context, A does have contributory empirical content. In contrast, E_n is a theory of measurement without standards, or rather one in which every event can itself be regarded as a standard. Where all events can be regarded as standards, it seems that the Archimedean condition adds no contributory content. This fits in with results Adams, Fagot, and Robinson (1970) stated, where it was found that Archimedean conditions add no empirical content to other systems of measurement in which all objects are standards.

Third, note that none of the nonnecessary conditions considered (namely universal equipartitionability, equipartitionability of the universe element, and the Koopman Archimedean condition) adds empirical content to the pure hypothesis of probabilistic representability with respect to either ordinal or inclusion data. This means that they satisfy what can be regarded as a "minimum requirement of acceptability" for nonnecessary conditions in axiom systems in fundamental measurement theory. Given that some of these must be included, if a representation theorem is to be proved, at least they should not be so strong that empirical data could be found that are consistent with the representability hypothesis but inconsistent with these axioms. Interestingly, although it might seem that certain axioms that have been formulated to the effect that domains of structures are *finite* (Suppes and Zinnes, 1963) do violate our acceptability requirement, Adams, Fagot, and Robinson (1970, p. 407) showed that, in the theories they considered, such axioms actually do satisfy it so long as they do not stipulate a fixed finite cardinality for the domain. This reflects the fact that all of the representations considered are essentially *linear,* which means that there are no "incommensurables" to worry about such as can occur with nonlinear representations (e.g., as in the analytic representation of synthetic plane geometry). The concluding subsection will make further comments on nonlinear representations.

The final remark to make on Theorem 2 is that it shows how theories of subjective probability can be fitted into Scott and Suppes' (1958) "representation" of theories of fundamental measurement, according to which these theories can be construed as classes of systems that are homomorphically embeddable in fixed, canonical relational systems. Here the fixed systems that we have considered are OBA(U) and OBA($U-$), and our study suggests, if it does not prove, that these systems might play a role in subjective probability theory similar to that which the reals or the positive reals under addition play to interval and extensive measurement.

Justification of Nonnecessary Axioms with Contributory Empirical Content

We will focus on two of these: namely Savage's axiom P6' and the equipartitionability axiom E_2. (We may ignore the fact that none of the theories to which Theorem 2 applies involves Savage's axiom; the points we will make do not depend on this.) Neither of these is a necessary condition for representability in any theory of which it is a part; both have contributory empirical content in their theoretical contexts, and both of them are consistent with any data whatever when considered by themselves outside of their theoretical contexts.

Savage (1954) himself offered a persuasive argument for P6':

> It seems to me rather easier to justify the assumption of P6',. . . . . . Suppose, for example, that you yourself consider B < C, that is, that you would definitely rather stake a gain in your fortune on C than on B. Consider the partition of your world into 2^n events each of which corresponds to a particular sequence of heads and tails, thrown by yourself, with a coin of your own choosing. It seems to me that you could easily choose such a coin and choose n sufficiently large so that you would continue to prefer to stake your gain on C, rather than on the union of B and any particular sequence of n heads and tails. (Savage, p. 38; this is essentially the quotation from Savage on p. 206 of Krantz et al., 1970).

Although this argument has something of an a priori flavor, given that the coin-tossing experiences on which it relies are not of a kind that can be subjected to standard sorts of experimental confirmation, it is clearly a posteriori. Obviously it is logically consistent to suppose that coins of the sort that Savage imagines do not exist and even that their existence would be contrary to laws of nature (imagine quantum laws of probability, according to which probabilities can only increase by discrete amounts). Thus, as is well known, although it may be that no data can be logically inconsistent with a law like P6', nevertheless it can be inductively confirmed and possibly also disconfirmed. Therefore, there is no difficulty in principle about empirically justifying such laws, although the fact that this kind of justification seems not to be reducible to standard techniques of experimentation does show that these laws have a rather special scientific status. All we would argue is that they should actually *be* justified.

A priori it would seem to be even simpler to justify E_2. Thus, to verify that any particular event x is equal 2–partitionable, it is only necessary to find two events y and z such that $y \cap z = 0$, $y \cup z = x$, and $y \sim z$; further, to inductively confirm E_2, it is only necessary to describe some systematic method for constructing these equipartitions. However, one feels uneasy about this, and the reason is easy to see. To establish that y and z equipartition x, we need to establish that they are subjectively equiprobable, not approximately but exactly, and one feels intuitively that that is beyond human capability. The problem here, however, is not with the *form* of E_2 but rather with the fact that we have assumed that the subjective equiprobability of y and z can be conclusively established on the basis of observational data. In fact we feel the same doubts about the status of certain purely universal laws.

Consider the *regularity* axiom, that $x \lesssim 0$ implies $x \subseteq 0$. We have assumed that it is possible to establish empirically that a subject regards an event x as no more likely than the impossible event 0 and, therefore, that this law is "empirically transparent." However, further consideration suggests that this must be an idealization, unless x itself is a logical contradiction. Furthermore, if we cannot *really* establish empirically that $x \lesssim 0$, then the regularity law cannot be regarded as empirical, and we must reconsider its justification and the justification of other idealizations like E_2 de novo. Part of this reconsideration involves examining the equivalences of theories involving these laws with respect to different *data*, to which we turn next.

Other Data, and a Generalization of the Theory

Obviously there is no a priori reason for taking just the formulas so far considered as expressing *the* data relative to which theories of subjective probability are to be tested. We have just seen that we may have included too much, and it is also possible that we have included too little. We will comment at the end of this subsection on possible extensions of the data, but first we will say something about a simple reduction—that is, to take only *negative* ordinal formulas of the form $x < y$ as ordinal data and not positive formulas of the form $x \lesssim y$. In effect this assumes that a person is able to judge that x is strictly *less* in probability than y, but if the person judges that x is *no greater* in probability than y, that can only be, because he or she actually judges that x is less probable than y. This adapts the approach to interval and extensive measurement taken in Adams (1965) to subjective probability theory, and it fits neatly into our present framework. What we should do is consider empirical equivalences not with respect to all ordinal data but rather with respect just to negative ordinal data. This cannot be entered into in detail, but certain implications may be noted.

With respect to negative ordinal data only, the theory P of Basic de Finetti Structures that are probabilistically representable is equivalent to the more general theory Q of structures for which there exist representations satisfying the unidirectional law: If $x < y$, then $p(x) < p(y)$, for some probability function p. However, the axioms for Basic de Finetti Structures are not necessary conditions for this kind of representability, and in fact the class of universal necessary conditions of representability in Q can be taken to be the subset of universal conditions of representability in P that are of the form $-(\phi \mathrel{\&} x_1 < y_1 \mathrel{\&} \ldots \mathrel{\&} x_n < y_n)$, where ϕ is a conjunction of inclusion formulas. Neither the transitivity nor the monotonicity axiom is included in this class, and we only have the following weakened versions:

$$-(x < y \ \& \ y < z \ \& \ z < x)$$

and

$$-(x \cap z \subseteq \varnothing \ \& \ y \cap z \subseteq \varnothing \ \& \ x < y \ \& \ (y \cup z) < (x \cup z)).$$

Roughly this is a theory that is *falsifiable* but that cannot make *predictions,* and it can begin to appear that, in order to attain predictive power, it is also necessary to include an element of idealization! How this idea can be formalized in a way that extends both the language and the data will be outlined below, although it will carry us far from our original concerns.

Adams (1965, p. 206) suggested that judgments of ordering relations are not simple observational data but rather that they are inductive inferences. In particular, the judgement that two events are equiprobable is an inference to the effect that *inequality* between them cannot be established. A way of formalizing this idea involves generalizing to a two-sorted language of a kind described in section 5.3 of Adams and Carlstrom (1979) in which the $x < y$ is subscripted with a *test variatle t*.[7] In this formalism, $x <_t y$ expresses the fact that x would be judged less probable than y by test t. Then $x < y$ can be construed as an abbreviation for $(t)(x <_t y)$ and $x \sim y$ as an abbreviation for $(t)(x \not<_t y \ \& \ y \not<_t x)$. If we assume that tests are *conclusive,* then $(x)(x <_t y)$ follows, if $x <_t y$ holds on any one test. On this assumption, $x < y$ (i.e., $(t)(x <_t y)$) can be regarded as "hard data." However, that does not mean that the *failure* of a test t to establish $x < y$ implies the failure of all tests to establish this, hence, $x \sim y$ would at best be an inductive inference and not hard data on this interpretation. Thus, in our extended two-sorted language, the data are no longer simple atomic formulas and their negations but rather are abbreviations for certain general formulas. However, which generalizations are properly considered as data and which require more complicated kinds of justification is something only detailed analysis of the theory can establish, and it is not a matter of form alone. This is something that lies far beyond our present aims to enter into, and instead we will conclude with a few remarks on mathematical method.

Mathematical Methods and Their Limits

The reader will have noted that the key step in the proofs of the equivalences in Theorem 2 was the reduction of the question of the consistency of data with theory to the question of the solvability of systems of linear inequalities. This permits conditions for the solvability of these systems that are standard in the

---

[7]Note that, if we change from tests t to *occasions o,* so that $x <_o y$ means that x is judged less probable than y on occasion o, then we move in the direction of theories of Stochastic Orderings such as are discussed in Roberts (1979).

mathematical literature (cf. Goldman, 1956) to be translated into syntactic conditions that data on qualitative probability orderings must satisfy if quantitative probability functions are to exist representing them.[8] What makes this reduction possible is the fact that the subjective probability representations we have been considering are *linearizable,* and the possibility of this kind of linearization defines the scope and limits of this approach to data analysis. We will make brief remarks on both the scope and the limits.

Given that most well known representations in the literature of fundamental measurement, including extensive, interval, and conjoint measurement, are essentially linear, our approach applies to those kinds of measurement as well, and in fact Adams, Fagot, and Robinson (1970) analyzed empirical equivalences (there called "data equivalences") in these theories in a manner that parallels our present treatment of theories of subjective probability. The same approach can be taken with theories of a still wider class, including utility theories like the von Neumann–Morgenstern (1944) theory, or Hausner's (1954) "multidimensional utilities" and certain sorts of "weak representations" like Holman's (1969) "weak extensive measurement," Savage's (1954) "almost agreeing subjective probability" representation, and the different weak interval and extensive representations studied in Adams (1965).

Our method does not apply to representations that are essentially nonlinear, including Tversky's (1967) polynomial conjoint representations, Jeffrey's (1965, 1983) and Bolker's (1967) mixture representation of utilities and subjective probabilities, or any "quantitative-analytic" representation of a "qualitative-synthetic" Euclidean geometry of dimension higher than 1 (cf. Hilbert, 1947). All of these cases involve what can be regarded as *polynomial* representations, in consequence of which qualitative data are translatable into inequalities between polynomials of degree higher than 1. The tantalizing thing is that Motzkin (1967) gave a beautiful generalization of standard conditions for the solvability of systems of linear inequalities, which applies to systems of polynomial inequalities. The problem that has so far resisted solution is that of translating Motzkin's conditions into syntactic conditions that data must satisfy in order to translate into solvable systems of polynomial inequalities.[9] It was this difficulty that ultimately led Domotor (1978) to his own amazingly ingenious approach to axiomatizing Jeffrey utilities. I regard the harnessing of Motzkin's methods as one of the really interesting, open technical problems of fundamental measurement theory.

---

[8]To the best of my knowledge, this method was developed independently by Adams (1965) and by Scott (1965) as a means of characterizing the classes of purely universal necessary conditions for representability in different fundamental measurement theories. Related methods are also used in the proof of Theorem 4.1 in Scott (1974).

[9]These conditions are based on the work of Abraham Robinson (1963), which, not surprisingly, traces back to Tarski's decision method for elementary algebra (Tarski & McKinsey, 1948).

REFERENCES

Adams, E. W. (1965). Elements of a theory of inexact measurement. *Philosophy of Science, 32,* 205–228.

Adams, E. W. (1974). The logic of "almost all." *Journal of Philosophical Logic, 3,* 3–17.

Adams, E. W. (1974). Model-theoretic aspects of fundamental measurement theory. In L. Henkin, J. Addison, C. C. Chang, W. Craig, D. Scott, & R. Vaught (Eds.), *Proceedings of the Tarski Symposium* (pp. 437–446). Providence, RI: American Mathematical Society.

Adams, E. W. (1986). Continuity and idealizability of approximate generalizations. *Synthese,* 439–476.

Adams, E. W., & Carlstrom, I. F. (1979). Representing approximate ordering and equivalence relations. *Journal of Mathematical Psychology, 19* (2), 182–207.

Adams, E. W., Fagot, R. F., & Robinson, R. E. (1970). On the empirical status of axioms in theories of fundamental measurement. *Journal of Mathematical Psychology, 7* (3), 379–409.

Bolker, E. D. (1967). A simultaneous axiomatization of utility and subjective probability. *Philosophy of Science, 34,* 333–340.

Davidson, D., Suppes, P., & Siegel, S. (1957). *Decision Making: an Experimental Approach.* Stanford, Stanford University Press.

de Finetti, B. (1937). "La prevision: Ses lois logiques, ses sources subjectives." ("Foresight: its logical laws, its subjective sources.") *Annales de l'Institut Henri Poincare, 7,* 93–158.

Domotor, Z. (1978). Axiomatizaton of Jeffrey utilities. *Synthese, 39,* 165–210.

Goldman, A. J. (1956). Resolution and separation theorems for polyhedral convex sets. In H. W. Kuhn & A. W. Tucker (Eds.), *Linear inequalities and related systems,* Annals of Mathematics Study, *38,* 41–51.

Hausner, M. (1954). "Multidimensional Utilities". In R. M. Thrall, C. H. Coombs, and R. L. Davis (Eds.), *Decision Processes.* New York, Wiley, pp. 167–180.

Hilbert, D. (1947). *The foundations of geometry.* LaSalle, IL: Open Court.

Holman, E. W. (1969). Strong and weak extensive measurement. *Journal of Mathematical Psychology, 6,* 286–293.

Jeffrey, R. C. (1965). *The logic of decision.* New York: McGraw-Hill. Second Edition 1983, University of Chicago Press.

Kolmogorov, A. N. (1956). *The foundations of probability.* New York: Chelsea.

Koopman, B. O. (1940). The axioms and algebra of intuitive probability. *Annals of Mathematics, 41,* 269–292.

Krantz, D. H., Luce, R. D., Suppes, P., & Tversky, A. (1970). *Foundations of measurement.* New York: Academic Press.

Lowenheim, L. (1915). Uber moglichkeiten im relativkalkul. ("On possibilities in the calculus of relations.") *Mathematische Annalen, 76,* 447–470.

Luce, R. D., & Galanter, E. (1963). Psychophysical scaling. In R. D. Luce, R. R. Bush, & E. Galanter (Eds.) *Handbook of Mathematical Psychology,* (Vol. 1, pp. 191–307). New York: Wiley.

Luce, R. D., & Suppes, P. (1969). Preference, utility, and subjective probability. In R. D. Luce, R. R. Bush, & E. Galanter (Eds.), *Handbook of Mathematical Psychology* (Vol. 3, pp. 249–410). New York: Wiley.

Manders, K. (1977). Necessary conditions of representability. Memorandum No. UCB/ERL/M77/3. Berkeley: College of Engineering, University of California.

Motzkin, T. S. (1967). Algebraic inequalities. In O. Shiska (Ed.), *Inequalities* (Vol. 1, pp. 199–203). New York: Academic Press.

Narens, L. (1985). *Abstract measurement theory.* Cambridge: MIT Press.

von Neumann, J., & Morgenstern, O. (1944). *Theory of games and economic behavior.* Princeton: Princeton University Press.

Pfanzagl, J. (1968). *Theory of measurement*. In cooperation with V. Baumann and H. Huber. New York: Wiley.

Roberts, F. S. (1979). *Measurement theory*. Reading: Addison-Wesley.

Robinson, A. (1963). *Introduction to model theory and the metamathematics of algebra*. Amsterdam: North-Holland.

Savage, L. J. (1954). *The foundations of statistics*. New York: Wiley.

Scott, D. (1965). Measurement structures and linear inequalities. *Journal of Mathematical Psychology, 1*, 233–247.

Scott, D. (1974). Completeness and axiomatizability in many-valued logic. In L. Henkin, J., Addison, C. C. Chang, W. Craig, D. Scott, & R. Vaught (Eds.), *Proceedings of the Tarski Symposium* (pp. 411–436). Providence, RI: American Mathematical Society.

Scott, D., & Suppes, P. (1958). Foundational aspects of theories of measurement. *Journal of Symbolic Logic, 23*, 113–128.

Stone, M. H. (1936). The representation theorem for boolean algebra. *Transactions of the American Mathematical Society, 40*, 37–111.

Suppes, P., & Zinnes, J. L. (1963). Basic measurement theory. In R. D. Luce, R. R. Bush, & E. Galanter (Eds.), *Handbook of Mathematical Psychology*. (Vol. 1, pp. 1–76). New York: Wiley.

Tarski, A., & McKinsey, J. C. C. (1948). *A decision method for elementary and geometry*. Santa Monica: RAND Corporation. Second revised edition, 1951, University of California Press.

Tversky, A. (1967). A general theory of polynomial conjoint measurement. *Journal of Mathematical Psychology, 4*, 1–20.

5 Measuring Errors of Measurement

Henry E. Kyburg, Jr.
University of Rochester

What is now considered classical measurement theory—which has nothing to do with the theory of making measurements—is concerned with specifying the homomorphisms of some "qualitative (or empirical) structure into a numerical one" (Narens 1985, p. 5). This view of classical measurement theory is referred to as the *representational theory,* because we are concerned with how to characterize the ways in which a *given* empirical structure can be *represented* in a numerical structure. This approach received a nearly definitive embodiment in Krantz, Luce, Suppes, and Tversky (1971). Narens (1984) provided further elegant mathematical elaborations and developments. However, one form of measurement has been conspicuously ignored in this modern view: the measurement of error. Narens' book does not contain the word "error" in its index. Krantz et al. (1971) provided two entries in the index. One concerns approximation and measurement by inequality relations and gives us no quantitative handle on error, and the other contains the following cryptic remark: "Today (1971), however, few error theories exist; what we know about them is described in Chapters 15–17" (Krantz et al., 1971).

A treatment of error was promised in chapters 15–17 of the second volume. The second volume has now appeared (Krantz et al., 1989). Consistently, it treats error as something that *other* people are subject to, and explores the question from point of view of an experimenter seeking to characterize objectively the error-behavior of subjects. Berka (1983, pp. 196–198) is not much more helpful; he no more than pays his respects to "systematic" and "accidental" errors.

The opposite extreme is represented by Barford (1985): He is concerned with teaching students that an experimentalist must learn to deal with error, and he provides a convenient guide to the mathematics of doing this. Mann (1949) does this same thing at a more sophisticated level, as does E. Bright Wilson (1952). These approaches provide us with the machinery for dealing with errors of measurement, but no philosophical analysis of the relation between measurement and error.

Norman Campbell (1920), the classical early work on measurement, has very little to say about the representation of error, or about dealing with it as a perennial problem of measurement. Brian Ellis (1968) takes an unusually deep and philosophical approach to measurement, but the word "error" doesn't even appear in his index.

Fred Roberts (1979) puts the matter this way: "In a situation of error or noise, some statistical discussion of goodness of fit of a measurement representation is called for. The literature of measurement theory has not been very helpful on the development of such statistical tests." (1979, p. 104)

It is my contention that a representational view of measurement renders a *quantitative* treatment of errors of measurement impossible. In order to argue for this, I must first say what I take a quantitative treatment of errors to be. Clearly it is not a treatment according to which we can apply a veracity-meter to the result of a given measurement and conclude that that measurement is in error by (say) +.13 millimeters. (Berka, 1983, p. 197, almost says this: "[W]e can determine its [the error's] approximate value!") In the first place, the theory must be statistical: What we learn about the errors of measurement associated with a certain measurement procedure is that they follow a certain statistical distribution. Such learning is fraught with problems; we will deal with some of them later, but, for the moment, let us leave these problems to one side.

Let us suppose we have a specific statistical theory of errors of measurement associated with a certain procedure of measurement. This is, after all, roughly what those scientists and engineers for whom measurement is part of their daily round tend to suppose. What do we say about the particular measurement of length? Not that it is in error by +.13 mm, for then we would just subtract .13 to the result of measurement to get the true value. What we might say is that 0.13 represents the *standard deviation* of the distribution of errors generated by the method of measurement employed.

However, this is clearly something that is not amenable to reconstruction according to the representational view. According to that view, we must have a collection of errors and a procedure for mapping them into the reals. The object of the theory, on this view, is to characterize *all* the ways of providing a homomorphism from the set of errors into the reals. Yet the best we can have is a *statistical* characterization of a distribution of errors. The only sense in which we can think of ourselves as *measuring* errors of measurement is collectively—by determining, in given units, the statistical distribution of errors produced by a certain procedure of measurement.

The point here is that we do not and cannot measure a single "error." There are exceptions to this—for example, when we are calibrating a measuring instrument; that will be discussed in due course, but it is not the common case of dealing with error. Furthermore, even in this case, we must *already* know something about the distribution of errors produced by comparisons with the standard.

I conclude that measuring error is not directly analogous to measuring length. There is no way in which we can say, "Here is a set of errors, and a collection of relations among them (some are larger than others); how best shall we represent this collection of objects and relations in the real numbers?" The representational theory simply does not apply without profound changes. And yet we know perfectly well that we *make* errors of measurement, and in fact we have a good sense of when we make large errors as opposed to small errors. How can this be?

WHAT ERRORS?

How do we know that any of our measurements are in error? In the first place, we don't. There is no reason—no a priori, irrefutable reason—to suppose that *any* of our measurements are in error. Suppose we measure the table five times and get five different results? Well no two of those measurements were made at the same time; so what is to say that the table hasn't changed length over time in such a way as to make all those measurements 100% accurate? What is to say? It is perfectly clear, once we ask the question. It is our vague and general (and perfectly well justified, within its limits) theory of physical objects, or our precise and technical theory of physical objects, if we have one. We *know,* and physics supports us in this, that objects like the table do not go around changing their lengths without reason. Without reason? Well except in response to such things as changes in temperature, humidity, physical stresses, and so on.

The most direct source of this knowledge that measurement admits of error is that we have all measured the same thing a number of times and obtained different measurements. Consider the following example: We measure the length of the table ten times, and we get seven or eight different results. "All within experimental error," shall we say? Not so fast—we do not *have* a theory of error, much less any way of determining what is and what is not "within experimental error."

This suggests a problem. If we construe our physics in a technical way, then the laws at issue—laws relating stress and strain, laws relating length to temperature or humidity—must be construed as "experimental laws." (If we were to construe them as deductive consequences of theoretical laws—a most implausible proposal—we would fact the same difficulties as we face in the case of experimental laws.) These experimental laws are obtained from measurement. To obtain the coefficient of thermal expansion (or contraction) for a kind of stuff, we perform laboratory experiments that involve careful measurement. If it were not for measurement—*and our understanding of errors of measurement*—we would not have the experimental laws that inform us that sometimes our measurements are in error.

I think it is no help to retreat to informal physics. It is quite true that we can come to know that most things expand when heated, or even that they don't change in length unless something happens to them (like being heated), but the procedure of measuring errors of measurement will be essentially the same: From vague and informal physical laws, we obtain vague and informal statistical theories of error. In general, large errors are rarer than small errors; there is no a priori limit on the size of an error; positive and negative errors both occur.

Many writers—Balzer, chapter 6, in the present volume; Berka (1983)—refer to "approximation," "fuzziness," and "inaccuracy" to paste over the difference between the crisp ideals of theory and the recalcitrant world of reality. Thank heaven the engineers who design our bridges are not content with such an informal treatment of error.

So it is our knowledge of physics, our knowledge of the way the world goes, that tells us that the table does not change its length, and, in consequence, that tells us that we have made some error or other when we measure the table a number of times and get different results. It is only through knowledge of the physical world, either in the form of common-sense knowledge or in the form of knowledge of the laws of physics that we know that there are any errors at all in our measurements.

However, "our knowledge of physics" is itself a rather vague notion. Exactly what it is about our knowledge of physics that tells us that our measurements are subject to error depends both on what we are trying to measure and what we are assuming belongs to our body of physical knowledge. We all know that the length of the table is essentially constant—that is, that its thermal expansions and contractions are orders of magnitude less than the variations in our measurements of the table. (We leave to one side expansions and contractions due to changes in pressure, magnetic fields, etc.)

It is only when we already have some physical knowledge that we can even begin to think of making measurements. So let us look at the foundations of elementary measurement and see what is required in the way of background knowledge before we can get the measurement business off the ground.

DERIVING ERROR DISTRIBUTIONS

To fix our ideas, let us look at the elementary measurement of length. We can see that some kinds of things change length easily, and other kinds of things do not. Worms, for example, change length easily and frequently. Ax handles do not. Trees change length (height), but they do so very slowly. This is where we start from. So let us look at things like ax handles. Some are longer than others (and stay that way!). Of some pairs of ax handles, one cannot say that one is longer than the other. Note that this is *not* the same as saying that they are the same length.

In fact, there is a tradeoff: If we are very cautious about judging that *A* is longer than *B*, there will be a large class of cases in which we suspend judgment about the relative lengths of things, but that class will not at all be an equivalence class. Just because I can't distinguish between *A* and *B*, and can't distinguish between *B* and *C* (in this cautious sense) doesn't mean that I can't distinguish between *A* and *C*. On the other hand, if I am less cautious about saying that *A* is longer than *B*, then there will be less things about whose relative lengths I suspend judgment, and we may expect that more of the pairs among the things indistinguishable in length from *B* will in turn be indistinguishable.

What is true of the relation "longer than?" We have just seen that its converse is not transitive. In order to assert that "*A* is not longer than *B*," and "*B* is not longer than *C*," imply "*A* is not longer than *C*," we must be infinitely cautious about asserting such statements as "*A* is not longer than *B*." Whether the relation of *not being longer than* is transitive in itself is another question.

We do not get measurement until we have equivalence classes corresponding to *being (truly) the same length as,* and these *require* the transitivity of *not being longer than.* The problems are the following two: How do we characterize such equivalence classes, and how do we come to have grounds for assigning objects to them? On the other hand, if we never have such grounds, how do we *use* these equivalence classes?

In the first place, it seems quite clear that we cannot characterize such equivalence classes in observational terms. As I point out (1984), the lengths that strictly satisfy the traditional formal axioms—especially the existential axioms such as the Archimedean axiom and the divisibility axiom—cannot be taken as empirical objects (or equivalently the functions that correspond to ideal measurement cannot be empirical functions). They are *ideal* objects. The *theory* of ideal length entails that every rigid body has a *true* length at a given time and further that that true length can be expressed in terms of whatever we have selected as the standard unit length. The selection of this standard, given the theory, gives all the equivalence classes we need.

It is not germane to our discussion of error to characterize the theory in general (although in fact it can have any one of a number of conventional formulations), nor to discuss the grounds for accepting such a theory, except to point out that it is *only* by admitting—"embracing"—the existence of error that we can possibly accept any such theory. Our problem is this: Given such a theory, and given the existence of error necessary to allow us to accept that theory, how can we go about *measuring* that error so that we can *use* the theory?

To begin with, let us consider two principles that I have defended elsewhere (1984). The first principle I call *the minimization principle;* the second I call *the distribution principle.* They can be illustrated in the very case I have just mentioned. Suppose we compare the lengths of a lot of objects. The transitivity principles only hold for rigid bodies; therefore, we had best include "x is a Rigid Body" among our predicates. So let us suppose that we have accumulated a number of statements of the following forms: "A is a rigid body;" "A is longer than B;" "A is not a rigid body;" and "A is not longer than B." Suppose, as seems natural, that this collection of statements is inconsistent with the following generalizations: "If x, y, and z are rigid bodies, then, if x is longer than y, and y is longer than z, x is longer than z;" and "If x, y, and z are rigid bodies, then, if x is not longer than y, and y is not longer than z, x is not longer than z." *Both* of course are required to generate equivalence classes of lengths. Further, it is also quite clear that we want to have the following as an a priori principle: "If x and y are rigid bodies, and x is longer than y, then y is not longer than x."

It follows that some of these statements, however firmly supported by observation, are false—How many? Which ones? There is no reason (unless we are in the unlikely situation of having both "x is longer than y," and "x is not longer than y" supported by observation) that *all* the statements cannot be false. But of course to reject them all, or to regard them all as unsupported, is gratuitous skepticism of the worst and most self-defeating sort.

"Which ones?" seems a question impossible to answer except arbitrarily. Fortunately we do not have to answer that question in order to use the conflicts as evidence for the frequency of error of judgments of the sorts considered. For that, we need only answer: "How many?"

"How many?" To avoid gratuitous skepticism, it seems quite clear that we should attribute no more error to our observations than we are *required* to attribute to them. So we should regard as erroneous the *minimum* number of statements that will render our body of observations consistent with the generalizations we have taken as a priori truths. (Note that this is different from minimizing the long run error rates; because we may plausibly regard the errors of observation of different sorts as stochastically independent, it is quite possible, as has been suggested, that the *estimated* long run error rates may differ from those that I have called minimal.)

This is the minimization principle: Do not regard any more statements as false than you need to in order to make your observations consistent with your body of knowledge.

But this principle doesn't give you error rates for particular *kinds* of observations. To get them, we need a supplementary principle: the distribution principle. What are the *kinds* of statements involved in our example? "x is longer than y;" "x is not longer than y;" "x is a rigid body;" "x is not a rigid body." The distribution principle tells us that the errors among these kinds of observation statements among those we have accepted as observational should be distributed as evenly as possible, *given* the satisfaction of the minimization principle.

This principle too, can be questioned. Perhaps negative judgments are intrinsically more (or less—I honestly do not know) reliable than positive judgments. But pending an argument to this effect, we had best stick to the even distribution.

This does not mean that each *kind* of observation will exhibit the same *frequency* of errors. We can have *no* grounds, in the situation described, to regard *any* of the statements of the form "*x* is not a rigid body" as false.

But some statements of the forms "*x* is a rigid body;" "*x* is longer than *y*;" and "*x* is not longer than *y*," *must* be wrong. Given the minimal *number* that must be wrong, there may well be various ways of distributing error among statements of these three kinds. Our second principle tells us to perform this distribution in the most democratic way possible. Note that this still gives us no way to settle on any *particular* statement as erroneous.

Now we can use this data—that so and so many of each kind of statement are erroneous—as data for a statistical inference. Given that the necessary conditions of randomness are met, we can infer with high probability that the error rate of observation statements of the various sorts is close to the error frequency we have derived from our sample of observations using the two principles of minimization and distribution. Needless to say, justifying this inference is another story entirely. We just assume that we may identify the minimal and most evenly distributed rejection rate as an observed *error* frequency, and use this observed error frequency as a basis from which to infer a long run error rate. From a finite body of (inconsistent) observation statements, we may, thus, infer (at a given level of confidence) long run error rates.

Our two principles lead to error rates for complex judgments that do not always depend directly on the error rates of their components. Statements like "*A* is a rigid body, and *B* is a rigid body, and *A* > *B*, and *B* > *A*" are subject to rejection rates of 100%.

MEASURING

Of course these principles do not apply directly to quantitative measurement. If we reject the minimal number of our measurements of the table we must reject in order to ensure that the table has a real-valued length, we must reject all but one or all but a small number. But this would only be the case if we construed our measurements as, in a sense, claiming "objective validity", and the true length of the table is not something we can claim to observe. Nevertheless we can apply quantitative analogs of the principles of minimum rejection and distribution.

First we must construct a meterstick. Consider Robinson Crusoe. He has all the physical knowledge needed to start measuring lengths, but he does not have a meterstick. However, Robinson can easily enough construct a stick that can be construed as the colinear juxtaposition of a large number of rigid bodies of the same length. Start with a handy rigid body. Mark what appears to be the midpoint. Use the principle (it follows from the generalizations already cited) that, if x, y, and z are rigid bodies, and x is the same length as y, and y is the same length as z, then x is the same length as z. We can find (or construct) an object the same length (so far as we can tell) as one half of our original rigid body and see how it fits on the other half. We can adjust the midpoint until the left half, right half, and test object are all in the same indifference class—that is, each bears the relation *not longer than* to the other two, so far as observation is concerned.

It is a fact about the world—about rigid objects—that we *can* do this. We can adjust three objects (two of them being parts of a single rigid body) so that no two of the three objects stand, so far as we can tell by direct observation, in the relation *longer than*. Now we repeat the process—that is, we can find a rigid body that is congruent to each of the four segments of the original body obtained by dividing each of the first two divisions in half. Again this reflects a fact about the world. The process can be continued until we have 1024 segments making up our original bistick (binary meterstick).

Note that we are not suggesting that each of these segments is *really* the same length. They are only indistinguishable from each other, and the indistinguishability is that transmitted through an auxilliary rigid body. We will see later how to refine the accuracy of our bistick.

If we can guess the midpoint of a rigid body, we can reasonably suppose that we can roughly judge the tenths of the rigid body. Thus, we can measure things with our bistick to within a ten-thousandth part of the unit length.

Let us now measure a rigid body with the bistick. For simplicity, let us take the original bistick as the standard unit length. If we do this a number of times, we get a number of different results: .5421, .5407, .5416, and so on. We cannot construe these measurements as purporting to be real congruences; the rigid body cannot be congruent to different fractions of the bistick. So what is the relation between these congruences and the true length of the body?

We have *true* lengths. These are provided by our abstract theory. We can *define* true lengths perfectly well. The true length of Robinson Crusoe's table is

$\lim_{m \to \infty} \dfrac{k}{m}$ bisticks if and only if the difference in length between the collinear juxtaposition of k bisticks and the collinear juxtaposition of m congruent tables can be made arbitrarily small by increasing m. What the measuring process does is to associate an abstract length with an object. The error associated with a measurement is reflected by the difference between the result of that measurement and the true value of the quantity being measured.

Just as the minimization principle, applied to categorical judgments, told us not to assume that any more are in error than we need to assume to be in error, so an analogous principle, applied to quantitative judgments, will tell us not to assume that any measurements are more in error than we need to assume they are. How shall we quantify this error? There are relatively compelling reasons for measuring it as the *square* of the difference between the observed measurement and the true value. The compelling reasons have more to do with analytic tractability than anything philosophically profound.

So what do we do in the case of measurements of a single object? We minimize the mean squared error. What this amounts to is that we take, as our estimate of the true value of the length of the object, the estimate of the mean of the distribution of measurements. The estimate of the variance of the measurements is exactly the estimate of the variance of the errors of measurement. Given the mean and variance of the distribution of errors of measurement, we can use our observations to make *probable* assertions concerning the true value: If the probability of making an error of less than size e is 0.99, and we observe a length of L, then (assuming appropriate conditions of randomness) the probability is 0.99 that the true value lies in the interval $L \pm e$. Of course, to implement these observations, we must have come to terms with statistical inference in general— but that is nothing special or peculiar to measurement. Jaech (1985) provides some practical guidance along these lines.

But we are not done yet. We have talked of the measurements of a single object. We have a distribution of errors of measurement for measurements of that object—we may suppose that we have inferred it to be roughly normal, with a mean of 0 and a variance roughly equal to the variance of the measurements we have made. How about other objects?

Well let us measure another object. We get another distribution of measurements. The mean may well be different, but the variance is quite likely to be about the same. Indeed, in accordance with the statistical principle of assuming no more populations than necessary, we may lump the second central moments of both sets of observations together to form an estimate of the variance of the measuring process. It *could* be the case of course that the numbers could render it *practically certain* that the two populations of measurements had different variances. In that case, the data could not be combined to obtain an estimate of the general variance. This again is a matter of statistical inference and not a matter that is peculiar to measurement.

It is part of our theory of measurement (a rather fundamental part of our theory of the measurement of length) that the true length of the collinear juxtaposition of x and y is the sum of the true length of x and the true length of y. How does this bear on our knowledge of the distribution of errors of measurement of length? It imposes a constraint on the true lengths, and that constraint in turn may require the attribution of more error to our measurements than would otherwise be required.

For example, suppose that measurements of x yield 3, 4, and 5 feet; measurements of y yield 7, 8, and 9 feet; and measurements of z yield 13, 14, and 15 feet. Minimum error would suggest that we have made six errors of one foot—the distribution of errors would have a mean close to 0 and a variance of close to ¾. But now let us also suppose that z is the collinear juxtaposition of x and y.

If x^*, y^*, and z^* are the true values of the lengths of x, y, and z, and z is the collinear justaposition of x and y, then we have $x^* + y^* = z^*$, and the total squared error of measurement is as follows:

$$E = (3 - x^*)^2 + (4 - x^*)^2 + (5 - x^*)^2 + (7 - y^*)^2 + (8 - y^*)^2 +$$
$$(9 - y^*)^2 + (13 - (x^* + y^*))^2 + (14 - (x^* + y^*))^2 + (15 - (x^*$$
$$+ y^*))^2$$

Elementary calculus shows that the least squares estimates for x^*, y^*, and z^* are now $4\frac{2}{3}$, $8\frac{2}{3}$, $13\frac{1}{3}$; the mean error in the sample is $\frac{2}{3}$ (mean squared error $\frac{4}{9}$), and the sample variance has increased from $\frac{3}{4}$ to $1\frac{1}{4} =$

$$\sum_{i=1}^{N} (E(X_i) - X_i)^2/(N - 1)$$

Abstractly the statistical problem is the following: Construe our measurements as measurements of $body_1$, $body_2$, . . . $body_n$. Consider the following constraints imposed by the axioms of our language: The transitivity of "longer than," the transitivity of "not longer than," the irreflexivity of "longer than" (but the last does not bear on our assessments of error directly). We want to estimate the mean of each subpopulation. We want to estimate the variance of this population (or these subpopulations). We find (at least within reasonably wide limits) that there is no reason to regard the variance as differing among the populations. We should also bear in mind the informational advantage in using a larger sample, which we can do if we lump each of the classes of measurement together.

Suppose we have this statistical problem solved. What have we then? We have precisely what we express only vaguely and approximately by saying that the distribution of errors is, within ordinary limits, normally distributed with variance s^2 and mean m. Note that m is rather unlikely to be *exactly* zero—we can define the error in such a way that its mean value is zero, if we are concerned only with independent measurements of one particular object. But if there are relations that have to be respected among objects (such as additivity of length), we can no longer guarantee that the minimum error principle will lead us to a mean error of zero.

The variance also must be taken to be larger, if we take the objects we are measuring to satisfy such conditions as additivity. These "analytic" constraints on length lead to the attribution of greater errors to the measurement of length than we would have without those constraints.

GENERALIZING

One of the factors that affects our measurements of length is temperature. If we take account of temperature, we find that we can improve the accuracy of our

measurements of length. What we need to do is to take account of the changes of
length of our standard bistick and of the object being measured as the temperature
changes. One way to do this is to take a look at the thermometer on the wall and
observe the length of its mercury column.

This suggests that we can't measure length accurately without measuring
temperature, and simultaneously that we can't measure temperature without measuring length. (Of course we can measure temperature by means of a bimetalic
strip connected to a spring and a dial, but then we are measuring around the
circumference of a circle, or we can measure by means of a digital readout
thermometer, but this involves even more theory than the law of thermal expansion.) However, when we read the thermometer, are we really *measuring* length?
I do not mean to raise labyrinthian questions of intentionality. Whatever my
intentions, whatever is going on in my mind, I am comparing one object (the
mercury column) with another (its holder) that is divided into collinear and
contiguous parts. If such comparisons are infected with some metaphysical dis-
ease, measurements of lengths and of temperatures will both be affected.

Clearly such relations do not undermine the possibility of taking account of
temperature in making accurate measurements of length. Equally clearly, however, both the theory of length (its additivity) and the theory of thermal expansion
(to a first approximation, its linearity) must be called on in determining the errors
of measurement of both temperature and length. The problem of sorting out the
errors in several kinds of measurements is discussed to some extent in *Theory
and measurement*. It suffices here to observe that, for example, the direct measurement of a temperature is taken to be more subject to error than the measurement of length. (In fact it is not clear what *is* error. There has to be some
indication that the law of linear thermal expansion is reasonably close to being
true before we can even construct a thermometer as a way of measuring *temperature*.) However, as soon as we have the law of linear thermal expansion (that
is, as soon as we have accepted it as part of our working practical/theoretical
machinery), we must allow temperature to play a role in determining the distribution of errors of measurement of length.

This is not hard, because that role will in general be to reduce errors: If we
take account of the temperature of our bistick and reduce its results to *standard*
temperature (and similarly for the objects we are measuring), we find the results
to be more closely clustered than they were otherwise. That is, we have succeeded in reducing the *variance* of the error distribution of length measurements.
But just as in the case of adopting the principle that length is additive, the
addition of a new *constraint* requires that we take account of more sources of
error. If we measure two temperatures and two lengths, and take for granted a
coefficient of thermal expansion, and the results do not fit the law of thermal
expansion, error must be imputed both to the temperature measurements and to
the length measurements.

If this sounds strange—to say that we are increasing error by adding a constraint (in the form of the law of thermal expansion) and decreasing error (by taking account of temperature in our measurements of length)—perhaps a more detailed treatment of the example will be helpful.

> Instruments: a mercury thermometer and our bistick.
>
> Objects: an assortment of rigid bodies composed of the same substance (different from that of the bistick) and having appropriate shapes; some are collinear juxtapositions of others.

Procedure 1: Ignore temperature. Measure an object a number of times with the bistick. Statistically infer a distribution of measurements with mean approximately m_1, and variance approximately $s_1{}^2$; assume that we need not bother with higher moments.

Conclusion 1: To minimize the sum of the squares of the errors of observation already made, take the true length of this object to be m_1, and the distribution of error to be given by the *same* distribution, with the exception that it is displaced by an amount m_1, so that its mean is 0. We could of course find ways of dividing these observations into groups: for example, those made on Mondays, those made on Tuesdays, and so on. However, we will (presumably) find no statistical justification for the hypothesis that these groups of observations come from different samples. (We can no doubt find "unnatural" groups of observations that would suggest that we are sampling from distinct populations; knowing what is unnatural and how to disregard it is a general problem of statistical inference and presents nothing special in the way of a problem for measurement.)

Procedure 2: Still ignoring temperature, we measure a lot of objects a lot of times. We assume that we can faultlessly reidentify objects. Thus, our measurements fall into clearcut groups, each identified with an object. Our measurements now have a general mean gm_2 and a very large *general* variance $gs_2{}^2$.

Conclusion 2: But now we have excellent statistical justification for taking our measurements to fall into different populations according to the object being measured. (In general, this is the case, although some pairs of objects may be so nearly the same length that the hypothesis that their measurements constitute a single population cannot be rejected by the data.) If we sort the data this way and then perform our statistical inferences in accord with the principle of minimizing past observational error, then we find that the general population of errors of measurement of each object has a distribution very much like the distribution of errors of measurement we uncovered in procedure 1: mean 0, variance about $s_1{}^2$. In fact, if we think of *error*, what we have is a set of distributions, all characterized by the same variance. We have no reason to regard any subsets of our general sample as coming from different populations so far as our inference regarding the variance (or higher order moments, for that matter) is concerned. (Of course we *might* have such reasons; if our original set of objects included very big ones and very tiny ones, and it were much more difficult to measure these accurately, we *would* have reasons, internal to our collected statistics, for dividing our sample of measurements to take account of different sample variances characterizing these cases.) This variance, s_2^2, is, we may suppose, about the same size as s_1^2 but, in virtue of the last observation, more accurately known.

Procedure 3: Now let us assume that some of the objects in our set are (faultlessly identifiable as) collinear juxtapositions of others, and let us impose the constraint that the length of the juxtaposition of two objects is the sum of the lengths of the two objects. As in Procedure 2, we make a lot of measurements of a lot of things—let us assume in fact that we make the same number of measurements of the same things. The observational basis of our conclusion will be the same as that of Conclusion 2.

Conclusion 3: From our assumptions, it follows now that the sum of the true values corresponding to the set of measurements of object x and the true value corresponding to the set of measurements of object y is the true value corresponding to the set of measurements of the collinear juxtaposition of x and y. This is to say that the means of the populations of the three kinds of measurement must bear the corresponding relation, if the mean errors are zero. As before, we minimize the sum of the squared errors of our actual (past) observations and, subject to this constraint, distribute our errors evenly. Since we have imposed this constraint at least *some* mean error estimates will not be 0. If the mean estimate is not 0, the variance will be larger than it was when the mean estimate was 0. However, we may still be able to use the whole population of performed measurements to estimate the variance of the error distribution, and overall the mean error will still be very close to zero. Thus we get a distribution of error that is *roughly* centered on 0 and has a variance s_3^2, a little bit larger than s_2^2. Taking account of a new constraint has required us to admit a wider range of error.

Procedure 4: Let us now suppose that we have a thermometer and that we know that the law of linear thermal expansion is true. To simplify matters, let us suppose that we also know the coefficient of thermal expansion of the substance of which all our objects (except for the bistick and the thermometer) are made. We also suppose ourselves to know the coefficient of thermal expansion of our bistick. Again let us make the same measurements, but now let us include with each measurement a temperature measurement. Assume that temperature measurement is without error.

Conclusion 4: Take t_0 as the reference temperature. Now the true value of the length of an object is to be construed as its length at t_0, and the error of *measurement* is as follows:

$$k \cdot (t - t_0)TL - ML,$$

where k is the coefficient of thermal expansion, t is the temperature, TL is the true length, and ML is the measured length (corrected for temperature—i.e., $M_0 \cdot k' \cdot (t - t_0)$, where k' is the coefficient of thermal expansion of our bistick). Now we choose the true lengths of the objects measured so as to minimize the squared error of our observations, subject to *two* constraints as follows: the additivity constraint and the thermal expansion constraint. However, in view of the fact that some of the variance $s_3{}^2$ of the third procedure was due variations in temperature, we may suppose that the variance $s_4{}^2$ is significantly smaller than $s_3{}^2$. The corrected readings are more closely packed about the mean values.

Procedure 5: Finally let us take account of the errors of measurement of temperature, just to show that it can be done. The circumstances are the same as in Procedure 4, except that we no longer assume that the measurement of temperature is error-free. The other data are the same as in Procedure 4.

Conclusion 5: Now our observations are construed as being of the following form:

$$TL \cdot k \cdot (Tt - t_0 + te) = M_0 \cdot k' \cdot (Tt - t_0 + te) + le,$$

where *le* is the error in the length measurement, *te* the error in the temperature measurement, and M_0 the observed measurement—the *reading*. Following the earlier principles, we choose *TL* and *Tt* to minimize squared error of past observations and to distribute the error as evenly as possible in the two categories.

This last exercise suggests a further one that might be made in the interest of realism, that we have also a class *L* of prior length measurements, from which we derive a prior distribution of errors of measurement of length. Let *S* be the set of observations that, in the absence of the law of thermal expansion as applied to our test object, gives us the distribution of errors of measurements of temperature. Thus, *L* and *S* give prior distributions of the respective errors, and when we combine observations of length and of temperature through the law of thermal expansion, the magnitude of the samples on which these error distributions are based is relevant. It is the *whole* set of observations whose observational error must be minimized and not just the joint ones we happen to make at the moment.

Of course we may no longer have individual records of these prior measurement observations. However, we can still compute them approximately, working backwards from interval estimates at given levels of confidence to approximate numbers and distributions. With a lot of history, we simply let the established error distributions dominate others: What we learn about new properties of matter will not (any longer) be taken to affect the distribution of errors of measurement with a meterstick.

The generalized lesson is that it is only *accepted theory* that gives us errors of measurement, where, in "accepted theory," I include everything from the additivity of length to relativity and biochemistry and even quantum mechanics. It is, therefore, only relative to accepted theory that we can derive a quantitative statistical theory of errors of measurement. And of course what theories are accepted depends on the results of quantitative tests—that is, on measurements—that is, in turn on the theory of measurement. Although there is no vicious circularity here, there is certainly something to be unpacked, analysed, and explained: the relationship between theories of error and the acceptability of theories. However, that does not concern the "measurement of errors of measurement;" it represents yet another "new" problem of induction.

We should also note that, despite the fact that, in some sense, the theory of errors of measurement of a certain sort—measurements of length performed by method M, say—depends on a variety of other theories, any well established method of measurement will be accompanied by a theory of error that is largely independent of recent results.

This is true for the three following reasons: First, current tests of theories involve more than a single quantity, and, as we saw in connection with the law of thermal expansion, the errors of measurement revealed by tests may be distributed among a number of different kinds of measurements. We may know more, on the basis of historical statistics, about the distribution of some of these errors than about the distribution of others. Thus, there may be much more room to impute error to the results of some measurements than to the results of others.

Second, if the test of a current theory yielded results that would require an unusual (particularly a strongly biassed) theory of errors of measurement, we would first note that the sample of errors obtained from those tests should be construed as being drawn from a *different population* than that from which the classical sample was drawn. This is based on *internal* statistical tests. We would then choose between our theory of measurement by method M that implies that M yields a population of errors that is homogeneous with respect to partitions defined by the particular theory T under investigation and the theory T itself. It is not surprising that we usually hang onto M and reject T—although the logical warrant for doing so has yet to be spelled out.

Third, by far the greatest mass of data relates to older and simpler theories than those currently being tested. It thus statistically swamps the results of current tests. This is so much the case that we base our estimates of error on classically established error distributions. Often we can obtain the parameters of the population of errors produced by a given method, or even a given instrument, by testing the method or instrument against certain *standard* quantities, and do so on the basis of relatively small samples.

CONCLUSIONS

The measurement of error is not like other measurement. Ordinarily, in measurement, we associate a particular number (or magnitude) with a particular object—for example, a "reading" of a measuring instrument is associated with the object measured. There is nothing corresponding to this in the measurement of error. The result of "measuring error" is a statistical distribution of errors to be associated with a method (or kind of instrument or instrument) M of making measurements. We do not generally observe or measure *particular* errors.

We might (absurdly but consistently) claim that all of our measurements were

100% accurate. That is, we might deny the existence of error. To maintain this, we would have to repudiate almost every bit of quantitative knowledge we take ourselves to have: not merely ordinary physics and engineering, but even such seemingly *a priori* principles as the transitivity "longer than." (Perhaps the simplest way to do this is to assume that the world is in a causal temporal flux, and that there is no measuring of time.) All of our physical laws would then have to be regarded as statistical laws relating varying quantities.) It should be noted that this procedure would render all representational theories of measurement mere superstition. We would have no reason to suppose any stable structure behind our statistics for the theories to "represent."

It is certainly more natural—and in accord with our qualitative knowledge of the world—to construe our measurements as measurements *of* an underlying reality. To do this, we must suppose the following two things: (a) that our measurements are prone to error, and (b) that the underlying reality has the structure we attribute to it. In order to *use* measurement, we must have some quantitative theory of errors of measurement. However, at the same time, the results of measurement surely are relevant to the structure we impute to the underlying reality.

Furthermore, it is not merely the internal structure of particular quantities (such as length) that is relevant to the derivation of the distribution of errors of measurement, but the structure of multiple quantities that are related by law—for example temperature and length as related by the law of thermal expansion, or pressure, volume, and temperature as related by the ideal gas law. As those who pursue the purely mathematical problems of representational measurement theory have realized—although mainly in connection with psychological magnitudes— conjoint measurement and scientific theory are intimately tied together. See, for example Narens (1985), Berka (1983), Krantz et al. (1971).

The statistical theories of error we emerge with depend not only on the structure we attribute to the magnitudes being measured but on the general structure of the world as captured by our assumed laws and theories connecting these magnitudes to other magnitudes.

In the actual process of evaluating the distributions of errors of measurement, this is easily seen. (See Jaech, 1985, for example, or Wilson, 1952.) What has been lacking is any work that brings the problem of measurement error to bear on the foundations of measurement. It is only the existence of error that allows us to believe in measurement, and it is only the knowledge of the distribution of error that allows us to use measurements in investigating and controlling the world.

REFERENCES

Barford, N. C. (1985). *Experimental measurements: Precision, error, and truth* (2nd ed.). New York: Wiley.

Berka, K. (1983). *Measurement.* Dordrecht: Reidel.

Campbell, N. R. (1952). *What is science?* New York: Dover. Original work published 1921.

Campbell, N. R. (1957). *Foundations of physics.* New York: Dover. Original work published 1920.

Ellis, B. (1968). *Basic concepts of measurement.* Cambridge: Cambridge University Press.

Jaech, J. L. (1985). *Statistical analysis of measurement errors.* New York: Wiley.

Krantz, D. H., Luce, R. D., Suppes, P., & Tversky, A. (1971). *Foundations of measurement.* New York: Academic Press.

Krantz, D. H., Luce, D. R., Suppes, P., & Tversky, A. (1989). *Foundations of Measurement, II.* New York: Academic Press.

Kyburg, H. E., Jr. (1984). *Theory and measurement.* Cambridge: Cambridge University Press.

Mann, H. B. (1949). *Analysis and design of experiments.* New York: Dover.

Narens, L. (1985). *Abstract measurement theory.* Cambridge: MIT Press.

Roberts, F. S. (1979). *Measurement Theory.* Reading, Massachusetts: Addison Wesley.

Wilson, E. B. (1952). *An introduction to scientific research.* New York: McGraw-Hill.

6

The Structuralist View of Measurement: An Extension of Received Measurement Theories

Wolfgang Balzer[1]
Seminar fur Philosophie, Logik, und Wissenschaftstheorie
Munchen, FRG

There is a vast literature on measurement and on the relation to theory of measurement, experience, evidence.[2] With few exceptions, these accounts have cases of simple, isolated, empirical, numerical hypotheses, like the ideal gas law, Ohm's law or Pythagoras' theorem, as their paradigm examples from which the general ideas are drawn and against which they are checked. However, scientific progress leads from those isolated beginnings to comprehensive networks of theories in which the systems originally studied form only small fragments. New devices of measurement are then introduced, and many (or even most) of the original methods of measurement are regarded as obsolete after a while. Such new devices of measurement often are quite different from the original methods. For instance, they often are "dependent" on the very same theory whose functions they determine—an idea hardly consistent with traditional concepts of measurement. The broader perspective of comprehensive theoretical networks and the practice of measurement in such broader contexts call for an extension of traditional views about measurement—an extension that may well necessitate some revision.

The term "measurement" in ordinary as well as in current scientific language is ambiguous. Sometimes counting is included, sometimes numerical calculations are excluded, sometimes concatenation, and sometimes experiment are regarded as necessary. A theory of measurement cannot perfectly match all these

---

[1]Much preliminary work from which the structuralist view of measurement presented here finally developed was done in DFG project Ba 678/1 and Ba 678/2. I am indebted to B. Lauth, R. Niederée, and R. D. Luce for critical comments and suggestions on the first draft.

[2]For a selection, see the references in Berka (1983) and Krantz et al. (1971).

usages, simply because they are inconsistent. I will not be concerned here with defending my special use of the word measurement. Rather I am interested in a theory about those kinds of scientific practice that aim at the determination of particular features, properties, relations attached to special, prepared objects or events. These kinds of scientific practice provide an array of phenomena rich enough to justify metascientific theorizing—maybe even too rich, given the lack of success up to now—and they include the phenomena studied by traditional theories of measurement.

This chapter is intended to sketch the basis for an extended concept of measurement that includes measurement in the context of big nets of theories as well as more "local," "fundamental," traditional situations. I cannot elaborate on the details and applications of this extended account; there are too many for this chapter.[3] Instead I will concentrate on the way this account relates to and extends traditional approaches.

I apologize for throwing together much outstanding and original work on measurement in one big pot to which the label "received view" is attributed, but I see no other possibility to arrive at a condensed, general comparison. Of course the particular label is chosen on purpose, although with a positive, "conservative" touch: What we received is a great heritage forming a solid *fundament* on which we can further build.

THE RECEIVED VIEW OF MEASUREMENT

Overview

According to the received view, measurement consists, very roughly, of an assignment of numbers to concrete, empirical objects or events such that the assigned numbers (together with suitable standard mathematical operations) *represent* the empirical objects or events (together with the empirical operations defined among them). In other words, for a given *empirical structure* consisting of a domain of concrete objects or events and concrete operations among these, measurement in a piecemeal fashion, establishes a mathematical structure consisting of a domain of numbers and abstract operations among these such that the mathematical structure represents the empirical one, which means that both structures are homomorphic or even isomorphic under a suitable mapping of empirical objects to mathematical objects. Often the empirical structure can be characterized by axioms expressing operationally testable propositions, and the existence of a homomorphism into a suitable mathematical structure can be proved from these axioms. The statement expressing the existence and uniqueness of such a homomorphism is then called a *representation theorem,* and the mapping

---

[3]Compare Balzer (1983, 1985b).

from objects to numbers (or the whole class of these) is termed a *scale*. Among the empirical operations there will usually be a relation of order, and classes of such orderings (subject to further conditions) are called *quantities*. I will say that the values of a numerical function *belong to* a quantity, if the function represents empirical structures of which the quantity's orderings are parts.

Historically this view may be traced back into antiquity. Euclid's axioms may be regarded as operationally testable statements about unspecified concrete operations. That is, they become testable once suitable operations are specified. In fact, these axioms miss only little of the axioms in D3 below. In modern times, things got started again when Hoelder produced the first mathematically sound representation theorem (Hölder, 1901), and this spread into applications of empirical sciences—most prominently of psychology. The classical modern formulation was achieved in *Foundations of measurement* by Krantz, Luce, Suppes, and Tversky (1971), which expresses a strong, progressive research program. Recent developments have focused on the study of interlocked concatenation, conjoint systems, and a generalized notion of scale type (e.g., Luce and Narens, 1985; Narens, 1985). I cannot do justice here to all the different individual contributions and expressions of the approach.

In spite of individual differences, all (or most) authors seem to agree on the distinctive feature that measurement yields numerical representations of empirical structures. For this reason, the received view of measurement is usually called the *representationalist* view.

This view of measurement is confirmed along several lines. First, numbers or mathematical objects allow for many manipulations that are impossible or at least difficult and inefficient to perform with concrete objects or events: Numbers can be compared according to their magnitude, and they can be added, multiplied, raised to the power, and so on. All this can be done without worrying about dimensions, about whether different numbers belong to the same quantity, and whether it makes sense to, say, add numbers belonging to different quantities. In this sense, numerical representations are an efficient means to unify and to make coherent scientific talk about and scientific practise dealing with concrete objects, events, and operations. Second, in several cases, historical developments in fact led to the establishment of numerical representations. This holds for geometry, chronometry, kinematics, gravitational and inertial mass and temperature, to mention some important cases in which numerical representation is crucial.[4] Third, it may be pointed out that numbers, after all, *are nothing but* "numerical representations" of empirical structures. So the representation of the latter in terms of numbers has a strong analytic flavor.[5]

---

[4]Other examples for which representation theorems can be proved but for which the empirical structures are less reliable are found, for instance, in Krantz et al. (1971).

[5]This view I share with perhaps few philosophers of mathematics. See Balzer (1979).

Fundamental Measurement

Fundamental measurement begins at the individual level of concrete systems. Let us look at one such system that conceptualizes or captures just one single process of measurement in the course of which one value, to be called the *measured value* in the following, is determined. A paradigm is measurement of distance by means of rigid rods, and the measurement of one distance-value is conceptualized as a process in which different copies of a unit-rod are put together (concatenated) until the two points in question can be connected by the concatenated sequence of units. The distance is then "read off" by counting the minimal number of unit rods necessary in order to establish a connection.

In general, such a system will involve concrete *objects* or *events* (like points marked on rigid bodies in the distance example, or processes in the measurement of time) as well as concrete operations among those objects or events (like concatenation and comparison of rigid rods). The operations can be classified into a certain, small number of *few* kinds, and by looking at many similar systems, several properties of the kinds of operations can be extracted and stated explicitly as axioms about the kinds of operations involved. These items, the *domain D* of objects, the *kinds of concrete operations* $o_1, \ldots, o_r$ involved, and the *axioms* characterizing these operations make up what is called an *empirical structure*. This is a structure $\langle D, o_1, \ldots, o_r \rangle$ satisfying the axioms.

However, in order to speak of measurement, representation is necessary. The empirical structure we find in some real system is matched by a *numerical structure* $\langle \mathbb{R}, m_1, \ldots, m_r \rangle$ where $\mathbb{R}$ is the set of real numbers, and each m_i ($i \leq r$) is a relation of the same type over $\mathbb{R}$ as is o_i over D. The numerical structure $\langle \mathbb{R}, m_1, \ldots, m_r \rangle$ is said to *represent* the empirical structure $\langle D, o_1, \ldots, o_r \rangle$, iff there is a mapping $\omega: D \rightarrow \mathbb{R}$, which is a homomorphism with respect to the relations on both sides. Altogether the conceptualization of a concrete system as a system capturing some process of measurement yields an entity of the following form:

$$\langle \langle D, o_1, \ldots, o_r \rangle, \langle \mathbb{R}, m_1, \ldots, m_r \rangle, \omega \rangle$$

(i.e., an empirical structure together with a numerical structure and some homomorphism ω between both). Let us call any such entity a *system of fundamental measurement*.

Here is a simple example.[6]

D1 (a). x is a *model of length measurement with units U* iff there exist D, $\leq$, o and ω such that $x = \langle \langle D, \leq, o \rangle, \langle \mathbb{R}, \leq, + \rangle, \omega \rangle$ and the following holds:

1. D is a set and $\varnothing \neq U \subseteq D$.
2. $\leq \subseteq D \times D$ is transitive, reflexive, and connected.

---

[6]In D1 and D3 below and the corresponding proofs, I use the following notation: "$a \equiv b$" for "$a \leq b$ and $b \leq a$," "$a < b$" for "$a \leq b$ and not $b \leq a$", "$x(\omega')$" for the result of substituting ω' in x for ω, and "na" for "$ao \ldots oa$" (n–times). $\mathbb{R}^+$ and $\mathbb{N}$ denote the sets of positive reals and of natural numbers respectively.

3. o is a partial function from $D \times D$ to D and is associative.

4. For all a, b, $c \in D$ for which $a \circ b$, $a \circ c$, $b \circ c$ are defined:
   $a < a \circ b$, and $(a \lesssim b$, iff $a \circ c \lesssim b \circ c$, iff $c \circ a \lesssim c \circ b)$

5. For all b, $b' \in U$: $b \equiv b'$.

6. For all $a \in D$, there exist $b_1, \ldots, b_n \in U$ such that $b_1 \circ \ldots \circ b_n$ is defined, and $b_1 \circ \ldots \circ b_n \equiv a$.

7. $\omega: D \to \mathbb{R}$ and the following holds for all a, $b \in D$:

   7.1. $a \lesssim b$, iff $\omega(a) \leq \omega(b)$.

   7.2. $\omega(a \circ b) = \omega(a) + \omega(b)$ (when $a \circ b$ is defined).

(b). x is a *model of length measurement* iff there exists some U such that x is a model of length measurement with units U.

T1 (a). If x is a model of length measurement with units U and with units U', then for all b, b': if $b \in U$ and $b' \in U'$ then $b \equiv b'$.

(b). If $x = \langle\langle D, \lesssim, \circ\rangle, \langle \mathbb{R}, \leq, +\rangle, \omega\rangle$ and $x' = \langle\langle D, \lesssim, \circ\rangle, \langle \mathbb{R}, \leq, +\rangle, \omega'\rangle$ are models of length measurement, then there exists $\alpha \in \mathbb{R}^+$ such that for all $a \in D$: $\omega(a) + \alpha \cdot \omega'(a)$.

(c). If $\langle D, \lesssim, \circ\rangle$ and U are such that D1a1 to 6 are satisfied, then there exists $\omega: D \to \mathbb{R}$ such that a–7 is satisfied and ω is uniquely determined up to some $\alpha \in \mathbb{R}^+$.

The proofs of this and the other theorems are given in the appendix.

Of course, by considering just one, single, real system, one hardly would end up with a system of fundamental measurement. In reality, many different but similar systems exist and are taken into consideration. Only on the basis of a large number of similar systems or situations is it possible to extract axioms for empirical structures that express observed regularities. The natural basis for the description of fundamental measurement, therefore, is given not by single systems but rather by classes of such systems. I will call them *fundamental measurement classes*.

D2 X is a *fundamental measurement class (with respect to transformations of type τ)*, iff there is a set-theoretic formula F such that the following holds:

1. F can be validated in structures of the form $\langle\langle D, o_1, \ldots, o_r\rangle, \langle \mathbb{R}, m_1, \ldots, m_r\rangle, \omega\rangle$ and F expresses (among other things) empirical regularities about $\langle D, o_1, \ldots, o_r\rangle$.

2. X is the class of all structures in which F is valid.

3. For all $D, o_1, \ldots, o_r, m_1, \ldots, m_r, \omega$, if $F(D, o_1, \ldots, o_r, m_1, \ldots, m_r, \omega)$, then the following holds:

   3.1. $o_1, \ldots, o_r$ can be interpreted by concrete operations.

   3.2. ω is a homomorphism from $\langle D, o_1, \ldots, o_r\rangle$ to $\langle \mathbb{R}, m_1, \ldots, m_r\rangle$.

   3.3. ω is uniquely determined up to transformations of type τ (that is, every other homomorphism from $\langle D, \ldots, o_r\rangle$ to $\langle \mathbb{R}, \ldots, m_r\rangle$ is obtained from ω by some transformation of type τ).

Condition (3.3) may seem redundant to some representationalists, because it usually follows as a theorem from appropriate axioms about $o_1, \ldots, o_r$. However, in the general case, there may be a considerable multiplicity of scales ω satisfying the other requirements of D2, that is, ω may be determined only up to rather general transformations. If we imagine a system of fundamental measurement to describe some real process of measurement, we expect specific numerical values to be produced. However, if ω is determined only up to very general transformations (like monotonic transformations), we will not get definite values. Some authors would still speak of measurement in such a case. What matters for them is representation, not determination. However, in practice, determination is most important, and D2 (3.3) may help to keep us aware of that.

Fundamental measurement classes have further interesting properties. Let us write D^x, o^x, ω^x, and so on for the various components of a system $x = \langle\langle D,o,\ldots,\omega \rangle$ and also U^x for the set of units occurring in D1. For a given fundamental measurement class X, let us define the *join* of X, $\cup X$, as the structure $\langle \bigcup_{x\in X} D^x, \bigcup_{x\in X} o^x,\ldots, \bigcup_{x\in X} \omega^x \rangle$. On the operational level, the join, of, say, two systems may simply be a conceptual artifact (think of two distance measurements in completely disjoint systems), or it may be an extension of the joined systems (e.g., if we measure by rigid rods the distance from e_1 to e_2 in one system s_1; from e_2 to e_3 in a second system s_2; and from e_1 to e_3 in the system s_3 obtained by joining s_1 and s_2). On the numerical level, the join of two systems yields an additional constraint on the choice of representing numbers; only those assignments are admissible that assign the same numbers to objects occurring simultaneously in different systems (the distance between e_1 and e_2 in s_1, for instance, must be the same as between e_1 and e_2 in the extended system s_3).

Formally such a constraint can be stated as a property of a fundamental measurement class X. X satisfies the constraint iff, for any two systems, $x=\langle\langle D,\ldots \rangle,\ldots,\omega\rangle$, $x'=\langle\langle D',\ldots \rangle,\ldots\omega' \rangle \in X$, the following holds: For all objects $a \in D \cap D'$, the representing numbers $\omega(a)$ and $\omega'(a)$ with respect to x and x' are the same—$\omega(a) = \omega'(a)$. In other words, the numerical representation $\omega(a)$ of an object a in a system x must not change when a is considered from the point of view of some other system x'. In measurement of distances, this amounts, among other things, to the requirement that some unit-rod in one system should also be a unit-rod in any other system. Expressed still differently, the constraint says that, in the join of any two systems $x, z \in X$, the numerical assignment $\omega^x \cup \omega^z$ in fact is a function: $\omega^x \cup \omega^z: D^x \cup D_z \to \mathbb{R}$. Similarly if we take the join of all of X, $\bigcup X$, we still have a function $\bigcup_{x\in X}\omega^x: \bigcup_{x\in X} D^x \to \mathbb{R}$.[7]

Usually the join $\cup X$ of a fundamental measurement class will not capture any

---

[7]See Balzer (1978), for applications of this kind and of other kinds of constraints to the case of geometry.

concrete process of measurement. Rather it captures a whole domain of objects to which some given measurement procedure can be applied. In the technical literature, such idealized universal systems play a dominant role for the standard, elegant representation theorems can be proved only for the idealized systems.[8] As a typical example, let us just cite the closed extensive positive systems of Krantz et al. (1971, p. 73).

D3 (a). x is a *closed extensive positive structure* iff there exist D, $\lesssim$, o such that $x = \langle D, \lesssim, \text{o} \rangle$ and the following holds:

    1. D is a nonempty set.

    2. $\lesssim \subseteq D \times D$ is transitive, reflexive, and connected.

    3. o: $D \times D \to D$ is associative.

    4. For all $a, b, c \in D$: $a < a \text{ o } b$, and ($a \lesssim b$ iff $a \text{ o } c \lesssim b \text{ o } c$ iff $c \text{ o } a \lesssim c \text{ o } b$).

    5. For all $a, b, c, d \in D$: if $a < b$, then there is $n \in \mathbb{N}$ such that $na \text{ o } c \lesssim nb \text{ o } d$.

  (b). x is an *idealized model of length measurement* iff there exist D, $\lesssim$, o and ω such that $x = \langle \langle D, \lesssim, \text{o} \rangle, \langle \mathbb{R}, \leq, + \rangle, \omega \rangle$ and the following holds:

    1. $\langle D, \lesssim, \text{o} \rangle$ is a closed extensive positive structure.

    2. $\omega: D \to \mathbb{R}$.

    3. For all $a, b \in D$: ($a \lesssim b$ iff $\omega(a) \leq \omega(b)$) and $\omega(a \text{ o } b) = \omega(a) + \omega(b)$.

T2 (a). If $\langle D, \lesssim, \text{o} \rangle$ is a closed extensive positive structure, then there exists ω such that $\langle \langle D, \lesssim, \text{o} \rangle, \langle \mathbb{R}, \leq, + \rangle, \omega \rangle$ is an idealized model of length measurement and ω is determined uniquely up to some $\alpha \in \mathbb{R}^+$.

  (b). If X is a class of models for length measurement such that the following holds: (i) for all $x, u \in X$, there exists a common extension[9] $z \in X$; (ii) for all $x \in X$ and all $a, b \in D$ such that $a < b$, there is some $u \in X$ such that u is an extension of x; and there is some $n \in \mathbb{N}$ such that, in u, $b \lesssim na$; (iii) $\bigcup_{x \in X} \text{o}^x$ is a total function, then $\bigcup X$ is an idealized model of length measurement.

Clearly closed extensive positive structures do not capture single processes of measurement. They are most naturally regarded as the join of an appropriate fundamental measurement class. In T2, some rather strong sufficient conditions for this are stated.[10]

---

[8]There are less elegant systems that apply also to unidealized finite systems, like the one in D1 above, or the one in Krantz et al. (1971, p. 103).

[9]That z is an *extension* of x means that $D^x \subseteq D^z$, and $\lesssim^x$ and o^x are the restrictions of $\lesssim^z$ and o^z to D^x respectively.

[10]It seems to be worthwhile studying this case and looking for weaker conditions that are necessary too.

Derived Measurement and the Structure of Science

Fundamental measurement occurs in science whenever a new range of phenomena for the first time is approached in a quantitative way. However, when one or several theories are established in some domain, new concepts of a theoretical nature will be introduced in order to get a more efficient organization of the available data. Often such new concepts will not be accessible to fundamental measurement in a straightforward way; they are determined by *derived* measurement. Derived measurement of a function simply consists of an explicit definition of this function in terms of other functions that are accessible to fundamental measurement, of measuring appropriate values of these latter functions, and of calculating the desired value(s) of the defined function from the measured values according to the given definition.

Consider the trivial example of velocity. The quantitative notion of velocity was introduced after quantitative concepts of spatial and temporal distance had developed. Velocity cannot be measured fundamentally—at least not in any straightforward way—and the same holds for mean velocity. The first step in the development of the notion was to define mean velocity as spatial distance travelled divided by time needed. In order to measure mean velocity, one has to measure (say, fundamentally) spatial and temporal distances and to apply the definition to the values, thus, obtained.

This account yields a nice and precise picture of the general structure of science: "Basic" terms, which can be fundamentally measured, are introduced in the beginning, and the vocabulary of science is enlarged step-by-step by introducing new terms definable by those that are antecendently available or by introducing new terms that can be fundamentally measured. Nice though it may be, this picture does not show how science actually develops. Usually new concepts are not explicitly defined, the previous example of velocity being one of the rare exceptions.[11] The discussions about theoretical terms in logical empiricism, as well as recent formal results about theoreticity[12] provide sufficient evidence here.

Recent work on measurement in conjoint systems[13] suggests that the question of definability in connection with derived measurement may be less central. The procedure just outlined might be replaced by some fundamental method directly producing the "defined" quantity; under suitable conditions, this direct representation can be decomposed multiplicatively. At present, there are only few, real-life examples of conjoint measurement, and these are mainly initiated by the development of the abstract notion. Still one could insist that derived measurement in principle might be replaced by conjoint measurement and that the dis-

---

[11]A more typical example is found in D4 below where the condition eligible for a definition (D4–a–5) does not guarantee uniqueness.

[12]See Balzer (1985a, 1986) and Gaehde (1983).

[13]Compare, for instance, Luce & Narens (1985), Narens & Luce (1986).

tance between scientific practice and the picture emerging from derived measurement, therefore, is artificial. However, replacing derived measurement by conjoint measurement would not bring us closer to scientific practise. In the natural sciences, there is a large class of methods of measurement that simply are not of the conjoint type.

In any case, the picture of the structure of science emerging from the representationalist view is not the most adequate one, and my claim is that the structuralist view of measurement provides a more adequate one.

THE STRUCTURALIST VIEW OF MEASUREMENT

Overview

According to the structuralist view, measurement consists in determining a *datum* (function value, truth value), which, on a regular pattern, is uniquely given by other, known, or available data. If all the data are represented as values of real valued functions, the regular pattern will usually be represented by a mathematical equation, and the determination of the value one is looking for (the measured value) amounts to its calculation from other, presupposed values by "solving the equation."

Let us start analyzing this picture at the level of single systems—as in the first case. What we have before us is a concrete process of measurement that, after some suitable preparations, consists of the development of a real system until the measured value is produced. Such a system is distinguished from it's environment as sharply as we are able to separate different systems in different situations—an ability that we may safely assume in the present context. Further, it usually is not too difficult to determine two instants marking the "beginning" and the "end" of the process of measurement (which need not be unique). If we start to conceptualize the system that is given by the process, we see that there are already some (one or several, but few) theoretical pictures, *theories,* that can be used for the conceptualization. We assume that the system at hand is a model of that theory or theories. Such a model *capturing* or *conceptualizing* or *describing* a real system that is given by some process of measurement I call a *measuring model.* Clearly, if a process of measurement involves more than one theory for its description, we may analyze it and deal with various subprocesses, each of which yields just one model of a theory (i.e., just one measuring model). I will not go into the question here of how to put together the various measuring models, thus, obtained in order to provide a complete description of the original process; in the following, I will deal only with processes that are governed or can be described by just one theory.[14]

As an example, let us consider the measurement of mass by means of colli-

---

[14]Compare Balzer (1985b) and Balzer and Wollmershaeuser (1986), for studies of more complex situations.

sions.[15] Consider three particles colliding with each other at one instant. Their velocities before and after the collision are approximately constant and are measured by suitable means. Furthermore, let us assume that the velocity vectors have some special geometrical configuration: the vectors of velocity differences (before and after the collision, for each particle) are such that it is not possible to have a plane passing through the origin of the three vectors and all three vectors lying on one side of the plane—D4(a)(6) below. In this situation, the law of conservation of total momentum—which is the central axiom of collision mechanics—allows us to calculate the particles' mass-ratios from their velocities.[16]

D4 (a). x is a *measuring model for mass by collisions* (*with respect to* p_1) iff there exist P, T, v, m such that $x = \langle P, T, \mathbb{R}, v, m \rangle$ and the following holds:

1. P is a three-element set (of "particles") and $p_1 \in P$ (we write $P = \{p_1, p_2, p_3\}$).
2. $T = \{b, a\}$ is a two-element set ("before" and "after").
3. $v: P \times T \to \mathbb{R}^3$ (velocity function).
4. $m: P \to \mathbb{R}^+$ (mass function).
5. $\Sigma_{p \in P} m(p)v(p, b) = \Sigma_{p \in P} m(p)v(p, a)$
    (law of conservation of momentum).
6. the subspace of $\mathbb{R}^3$ generated by w_1, w_2, w_3 has two dimensions and there is no $u \in \mathbb{R}^3$ such that the following holds:

    6.1. For all $i \in \{1, 2, 3\}$: $w * u \geq 0$.
    6.2. There is some $i \in \{1, 2, 3\}$ such that $w * u > 0$.
7. $m(p_1) = 1$.

(b). x is a *measuring model for mass-ratios by collision* iff $x = \langle P, T, \mathbb{R}, v, m \rangle$ is, as in part a) and D4 (a) (1) to (a) (6), are satisfied with respect to some p_1.

T3 (a). If $\langle P, T, \mathbb{R}, v, m \rangle$ and $\langle P, T, \mathbb{R}, v, m* \rangle$ are measuring models for mass by collisions with respect to p_1, then $m = m*$.

(b). If $\langle P, T, \mathbb{R}, v, m \rangle$ and $\langle P, T, \mathbb{R}, v, m* \rangle$ are measuring models for mass-ratios by collisions then there is an $\alpha \in \mathbb{R}^+$ such that for all $p \in P$: $m(p) = \alpha \cdot m*(p)$.

Measuring Models

In general, the idea of a measuring model comprises five features—all present in the previous example. First, the system captured by the measuring model satis-

---

[15]See Balzer & Muehlhoelzer (1982), for a complete survey of all possible measuring models for mass in collision mechanics. The simplest case of collision along a straight line is avoided on purpose.

[16]In D4 and the corresponding proofs, I write w_i, for $v(p_i, a) - v(p_i, b)$, $i = 1, 2, 3$, and $u*s$ for $\Sigma_{i \leq 3} u_i s_i$ where $u = \langle u_1, u_2, u_3 \rangle$ and $s = \langle s_1, s_2, s_3 \rangle$.

fies some law—like the law of conservation of total momentum in D4 (a) (5). In general, we may suppose that the system under consideration gives rise to a structure x of the following form:

$$\langle D_1, \ldots, D_k; A_1, \ldots, A_m; R_1, \ldots, R_n \rangle,$$

where $D_1, \ldots, D_k$ are sets of objects, $A_1, \ldots, A_m$ are sets of mathematical entities (like real numbers), and $R_1, \ldots, R_n$ are relations "over" $D_1, \ldots, D_k$, $A_1, \ldots, A_m$,[17] that is, x is a structure of type $\langle k, m, \sigma_1, \ldots, \sigma_n \rangle$. The law that holds in the given system may be expressed by some set-theoretic formula $B(z_1, \ldots, z_{k+m+n})$ containing at least the free variables $z_1, \ldots, z_{k+m+n}$ such that $D_1, \ldots, D_k, A_1, \ldots, A_m, R_1, \ldots, R_n$ are of the same types as $z_1, \ldots, z_{k+m+n}$ respectively. We then say that B has the type of x and B's validity in x then simply is stated by $B(x)$ or $B(D_1, \ldots, R_n)$.[18]

Second, in each measuring model, the function one wants to measure is uniquely determined by means of the other "parts" (functions and sets of objects) of the model and by the law that holds in the model. In the last example, this condition is expressed by T3 (a). It may be still further formalized by letting "$B(P, T, \mathbb{R}, v, m)$" stand for "$\langle P, \ldots, m \rangle$ is a measuring model for mass by collisions." That m is uniquely determined by $P, T, \mathbb{R}, v$, and statement B then amounts to[19] the following:

$$\forall\, m\, \forall\, m* \; (B(P, \ldots, v, m) \wedge B(P, \ldots, v, m*) \to m = m*)^{[20]} \qquad (1)$$

---

[17]For each $r \in \mathbb{N}$, we define syntactic r-*types* by induction: For each $i \in \mathbb{N}$, $i \leq r$, we let $[i]$ be an r-type, and, if τ_1, τ_2 are r-types, then so are $(\tau_1 \otimes \tau_2)$ and $(\mathrm{pow}\tau_1)$. For each r-type, τ and given sets $S_1, \ldots, S_r$, we define the *echelon set* $\tau(S_1, \ldots, S_r)$ by induction. If τ is some $[i]$, then $\tau(S_1, \ldots, S_r)$ is S_i, and, if $\tau_j(S_1, \ldots, S_r)$ is already defined for $j = 1, 2$, then $(\tau_1 \otimes \tau_2)(S_1, \ldots, S_r)$ is $\tau_1(S_1, \ldots, S_r) \times \tau_2(S_1, \ldots, S_r)$, and $(\mathrm{pow}\, \tau_1)(S_1, \ldots, S_r)$ is $\mathrm{PO}(\tau_1(S_1, \ldots, S_r))$. R is a relation *over* $S_1, \ldots, S_r$, iff there is some r-type τ such that $R \subseteq (\mathrm{pow}\tau)(S_1, \ldots, S_r)$. x is a *structure of type* $\langle k, m, \sigma_1, \ldots, \sigma_n \rangle$, iff k, m $\in \mathbb{N}$, $n \geq 1$, $\sigma_1, \ldots, \sigma_n$ are $(k + m)$-types, and $x = \langle D_1, \ldots, D_k; A_1, \ldots, A_m; R_1, \ldots, R_n \rangle$ where $D_1, \ldots, D_k$ are sets, $A_1, \ldots, A_m$ are sets of mathematical objects, and each R_i is a relation over $D_1, \ldots, D_k, A_1, \ldots, A_m$.

These definitions originally are found—with small deviations and in different notation—in Bourbaki (1968, pp. 259). In the following, for $x = \langle D_1, \ldots, D_k; A_1, \ldots, A_m; R_1, \ldots, R_n \rangle$, and $i \leq n$, we write x_{-i} for the result of omitting R_i in x, and $x_{-i}[R]$ for the result of substituting R_i in x by R (provided always that R_i and R are of the same $(k + m)$-type). Also we write R_i^x in order to denote the ith relation R_i occurring in x.

[18]Allowing for higher-order relations R covers those cases that in first-order formulations involve infinitely many axioms or that in infinitary logic involve infinitely long "formulas." The distinction between "proper objects" and "mathematical entities" represented by $D_1, \ldots, D_k$ and $A_1, \ldots, A_m$ respectively is taken from Bourbaki and is mainly of practical importance here. Compare Balzer (1985b, chap. II).

[19]$P, T, \mathbb{R}$, and v may be set theoretically regarded as free variables.

[20]Note that, in general, this condition is quite different from the one stating that m is a function that is formalized by $\forall\, p, p' \in P(p = p' \to m(p) = m(p'))$, or, more explicitly

(1*) $\forall\, p, p' \in P\, \forall\, \alpha, \beta \in \mathbb{R}\,(\langle p, \alpha \rangle \in m \wedge \langle p', \beta \rangle \in m \wedge p = p' \to \alpha = \beta)$. It is only in the "limit case" of P being a singleton that (1) follows from (1*). Intuitively (1) states the uniqueness of a set (of pairs of arguments and function values), whereas (1*) states the

In the general notation used previously, uniqueness of R_i in structure $x = \langle D_1, \ldots, R_n \rangle$ is expressed as follows:

$$\forall R^*(B(D_1, \ldots, R_n) \wedge B(D_1, \ldots, R_{i-1}, R^*, R_{i+1}, \ldots, R_n) \rightarrow R_i = R^*). \tag{2}$$

If it is relation R_i (which I always take to be a function, if necessary by switching to the characteristic function) that is uniquely determined in the measuring model x, I will say that x is a measuring model *for the i–th relation* ($i \leq n$).

A third feature common to measuring models is that the function to be measured is determined uniquely only up to certain transformations by the law involved. In the example of D4 (a) above, one particle was required to have unit mass, D4 (a) (7). Usually, such requirements that refer to units or origins simply are omitted in the description of a measuring model with the effect that the function under consideration no longer is uniquely determined. The effect for uniqueness of omitting reference to units can be accounted for by weakening uniqueness to uniqueness-up-to-transformations-of-scale of a predetermined type. In the example of D4, the effect for uniqueness of dropping reference to a unit-mass, D4 (a) (7), is that the mass function m is no longer uniquely determined but is determined only up to a positive real number, T3 (b). The measuring model for mass-ratios by collision, D4 (b), thus, obtained is more realistic with respect to scientific practice, because it also covers those cases in which the process of measurement—the process of collision—does not involve a unit mass. This situation is acceptable, because still something reasonably accessible is uniquely determined: mass-ratios. If mass-ratios can be determined from velocities, one may eventually obtain "absolute" mass values by measuring the mass of one of the particles involved by means of another measuring model, different from the one at hand.

Here the general problem arises of what to regard as the right transformation of scale. There are quite a number of different, "established" transformations to be found in the literature. Obviously, the more general transformations for a function we admit, the less determination of that function we can achieve in a measuring model. For the time being, I will restrict considerations to linear transformations (more on this below). If $f: D \rightarrow N$, and $f': D' \rightarrow N'$, we say that f' *is obtained from f by a linear transformation*[21] (abbreviated by $f' \approx f$), iff either ($D = D', N = N'$, and there exist $\alpha, \beta \in \mathbb{R}$, $\alpha > 0$ such that, for all $a \in D$: $f'(a) = \alpha \cdot f(a) + \beta$) or $f = f'$. The weaker condition of uniqueness that results from (2) above, thus, is the following:

$$\forall R^*(B(D_1, \ldots, R_n) \wedge B(D_1, \ldots, R_{i-1}, R^*, R_{i+1}, \ldots, R_n) \rightarrow R_i \approx R^*) \tag{3}$$

---

uniqueness of function values—which may be construed as components of elements of the sets occurring in (1).

[21]This definition can be easily extended to functions taking values in vector spaces over ordered fields.

That is, if $\langle D_1, \ldots, R_n \rangle$ is a measuring model for the i-th relation, and, if, by replacing R_i by some R^*, we still have a measuring model for the i-th relation, then R^* is obtained from R_i by a linear transformation. In other words, the function R_i to be determined in measuring model $\langle D_1, \ldots, R_n \rangle$ is determined by the law B and by the other "parts" $D_1, \ldots, R_{i-1}, R_{i+1}, R_n$ of the measuring model up to a linear transformation.

The fourth feature inherent in measuring models is that the measured value, or more generally, the function of which this value is a function value, can be *computed* from the other "parts" of the measuring model. This means that, for each argument a, the function value $R_i(a)$ can be computed from appropriate values of the other functions $R_1, \ldots, R_{i-1}, R_{i+1}, \ldots, R_n$. The computation has to start with a finite input; thus, only finitely many values $R_j(a_s)$ ($j = 1, \ldots, n$, $j \neq i$, $s \leq t$ for some $t \in \mathbb{N}$) will be needed. That is, the computation of the measured value does not really use "all of" the other functions but only some finite parts of them. This idea may be formalized by means of a rather general notion of a substructure. If $x = \langle D_1, \ldots, D_k; A_1, \ldots, A_m; R_1, \ldots, R_n \rangle$ is a structure of type $\tau = \langle k, m, \sigma_1, \ldots, \sigma_n \rangle$, then $z = \langle D'_1, \ldots, D'_k; A'_1, \ldots, A'_m; R'_1, \ldots, R'_n \rangle$ is a *substructure of* x iff for all i $\leq$ k: $D'_i \subseteq D_i$; for all $i \leq m$: $A'_i \subseteq A_i$; and for all $i \leq$ n: $R'_i \subseteq R_i$, and z again is a structure of type τ. The requirement of computability of the measured value in a measuring model $x = \langle D_1, \ldots, R_n \rangle$ for the i-th relation then can be stated as follows. For each a in the domain of R_i, there is a finite substructure z_a of x_i (see footnote 17) such that $R_i(a)$ is computable from z_a. In order to link this notion to the standard notion of computability, some further encoding of $R_i(a)$ and of z_a will be necessary, but it will depend on the particular case, and not much can be said about it in general.

Usually the computations arise in a natural way from the law B that governs the measuring model. Often this law consists of a simple equation that can be solved for the measured value $R_i(a)$ (as in the example of weight measurement following). In other cases, the computation may involve some mathematics. The computation of mass values in the case of the example from D4 involves linear algebra in order to solve the system of linear equations given by the basic law (see the proof of T4).

A final feature of measuring models is that the measured value in fact depends on the other parts of the model. In the conceptual frame used here, function R_i might be defined in a purely mathematical way. A real valued function $R_i: D_1 \to \mathbb{R}$ could be defined, for example, by: $R_i(a) = 5$ for all $a \in D$. Such an R_i would satisfy the requirement of uniqueness, but the measured value $R_i(a)$ would be mathematically defined, and there would be no need for measurement. Such cases are excluded by requiring that R_i in fact changes when the other parts of the model change. Here topological concepts come into play. Consider the following relation θ_B given by the formula B that characterizes a measuring model: $\theta_B(u, v)$, iff there is x such that $B(x)$, $u = x_{-i}$ and $v = R_i^x$. Factorizing θ_B modulo $\approx$ in its second argument yields a relation $\theta_B^{\approx}$ given by $\theta_B^{\approx}(u, v)$ iff there is x such that $B(x)$, $u = x_{-i}$ and $R_i^x \in v$. If B determines R_i in x up to linear transformations, then $\theta_B^{\approx}$ will be a function. Now purely mathematical definitions of R_i as the one mentioned above might be excluded just by saying that $\theta_B^{\approx}$ is not constant. Still, this seems to leave room for *ad hoc* definitions that really do not involve measurement. A stronger and more adequate requirement is that $\theta_B^{\approx}$ be a continuous, nonconstant function, continuity being defined relative to some natural topologies introduced on the domain and range of $\theta_B^{\approx}$ by a given topology on the class $\{x/B(x)\}$ of all measuring models given by B. In the example of D4, such topologies are given by the distances of the function values $|v^x(p, a) - v^z(p, a)|$ and $|m^x(p) - m^z(p)|$ for the v- and m-functions in different models x, z (in which the sets P and T are the same).

Summing up these features, we obtain the following:

D5   (a). x is a *measuring model (for the i–th relation) characterized by B and ψ* iff
there exist $D_1, \ldots, D_k, A_1, \ldots, A_m, R_1, \ldots, R_n$ such that $x = \langle D_1, \ldots, D_k, A_1, \ldots, A_m, R_1, \ldots, R_n \rangle$ and the following holds:

1. $i \leq n$.
2. B is a set theoretic statement of a law; B is of the type of x and B is valid in x.
3. ψ is a topology on $\{x/B(x)\}$.
4.   For all R^*: if $B(D_1, \ldots, R_n)$ and
$B(D_1, \ldots, R_{i-1}, R_*, R_{i+1}, \ldots, R_n)$, then $R_i \approx R^*$.
5.   For all a in the domain of R, there is a finite substructure z_a of $\langle D_1, \ldots, R_{i-1}, R_{i+1}, \ldots, R_n \rangle$ such that $R_i(a)$ is computable "up to $\approx$" from z_a (after appropriate encoding).
6.   relation $\theta_B^{\approx}$ is a continuous function (relative to suitable topologies induced by ψ) and not constant.

   (b). x is a *measuring model (for the i–th relation)* iff there exist B and ψ such that x is a measuring model (for the i–th relation) characterized by B and ψ.

Methods of Measurement

As before, consideration of a single system is unlikely to lead us to a measuring model, because it will hardly reveal law-like features as required in D5 (a) (2). In reality a large number of real systems has to be studied and compared with each other so that a regularity can be detected and a law formulated correspondingly. A more natural basis for the definition of measuring models, therefore, is given by a class of systems or, after conceptualization, by a class of structures.

D6 $\mathcal{L}$ is a *method of measurement (for the i–th relation)* iff there exist B and ψ such that the following holds:

1. B is a set theoretic formula that can be interpreted in structures of the form

$\langle D_1, \ldots, D_k; A_1, \ldots, A_m; R_1, \ldots, R_n \rangle$, $i \leq n$, and B expresses a law.

2. $\mathcal{L}$ is the class of all structures in which B is valid.

3. Each $x \in B$ is a measuring model for the i–th relation characterized by B and ψ.

4. $\mathcal{L}$ contains (descriptions of) many real systems.

D6 (1) and (3) just rephrase D5. D6 (4) is intended to exclude contrived, abstract examples. We speak of a method here in the following, derived sense. For each proper method of measurement, we can think of the class of all cases in which the method might be applied successfully. Each such case would yield a real system, given either by the process of applying the method or by the result of having the method applied. In this way, each method of measurement corresponds to a class of systems, and we decide to call this class itself a method of measurement.

Obviously the requirements of B being a law and of $\mathcal{L}$ containing many real systems cannot be formalized. They tie the notion of a method of measurement to pragmatics and to "reality." What is a law can only be made out on the basis of theoretically minded human interaction, and what is a (description of a) real system can be made out only by some reference to experience. We cannot expect the notion of a method of measurement to be definable more formally than the notion of an empirical theory, simply because we want methods of measurement to cover cases governed by proper theoretical laws (which occur in established theories) as well as cases of fundamental measurement in which the law characterizing the measuring models is not a law of any established theory.

Examples

1. The classes $\mathcal{L}_1$ and $\mathcal{L}_2$ of all measuring models for mass and mass-ratios by collisions are methods of measurement (for the second relation).

2. If we rearrange the components in models of length measurement like this: $\langle D; \mathbb{R}; \leq, +, \lesssim, \mathbf{o}, \omega \rangle$, the class of all models of length measurement yields a method of measurement $\mathcal{L}_3$ for the fifth relation.

3. Let $\mathcal{L}_4$ be the class of all structures $\langle P; T, \mathbb{R}; s, m, f_1, \ldots, f_n \rangle$ for which there exist p_1, p_2, p_3 ("earth," "particle the weight of which is measured," "particle marking the origin"), all distinct, such that the following: (a) $P = \{p_1, p_2, p_3\}$; (b) $T \subseteq \mathbb{R}$ is an open interval (set of "instants"); (c) $s: P \times T \to \mathbb{R}^3$ is smooth ("position function"); (d) $m: P \to \mathbb{R}^+$ ("mass function"); (e) for all $i \leq n: f_i: P \times T \to \mathbb{R}^3$ ("force functions"); (f) there is $k \in \mathbb{R}^+$ such that, for all $t \in T: f_1(p_2, t) = -k(s(p_3, t) - s(p_2, t))$ ("Hooke's law"); (g) for all $t \in T: f_1(p_2, t) = -f_2(p_2, t)$ ("actio-reactio law," specialized to p_2); (h) for all $t \in T: f_2(p_1, t) = f_2(p_3, t) = 0$. Elements of $\mathcal{L}_4$ capture measurements of weight ($= f_2(p_2, t)$) under

the following interpretation:[22] f_1 denotes gravitational force and f_2 Hooke's force exerted in a system in which p_2 (some object) is hung on a spring balance (where p_3 marks the end of the spring in the unextended case). Clearly function f_2 is uniquely determined in members of $\mathcal{L}_4$, and $\mathcal{L}_4$ is a method of measurement (for the fourth relation).

Note that the class of all closed extensive positive structures would not be a good candidate for a method of measurement because of D6 (4). There are no real systems that can be described in terms of D4.

Unlike the notion of fundamental measurement, the notions of a measuring model and of a method of measurement are neutral with respect to the structure of science. They fit in naturally into the picture of science as a web or a net of structures, models, or theories. Measuring models can be treated on a par with models of theories, and methods of measurement on a par with classes of models of theories. According to the most sophisticated notion available,[23] one main constituent of an empirical theory is a net consisting of a class of models and of various subclasses, ("specializations"). Methods of measurement are just a particular kind of such specializations. In this picture, no priority is given to "direct observation" or to distinguished forms of measurement.

COMPARISON

Having outlined the basic features of the representationalist and the structuralist view of measurement, we now can compare the two.

First, let us compare the notions of a fundamental measurement class and of a method of measurement as given by D2 and D6. A fundamental measurement class is a class of systems of fundamental measurement; that is, a class of structures characterized by certain axioms and so is a method of measurement (D2 (2) and D6 (2)). The axioms for empirical structures in systems of fundamental measurement have to be grounded in empirical regularities and so have the axioms characterizing the measuring models D2 (1) and D6 (1). In systems of fundamental measurement, there is the representing homomorphism ω that is determined uniquely up to specified transformations. In measuring models, there is the corresponding requirement that the function to be measured be determined uniquely up to some specified transformation D2 (3.3) and D6 (3). The requirements of computability and of proper dependence inherent in D6 (3) usually also are satisfied in systems of fundamental measurement—although not required explicitly.

Besides these correspondences, there are the following differences. Systems

---

[22]See Balzer and Moulines (1980).
[23](Balzer, Moulines, & Sneed, 1987, chap. IV).

of fundamental measurement have an inner structure more specific than that of measuring models. They have to consist of two "smaller" structures (the empirical and the mathematical one) and a homomorphism between those. No such requirement is present for measuring models. In this respect, measuring models are much more general. Furthermore, the empirical relations in systems of fundamental measurement have to represent concrete operations, whereas, on the side of measuring models, no distinction among the relations $R_1, \ldots, R_n$ (like observational-theoretical or concrete-abstract) is required. In this respect also, measuring models are more general.

This indicates that methods of measurement are more general than systems of fundamental measurement. There is, however, a little difficulty. As noted previously, the idealized systems of fundamental measurement do not describe real systems, and if we consider corresponding classes of such systems as candidates for methods of measurement, usually D6 (4) will not be satisfied. There are two remarks to that point. First, one might simply drop D6 (4) and, thus, eliminate the difficulty. This might be justified by saying that, for the sake of comparison, we are primarily interested in the conceptual structure of measuring models. I do not regard this as an adequate reaction. Rather I would remark secondly that the transition from the representationalist to the structuralist view is not completely smooth. It seems to involve a kind of "Kuhn-loss," and what is lost are precisely those superidealized structures that have no real applications. As soon as approximation is brought into play, an analogue to approximative reduction perhaps would be appropriate to describe the relation between the two approaches.

A second dimension of comparison is that of implications for the structure of science. It seems that the structuralist view fits better with the actual, overall structure of empirical science than does the received view that has some difficulties "getting off the ground" of empirical structures and systems of fundamental measurement. We may say that the structuralist view frees philosophy of science from dogmatic assumptions of logical empiricism without loss of potential of drawing a fine-grained picture of science.[24]

Finally it has to be stressed that the structuralist view covers both kinds of representationalist measurement: fundamental as well as derived (or conjoint) measurement. It does so by substantial generalization. In connection with fundamental measurement, one result of this generalization is that the distinction between a qualitative ("empirical") and a quantitative (numerical) level vanishes. In connection with derived measurement, the greater generality of measuring models is obvious. Derived measurement requires a definition, whereas, in measuring models, only some law-like connection is required. The law B in a measuring model need not be suited as a general definition of the term to be measured.

---

[24]It is not difficult, for instance, to draw the hierarchical picture of science within the structuralist view.

If we use the term "extension" in a broad way that does not allow "parts" of the representationalist account to be properly included in the extended account but to be only captured by the structuralist view in the limit, then these considerations may be summarized by stating that the structuralist view is a proper and essential extension of the representationalist view of measurement.

PERSPECTIVES AND PROBLEMS

In the section, The Structuralist View of Measurement, only the most basic features of the structuralist view were sketched. When implemented in the semantic or the structuralist approach to theories, the structuralist view of measurement opens up a wide range of applications. In this final section, I want at least briefly to touch on some achievements, possibilities, and problems of this view.

Its most definite achievement consists in the development of a formal definition of theoreticity that yields a formal distinction between T–theoretical and T–nontheoretical terms in any axiomatized theory T. The definition evolved from investigations of measurement under the structuralist view, and it yields the expected distinctions when applied to axiomatized versions of real-life theories. Moreover, this definition for the first time opens a way for empirical and precise studies of the global structure of science—in contrast to logical empiricism or the received view that both simply postulate and presuppose a hierarchical structure. The new definition of theoreticity being available in the literature, there is no need to go into the details here (see footnote 12).

A second achievement consists in complete accounts of complicated measurements involving several intermediate steps (preliminary measured values) and several different theories to account for these steps. A simple example is provided by the measurement of mass by collisions: In order to obtain the desired mass-values, we have to measure velocities, that is, intervals of space and time. So the whole process of measurement may be divided into several subprocesses: one for each measurement of a distance in space or time, and one consisting of the whole process. In total, three different kinds of phenomena and three corresponding theories are involved: phenomena of spatial distance, of distance in time, and of the inertial behavior of moving particles. The masses are calculated from "presupposed" values of velocities by means of collision mechanics, whereas the presupposed velocity values themselves are calculated from other, "presupposed" values of distances and times, which in turn are measured by means of geometric and chronometric devises (i.e., by means involving geometry and chronometry). A full analysis yields a whole chain of values obtained from iterated calculations of measured values from presupposed values.

The idea of a chain of values is not very original. Furthermore, it does not give a satisfactory account of the respective measurement, for it does not contain any information about the theories involved. Let me call a description of some process of measurement *complete,* only if it gives the relevant sequence of measured values plus the equations (theories) that are applied in each step of the calculation. Again this idea of a complete description does not seem to be very original. However, it did not appear in the literature up to now, and mainly so for one reason (now becoming obvious): a prejudiced view of measurement that dissociates measurement too much from theory. Within the structuralist view, complete descriptions of measurement can be given easily. The concept of a *chain of measurements* and of a *measurement graph* (a sequence, respectively a graph of interrelated measuring models) provide simple and powerful descriptive tools.[25]

It may be objected here that there is a still more strict notion of a complete description capturing also errors of measurement and experimental design. The important topic of errors of measurement has not yet been addressed from the structuralist point of view. It seems possible, however, to reformulate existing accounts in terms of measuring models and substructures. Such a reformulation might prove helpful, especially in cases of measurement in highly developed theories that may involve features of theory dynamics and of approximate comparison of theories. The subtle picture of how errors of measurement come up together with theory provided by H. E. Kyburg Jr.[26] is of particular relevance here. Furthermore, some general structuralist apparatus might be helpful.[27] As far as experimental design is concerned, I do not think that this can be included in a systematic description of measurement. All the *systematic* features are somehow captured by the theories governing the process of measurement, any further features of special design being attached to special cases and in this sense being unsystematic.

A third achievement of the structuralist view—closely related to the second one—is that it treats measurement and theory in the same model-theoretic way. The basic units of analysis are systems (represented by models), and investigations aim at revealing their inner structure (represented by types and axioms) as well as their outer relations to other systems. In addition to "mere" models, measuring models are distinguished by their uniqueness properties. However, this does not prevent them from functioning in the network of theories much like ordinary models. This perspective is likely to prevent us from ascribing to measured values a *preferred* status of given, nonhypothetical items against which theories are tested, and it yields a better starting point for the investigation and understanding of how theory and measurement function and develop together. So much has become clear by now: The development and test of comprehensive theoretical networks do not fit into the simple picture of collecting independent

---

[25]See (Balzer, 1985b, chap. IV) and (Balzer & Wollmershaeuser, 1986).

[26]See (Kyburg, 1984) and his contribution to this volume. Although his two rules may be still controversial, the basic picture he provides is not.

[27]See (Balzer et al. 1987, chap. VII).

data and then theoretically organizing them. There is much interplay between the development of theoretical pictures and what counts as data in a given state of the development. This interplay can be structured best when theory and data (measurement) are represented in the same way, as having equal rights.

This brings me to some further topics not yet worked out, for the treatment of which the structuralist view seems to be promising. The first topic is theory development including features of measurement, test, and approximation. Up to now, pictures of theory development do not capture aspects of measurement, and if they include features of approximation at all, they do so (see footnote 27) just by blurring the idealized theoretical pictures. However, the real source of such fuzziness is of course the impossibility of exactly measuring numerical functions. The inclusion of measurement into the diachronic picture of theoretical development, therefore, not only will yield an explanation of why theories are only approximately true; it also will provide a frame for depicting the origins and changes of the degrees of accuracy relevant for each application of a theory at a given time.

A second promising topic is confirmation. There are the classical ideas about a choice between alternative hypotheses attached to the names of Bacon, Nicod, and Popper, and the ideas of Carnap and Hempel about degrees of confirmation of a hypothesis (theory) in a given structure. However, these ideas are intended to apply to one isolated hypothesis that is matched against an independently given data-base and given alternative hypotheses. Philosophers abandoned these ideas as inadequate for more comprehensive arrays of theory long ago, but only recently did some positive move occur, in the form of the "bootstrap view" of confirmation Glymour (1980) has put forward. Although this account in fact hits the central pattern underlying confirmation in large theoretical networks, it falls short of providing a global analogue to the idea of a degree of confirmation. The reason for this limitation again is the conceptual separation of measurement from theory. Glymour represented measurement by "computations," sequences of presupposed and measured values, the theories underlying the various steps being ignored. Yet as soon as theories are properly included in the picture—which means that measurement is treated within the structuralist view—the notion of a degree of confirmation for more comprehensive theoretical arrays can be attacked once again by combining bootstrap ideas with those of partial implication.[28]

A third promising topic is reference. Up to now, reference has been approached merely from the side of philosophy and philosophy of language. The structuralist view of measurement yields an elegant conceptual frame for defining the referents of terms of scientific, extensional theories. This may form the basis for a precise, detailed theory of reference for empirical, extensional theories, that is, for a theory of reference suited for the philosophy of science. For example,

---

[28]For the purely theoretical side of the issue that also is one-sided by neglecting measurement, see (Balzer et al., 1987, chap. VIII).

the referent of a numerical function in a theory is given as that assignment of numbers to real objects (which are represented by appropriate arguments in models of real systems) that is determined by the theoretical axioms, constraints, and interrelations as well as by the real systems to which the theory applies. The fact that, among the real systems, there usually are many measuring models for the function in question will often guarantee a unique referent, whereas the theoretical constraints provide for coherence.[29]

I want to close by pointing to a problem central to the present account, namely that of drawing a demarcation between "mere" models of a theory and measuring models for some term of the theory. The crucial condition distinguishing measuring models from mere models is that of uniqueness of the function to be measured. However, as already noted, to require strict uniqueness would deprive the notion of a measuring model of practical interest, because usually the theoretical laws alone do not imply such strict uniqueness. An adequate concept of a measuring model has to be formulated with a requirement of uniqueness up to some kind of transformation. There are different kinds of transformations one may consider; thus, the problem is to choose the "right" kind of transformation to be employed in the definition of a measuring model. This really is a problem of demarcation, because, if the transformations chosen are too general, we will not be able to determine the function considered in any interesting sense, and, therefore, we will not have a *measuring* model before us. If the transformations are chosen very narrowly, we may have a measuring model but one that is not interesting in connection with its corresponding theory, because it applies only to few and uninteresting real systems.

In the section, Structuralist View of Measurement, this problem was "solved", or rather suppressed, by pretending an absolutely adequate class of transformations, adequate for all numerical functions—linear transformations. However, inspection of examples shows that each theory has its own adequate class of transformations. When determining distances in affine geometry, only dilatations are meaningful, whereas, in a fundamental determination of temperature, the full class of linear transformations is appropriate. In a determination of positions by means of classical mechanics, Galilei transformations might be suggested, because such transformations connect different frames of reference. In utility theory, the determination of utility in standard approaches[30] proceeds

---

[29]Compare (Balzer, 1985b, Sec. 23, 1987), and (Balzer, Lauth, Zoubek, 1989).

[30]By "standard approaches," I here mean those exemplified in traditional economic literature like, (Henderson & Quandt, 1958). There is another approach originating from v. Neumann & Morgenstern (1947) regarding utilities as determined by preferences and probabilities ("beliefs") up to linear transformations that now has started to penetrate "standard" economic literature. Still a third view, represented by (Jeffrey, 1965), is worth mentioning (in order to show that the issue really is not settled) according to which utility together with probability are determined by means of preferences up to so-called "Goedel–Bolker" transformations.

only up to monotone transformations: By such procedures, only an ordering of the alternatives can be achieved, and the numerical values for utility are really not determined at all. From these considerations, one is tempted to jump to the conclusion that each theory for each of its terms determines the appropriate class of transformations to be used in the definition of the measuring models for that term. However, this view deprives the condition of uniqueness of any content. Each R_i is unique up to natural transformations, if by natural transformations we mean those that preserve the property of being a measuring model. Uniqueness is central to measurement proper; thus, a criterion is necessary that prevents the condition of uniqueness from becoming trivial.

There are two lines of attacking the problem. First, formal considerations may be used to exclude certain kinds of transformations or invariances as inadmissible for a given method of measurement. Recently Luce and Narens[31] achieved progress here. By introducing the concept of a scale type as consisting of a degree of uniqueness and a degree of homogeneity, they were able to show that, under special conditions (like the presence of a concatenation operation or the existence of some representation onto the reals), only certain, few scale types are possible.

Second, by concentrating on the "positive", real-life cases of measurement up to certain transformations of scale, those cases in which no doubt is likely to occur, we see that there the transformations are completely determined by finitely many—actually very few—parameters, like two numbers in the case of linear transformations. Moreover, giving some particular value to any of these parameters has a straightforward, empirical meaning like choosing a particular object as unit or as origin. We, therefore, might say that some class of transformations is *admissible*, iff it is determined by finitely many parameters, and if the choice of each parameter corresponds to a choice of some basic object in the model, that is, of some element of the base sets $D_1, \ldots, D_k$ of the model. Of course the meaning of "corresponds" here needs further elaboration, and a little reflection shows that a kind of reduction to qualitative comparison lurks behind it—much like that underlying the representationalist view.

APPENDIX

Proof of T1: (a) Let $b \in U$, $b' \in U'$. By D1 (a) (6), there are $b_1, \ldots, b_n \in U$ such that $b_1 \circ \ldots \circ b_n \equiv b'$. Suppose $n \geq 1$. Then, for all $i \leq n$: $b_i < b'$ by D1 (a) (4) and (2). But also, by D1 (a) (6), there are $b'_1, \ldots, b'_m \in U'$ such that $b'_1 \circ \ldots \circ b'_m \equiv b$, which implies $b'_j \lesssim b$ by D1 (a) (2) and (4). So $b'_1 \lesssim b \equiv b_i < b' \equiv b'_1$ by D1 (a) (5), (i.e., $b'_1 < b'_1$), which yields a contradiction with D1 (a) (2). So $n = 1$, (i.e., $b \equiv b_1 \equiv b'$), from which we obtain $b \equiv b'$ #.
(b) Let x be a model with units U and x' a model with units U'.

---

[31]Compare (Luce & Narens, 1985) and (Narens, 1985).

Lemma 1   For all $b_1, \ldots, b_n, b'_1, \ldots, b'_m \in U$:

$$b_1 \circ \ldots \circ b_n \equiv b'_1 \circ \ldots \circ b'_m \text{ iff } n = m.$$

Proof of the Lemma: If $n = m$, the left-hand side follows from D1 (a) (2), (4), and (5) by induction with respect to n. Conversely, if without loss of generality $m < n$, then $b'_1 \circ \ldots \circ b'_m \equiv b_1 \circ \ldots \circ b_m < (b_1 \circ \ldots \circ b_m) \circ (b_{m+1} \circ \ldots \circ b_n) \equiv b_1 \circ \ldots \circ b_n$, by the first part of the proof, and by D1 (a) (2) and (4)#.

Now let $b \in U$, $\omega(b) = \beta$, $\omega'(b) = \tau$, and $\alpha := \beta/\tau > 0$. Let $a \in D$. By D1 (a) (5), there exist $b_1, \ldots, b_n \in U$ and $b'_1, \ldots, b'_m \in U'$ such that (1) $b_1 \circ \ldots \circ b_n \equiv a \equiv b'_1 \circ \ldots \circ b'_m$. By D1 (a) (7.1) and part (a): $\omega(b_i) = \omega(b'_j)$ and $\omega'(b_i) = \omega'(b'_j)$ for all $i \leq n$ and $j \leq m$. This, together with (1) and D1 (a) (7.2), yields $\omega(a) = n\,\beta = n\,\omega(b_1)$ and $\omega'(a) = m\omega'(b) = m\tau$.

Applying Lemma 1 to $U \cup U'$, we obtain from (1): $n = m$, so $\omega(a) = n\,\beta = n\,\alpha\tau = \alpha\,n\tau = \alpha\,\omega'\,(a)$#.

(c) Define ω by $\omega(b) = 1$ for all $b \in U$ and $\omega(a) = n$, iff $a \equiv b_1 \circ \ldots \circ b_n$, according to D1 (a) (6). Then D1 (a) (7) follows from D1 (a) (6) and Lemma 1, and uniqueness follows from (b) #.

Proof of T2: (a) See (Krantz et al., 1971), T1 p. 74 #.

(b) We first need Lemma 2.

Lemma 2   If D3 (a) (1) to (4) hold, then $\circ$ is commutative.

Proof: (Krantz et al., 1971), p. 78, lemma 3#.

D3 (a) (2) follows from (i) and D1 (a) (2). By (iii), $\cup \circ$ is total, and associativity follows from (i) and D1 (a) (3). D3 (a) (4) follows from (i), (iii) and D1 (a) (4). In order to prove D3 (a) (5) let $a, b, c, d \in D^{\cup X}$ such that $a < b$. If $c \lesssim d$, (5) holds for $n = 1$ by D3 (a) (4). So let $d < c$. If $a \circ c < b \circ d$, (5) holds for $n = 1$. Otherwise $a \circ c > b \circ d$ (by D3 (a) (1) to (4), which are already proved. By (i), there is an $x \in X$ such that $a, b, c, d \in D^x$, and, by D1 (a) (6), there are $a_1, \ldots, a_{n(a)}, b_1, \ldots, b_{n(b)}, c_1, \ldots, c_{n(c)}, d_1, \ldots, d_{n(d)} \in U^x$ such that $a_1 \circ \ldots \circ a_{n(a)} \equiv a$ and similarly for b, c, d. From $a < b$, it follows that $a <^x b$, and from Lemma 1, we obtain that $n(a) < n(b)$, i.e. $b \equiv^x a_1 \circ \ldots \circ a_{n(a)} \circ b_{n(a)+1} \circ \ldots \circ b_{n(b)}$, and similarly from $d < c$, we obtain $n(d) < n(c)$, i.e. $c \equiv^x d_1 \circ \ldots \circ d_{n(d)} \circ c_{n(d)+1} \circ \ldots \circ c_{n(c)}$. Now let $c - d := c_{n(d)+1} \circ \ldots \circ c_{n(c)}$ and $b - a := b_{n(a)+1} \circ \ldots \circ b_{n(b)}$. From $a \circ c > b \circ d$, Lemma 2, and D1 (a) (4), we obtain that $c - d > b - a$. By (ii), there is an extension $z \in X$ of x and some $n \in \mathbb{N}$ such that $n(b - a)$ is defined in z, and $c - d \lesssim^z n(b - a)$. By (iii) and (i), we find some extension u of z such that na and nb also are defined in u. From D3 (a) (1) to (4), Lemma 2, it follows, by straightforward calculation, that $n(b - a) \equiv nb - na$ where the latter entity is constructed like $b - a$ above. In u, we then have $c - d \lesssim^u nb - na$ which, by Lemma 2, implies $na \circ c \lesssim^u nb \circ d$. But then $na \circ c \lesssim nb \circ d$, by the definition of $\cup X$#.

Proof of T3:

(b) Let $m_i := m(p_i)$ for $i = 1, 2, 3$, Then D4 (a) (5) can be rewritten as $\sum_{i \leq 3} m_i w_i$

(1)

$= 0$. This is a homogeneous system of linear equations. Let W be the matrix $(w_1,$
$w_2, w_3)$, $Z: = \{\langle m_1, m_2, m_3 \rangle \in \mathbb{R}^3 / m_i > 0 \text{ for } 1 \leq i \leq 3\}$ and $L: = Z \cap \text{Kernel}$
(W). By a theorem by Tucker (Tucker, 1956), Corollary 1A, D4 (a) (6) implies
(2): The existence of a positive solution of (1). Now (1) has a unique (up to a
positive factor) and positive solution iff $\text{Dim}(L) = 1$, but L is an open subset of
Kernel (W), so $\text{Dim}(L) = \text{Dim}(\text{Kernel } (W))$. Therefore, (1) has a unique and
positive solution, iff $\text{Dim}(\text{Kernel } (W)) = 1$. By a well known theorem of linear
algebra: $\text{Dim}(\text{Kernel } (W)) + \text{Rank}(W) = 3$. So (3): (1) has a unique positive
solution, iff $\text{Rank}(W) = 2$. By D4 (a) (6), Part 1, we have $\text{Rank}(W) = 2$, and
from (3) and (2), we obtain that the solution of (1) is unique up to a positive
factor#.
Part (a) now follows from D4 (a) (7)#.

REFERENCES

Balzer, W. (1978). *Empirische Geometrie und Raum-Zeit-Theorie in mengentheoretischer Dar-
    stellung*. ("Empirical Geometry and Space-Time Theory in Set Theoretic Formulation") Kron-
    berg: Scriptor Verlag.
Balzer, W. (1979). On the status of arithmetic. *Erkenntnis, 14,* 57–85.
Balzer, W. (1983). Theory and measurement. *Erkenntnis, 19,* 3–25.
Balzer, W. (1985a). On a new definition of theoreticity. *Dialectica, 39,* 127–145.
Balzer W. (1985b). *Theorie und Messung*. Berlin: Springer Verlag.
Balzer, W. (1986). Theoretical terms: A new perspective. *The Journal of Philosophy, 83,* 71–90.
Balzer, W. (1987). Reference and the development of theories. In: P. Weingartner & G. Schurz
    (Eds.), *Logic, philosophy of science and epistemology*. Proceedings of the 11th International
    Wittgenstein Symposium. Vienna: Hoelder-Pichler-Tempski. 213–24.
Balzer, W., Lauth, B., & Zoubek, G. (1989). A Static Theory of Reference in Science, *Synthese,
    79,* 319–60.
Balzer, W., & Moulines, C. U. (1980). On theoreticity. *Synthese, 44,* 467–494.
Balzer, W., Moulines, C. U., & Sneed, J. D. (1987). *An architectonic for science*. Dordrecht:
    Reidel.
Balzer, W., & Muehlhoelzer, F. (1982). Klassische Stossmechanik. ("Classical Collision Mechan-
    ics") *Zeitschrift fuer allgemeine Wissenschaftstheorie, 13,* 22–39.
Balzer, W., & Wollmershaeuser, F. R. (1986). Chains of measurement in Roemer's determination of
    the velocity of light. *Erkenntnis, 25,* 323–344.
Berka, K. (1983). *Measurement*. Dordrecht: Reidel.
Bourbaki, N. (1968). *Theory of sets*. Paris: Hermann.
Gaehde, U. (1983). *T–Theoretizitaet und Holismus*. ("T-Theoreticity and Holism.") Frankfurt: Pe-
    ter Lang Verlag.
Glymour, C. (1980). *Theory and evidence*. Princeton: Princeton University Press.
Henderson, J. M., & Quandt, R. E. (1958). *Microeconomic theory, A mathematical approach*.
    New York: McGraw-Hill.
Hölder, O. (1901). "Die Axiome der Quantitaet und die Lehre vom Mass. ("The Axioms of Quan-
    tity and the Science of the Measure.") *Verh. kgl. saechs. Ges. f. Wiss., Math.-Phys. Klasse,
    Leipzig 53,* 1–64.
Jeffrey, R. C. (1965). *The logic of decision*. New York: McGraw-Hill.

Krantz, D. H., Luce, R. D., Suppes, P., & Tversky, A. (1971). *Foundations of measurement.* New York: Academic Press.

Kyburg, H. E., Jr. (1984). *Theory and measurement.* Cambridge: Cambridge University Press.

Luce, R. D., & Narens, L. (1985). Classification of concatenation measurement structures according to scale type. *Journal of Mathematical Psychology, 29,* 1–72.

Narens, L. (1985). *Abstract measurement theory.* Cambridge: Cambridge University Press.

Narens, L., & Luce, R. D. (1986). Measurement: The theory of numerical assignments. *Psychological Bulletin, 99,* 166–180.

von Neumann, J., & Morgenstern, O. (1947). *Theory of games and of economic behaviour.* Princeton: Princeton University Press.

Tucker, A. W. (1956). Dual systems of homogeneous linear equations. *Annals of Mathematics Studies, 38.*

7 Synthetic Physics and Nominalist Realism

John P. Burgess
Princeton University

> 'Words do not reflect the world, not because there is no world, but because words are not mirrors.'
>
> —Roger Shattuck

In mathematical as opposed to philosophical usage, geometry in the style of Euclid and physics in the style of Archimedes are called *synthetic*, whereas geometry in the style of Descartes and physics in the style of Laplace are called *analytic*. Analytically formulated theories differ from synthetically formulated theories in two respects. First, they involve the *representation* of spatial and temporal *position* by real-number *coordinates* and of extensive and intensive *magnitudes* by real-number *measures* of extent and intensity. Second, they involve the application of (*algebra* and) *analysis*, theorems and techniques pertaining to operations on (real numbers and) functions from and to real numbers.

These mathematical methods were creations of the seventeenth century, the first being associated with the names of Descartes and Fermat, the second with the names of Newton and Leibnitz. Analytic methods were important if not essential to the progress of physics in the seventeenth century and to Newton's development of classical gravitational theory. However, when writing up his results for publication in the *Principia*, Newton attempted an exposition in a more synthetic style. This was perhaps in part because he himself viewed the older methods as more elegant, and was surely in part because he wished to avoid controversy with those who viewed the newer methods as less legitimate. Whatever its motives Newton's procedure was not followed by his most important successors. Since the eighteenth century, modern physics has been analytic physics.

Whether it is formulated in synthetic or in analytic style, classical gravitational theory requires implicit or explicit use of notions pertaining to limits. No rigorous treatment of such notions, whether of the limiting position of a figure or of the limiting value of a function, was available in the seventeenth or eighteenth century. It is not for their rigor that the works of Newton and Laplace are admired. By now a rigorous formulation of classical gravitational theory in analytic style has long been available. To make available a rigorous formulation of classical gravitational theory in synthetic style, to do for the *Principia* what has long since been done for the *Mécanique Céleste,* was the goal of the recent book of Hartry Field (1980).[1]

A general method for transforming analytic formulations into synthetic reformulations, applicable to any theory of a type common in pregeneral-relativistic, prequantum physics (any theory of one or more scalar- and/or vector-fields on a flat space-time) is implicit in Field's book, and a modification thereof was made explicit in a recent paper of mine (Burgess, 1984).[2] In the section on Synthetic Physics in this chapter, a further modification thereof will be outlined (without proofs).

In this version, the process of transforming an analytic formulation into a synthetic reformulation is decomposed into three stages. In the first section, it is indicated how to formalize (using only elementary logic) a preformal analytic physical theory together with the pure analysis applied therein. In the section Invariantizing Ideology, it is indicated how to achieve *invariance* in the "ideology" of the theory, how to transform it so as to eliminate *arbitrariness* of the kind involved in fixing a *frame* of coordinates or *scale* of measurement. In the section Denumericalizing Ontology, it is indicated how to achieve *non-numericality* in the "ontology" of the theory, how to further transform it so as to eliminate numbers, functions from and to numbers, and sets of numbers. At both stages, the method involves *coding:* When objects of one sort are systematically related to objects of another sort, so that a p–tuple of the latter suffices to determine uniquely one of the former, then quantification over the former can be eliminated in favor of p–fold quantification over the latter.

For Field, denumericalization was the primary technical goal, and invariantization was a secondary technical goal. The two goals are independent and can be achieved in either order, although the order adopted here, invariantizing before denumericalizing, is perhaps the easier.[3] In any case, neither technical goal is very difficult to achieve. However, Field had also the intuitive goal of

---

[1]Field wrote of "platonist" versus "nominalist" rather than "analytic" versus "synthetic" physics, but alluded to the analogy with analytic versus synthetic geometry on p. 44.

[2]More proofs are provided there than here.

[3]For the importance Field attaches to *invariance* (and the closely related feature of *intrinsicness*), see the many passages listed in the index to his book. He alluded to the possibility of invariantizing without denumericalizing on p. 49.

achieving these technical goals in an *attractively natural* manner. In the third section, it is indicated how to yet further transform the theory so as to obtain a less repellently artificial list of primitives and postulates.

At this stage, the method draws on a traditional interpretation of algebra and analysis in classical synthetic geometry (briefly *geometric algebra*), on which real numbers are identified not with elements of a set-theoretic structure but rather with *ratios* of magnitudes. (Contrast the contemporary interpretation of classical synthetic geometry in algebra and analysis (briefly *algebraic geometry*), on which points are identified not with minimal parts of physical space but rather with *p*–tuples of real numbers.) In the seventeenth century, geometric algebra was viewed as foundationally significant, because the foundations of classical synthetic geometry were viewed as more secure than the foundations of algebra and analysis. It was advocated (somewhat obscurely and confusedly) in the *Géometrie* of Descartes and (quite clearly and distinctly) in the *Universal Arithmetick* of Newton. In the nineteenth century, with the introduction of nonclassical geometries and of set theory, there may have been less confidence in its foundational significance, but there was more work on its rigorous development. How much had been achieved by 1900 can be seen from the work cited by Field in this connection, Hilbert's *Grundlagen der Geometrie.*

Frege (1960), in *Grundlagen der Arithmetik,* criticized geometric algebra for presupposing and not explicating such notions as the following:

1. There exist only finitely many $\mathcal{L}$s.
2. There exist exactly as many $\mathcal{L}$s as $\mathcal{G}$s.

Frege proposed to define such notions in terms of classes or concepts. In his book, Field proposed to take them as primitives, and this invocation of logical primitives outside, above, and beyond those of elementary logic has occasioned much philosophical controversy and some technical confusion in the literature. In the fourth section, it is explained why no such auxiliary apparatus as Frege's classes or concepts or Field's nonelementary logical primitives is needed.[4]

My hope in offering a new version of an old method is to settle questions as to the *technical possibility* of producing synthetic alternatives to analytic originals in the case of theories from turn-of-the-century physics. Then assuming for the sake of argument that the method can be adapted to theories from up-to-date physics,[5] discussion can proceed to questions of its *philosophical significance.*

Field's view on such philosophical questions was roughly as follows.[6] He

---

[4]The above (finite) cardinality-comparison quantifiers are by no means the only items of nonelementary logical apparatus invoked by Field, but they are the only ones that will be discussed in the present chapter. Field himself contemplated dropping them in his book (chapter 9, Part II).

[5]Field offered some hints for adaptation to the general-relativistic case in his book (p. 123).

[6]See his book, "Preliminary Remarks," pp. 1–6.

wished to defend *nominalism,* in the sense of disbelief in numbers, functions, and sets, against W. V. Quine. However, unlike some other nominalists, he agreed with Quine on several issues. He conceded that disbelieving in numbers, functions, and sets obliges one to disbelieve current analytic physics. He conceded that the use of current analytic physics is in practice indispensable, and he conceded that it is impermissible to use current analytic physics in practice while professing to disbelieve it in principle, *unless* one believes some alternative physics whose truth would explain the utility of current analytic physics—hence, the significance for Field of producing a synthetic alternative physics.

Field's view was that, if a synthetic alternative can be produced, then belief in current analytic physics will be unjustifiable. In another recent paper (Burgess, 1983), I argued that such a view cannot be justified by appeal to any recognized or recognizably *scientific* criteria for the justification of belief but rather must rest on some nonscientific or antiscientific *philosophical* criterion.[7] In the section Nominalist Realism of the present chapter, I attempt to uncover what this underlying philosophical criterion may be. I suggest that it may be not an indiscriminate preference for eliminating whatever is eliminable but rather a more discriminating preference for eliminating whatever seems to be "merely contributed by language" and not "a genuine reflection of reality." It may be *realism* in the sense in which it is understood and opposed by Quine.

SYNTHETIC PHYSICS

Analysis and Analytic Physics

The pure analysis applied in physics can be formalized (in elementary logic) as follows. The language $\mathcal{L}_0$ has the following two sorts of variables:

$\xi, \upsilon, \ldots$ for real numbers

$\Xi, Y, \ldots$ for sets of real numbers

It has the following primitives:

$\xi < \upsilon$ ξ is less than υ

$\oplus\xi\upsilon\zeta$ ζ is the sum of ξ and υ

$\otimes\xi\upsilon\zeta$ ζ is the product of ξ and υ

$\xi \in \Xi$ ξ is an element of Ξ

---

[7]Especially Part 4, "Revolutionary Nominalism." The judgment that theories of one type are superior to theories of another type by scientific criteria has revisionary implications for the practice of (education and research in pure) science: In branches where a theory of the type judged superior have been found, it will be taught; in branches where a theory of the type judged superior has not yet been found, one will be sought. Field seems to have disclaimed revisionary implications for the practice of science in his book (p. 90).

The theory $\mathscr{A}_0$ has the following postulates:

A1. *Number-Order, Sum, Product Axioms:* The numbers under $<$, $\oplus$, $\otimes$ form an *ordered field*.

A2. *Set-Extensionality Axiom:* Sets having exactly the same numbers as elements are identical.

A3. *Set-Comprehension Scheme:* For each formula, the following axiom: There exists a set having exactly those points satisfying the formula as elements.

A4. *Set-Completeness Axiom:* Any set contained in an interval (i.e., having lower and upper bounds) is contained in a minimal interval (i.e., has a greatest lower and a least upper bound).

An analytical physical theory of m scalar- and n vector-fields on a flat space-time can be formalized (in elementary logic) as follows. The language $\mathscr{L}$ adds to $\mathscr{L}_0$ two further sorts of variables:

x,y, . . .   for points of space-time

X,Y, . . .   for regions of space-time

and the following further primitives,

$z \lhd Z$	z lies in Z
$\langle z, \zeta \rangle_i$ (i = 1,2,3)	ζ is the ith spatial coordinate of z
$\langle z, \zeta \rangle_4$	ζ is the temporal coordinate of z
$|z, \zeta|^j$ ($l \leq j \leq m$)	ζ is the measure of the intensity of the jth scalar-field at z
$|z, \zeta|_i^k$ ($l \leq k \leq n$)	ζ is the measure of the intensity in the direction of the ith spatial coordinate axis of the kth vector-field at z

The theory $\mathscr{A}$ adds to $\mathscr{A}_0$ the following further postulates:

A5. *Region-Extensionality Axiom:* Regions having exactly the same points lying in them are identical.

A6. *Region-Comprehension Scheme:* For each formula, the following axiom: There exists a region having exactly the points satisfying the formula lying in it.

A7. *Coordinate Axioms:* Trivial axioms, the same for all theories in the present format, about $\langle \, \rangle$: the existence and uniqueness of the coordinates of any given point, and of the point having any given numbers as coordinates.

A8. *Intensity Axioms:* Trivial axioms, the same for all theories in the present format, about $|\;|$: the existence and uniqueness of the measure of intensity of any given scalar-field at any given point, and the existence for any given scalar-field of points at which these measures of intensity are distinct and similarly for vector-fields.

A9. *Special Axioms:* Nontrivial axioms, different for each theory in the present format, typically formalizations of differential equations.

Henceforth, to simplify exposition, it will be pretended that $m = 1$ and $n = 0$, and *measure of intensity of the scalar-field* will be abbreviated *intensity;* also it will be assumed that the theory takes space-time to be *nonrelativistic* (rather than *special-relativistic*) and the scalar-field to be of *interval type* (rather than of *ratio type* or some other type).

Invariantizing Ideology

Informally the goal of the present section and the strategy for achieving it may be described as follows: The symbols $\langle\rangle$ and $||$ must be read as "coordinate" and "intensity" relative to some one frame of coordinates and scale of intensity, unspecified but fixed. However, for each theory in the present format, there will be many *admissible* frames and scales, frames and scales on which the postulates are satisfied. (Which frames and scales will be admissible depends on the mathematical form of the special axioms, which distinguishes the nonrelativistic from the special-relativistic, and the interval- from the ratio-type cases.) The choice of any one out of the many admissible frames and scales is arbitrary. The goal is to eliminate such arbitrary choices.

A formula $\mathcal{P}$ with $p \geq 0$ free variables will be termed *invariant,* if and only if, for any p objects and any two admissible frames or scales, the objects either satisfy the formula on *both* frames or scales, or else they satisfy the formula on *neither* of the frames or scales: Whether or not the objects satisfy the formula is *independent* of which frame or scale is fixed. The goal is to produce a language $\mathcal{L}'$ and a theory $\mathcal{A}'$ such that the following hold:

I1. The primitives of $\mathcal{L}'$ are definable in $\mathcal{L}$ and are invariant.

I2. For any invariant formula of $\mathcal{L}$, there is a formula of $\mathcal{L}'$ such that the equivalence of the two formulas is deducible in $\mathcal{A}$.

I3. The postulates of $\mathcal{A}'$ are deducible in $\mathcal{A}$.

I4. Any sentence of $\mathcal{L}'$ that is deducible in $\mathcal{A}$ is deducible in $\mathcal{A}'$.

Thus, $\mathcal{L}'$ and $\mathcal{A}$ are to capture the invariant content of $\mathcal{L}$ and $\mathcal{A}$.

The strategy will be to replace postulates asserting that certain conditions hold on some one, arbitrarily chosen frame or scale by postulates asserting that these conditions hold on *any admissible* frame or scale. Frames and scales cannot be quantified over directly in the formalism; therefore, they must be coded by

objects . . . that can be.[8] However, then the coding must be such that the following are expressible by invariant formulas:

$\downarrow$ (. . .)	. . . code an admissible frame
$\uparrow$ (. . .)	. . . code an admissible scale
$\langle z, \zeta, \ldots \rangle'_i$	ζ is the ith coordinate of z on the frame coded by . . .
$\lvert z, \zeta, \ldots \rvert'$	ζ is the intensity at z on the scale coded by . . .

Formally a change of coordinates from the original, arbitrarily chosen frame
to an alternative frame can be represented by a 5–by–4 matrix $\xi = (\xi_{ij})$ $(0 \le i \le 4;\ 1 \le j \le 4)$ such that

1. The submatrix (ξ_{ij}) $(1 \le i,j \le 4)$ is nonsingular.

If the χ'_i are the coordinates of x on the original frame, then the coordinates of
x on the alternative frame will be the χ_j given by the following:

$$\chi_j = \xi_{0j} + \Sigma^4_{i=1} (\xi_{ij} \cdot \chi'_i)$$

In the nonrelativistic case, the change of coordinates will be admissible if and
only if the *Galilean* conditions hold:

2. (a) $\xi_{14} = \xi_{24} = \xi_{34} = \xi_{41} = \xi_{42} = \xi_{43} = 0$
   (b) $\xi_{44} \ne 0$, and the submatrix (ξ_{ij}) $(1 \le i,j \le 3)$ is *orthogonal*.

A change of (measure of the) intensity (of the scalar-field) from the original,
arbitrarily chosen scale to an alternative scale can be represented by a 2–by–1
matrix $\upsilon = (\upsilon_k)$ $(k = 0,1)$ such that

3. $\upsilon_1 \ne 0$

If η' is the intensity at y on the original scale, then the intensity at y on the
alternative scale will be η, given by the following:

$$\eta = \upsilon_0 + \upsilon_1 \cdot \eta'$$

In the interval-type case, the change of intensity will be admissible if and only if

4. $\upsilon_1 > 0$

The coding of a frame or scale by a matrix ξ or υ only indicates how it is
obtained from the original, arbitrarily chosen frame or scale. Thus, the following
cannot be expressed by invariant formulas:

ζ is the ith coordinate of z on the frame coded by ξ.
ζ is the intensity at z on the scale coded by υ.

---

[8]The strategy is, thus, to *introduce parameters* (. . . coding frames and scales) and then *quantify
out*. Field made occasional use of this strategy in his book (e.g. bottom p. 76 to top p. 77–where the
parameters a,b,c and a',b',c' in effect determine a frame).

However, another coding is available, based on the observation that a frame or scale can be determined uniquely by the matrix χ or η of coordinates or intensities at a quintuple $\underset{\sim}{\chi}$ or pair $\underset{\sim}{y}$ of suitable points. Writing out quantification over p–by–q matrices as pq–fold quantification over numbers, the following can be expressed by invariant formulas:

$\downarrow_0(\underset{\sim}{x},\chi)$ There exists a unique $\underset{\sim}{\xi}$ satisfying (1) such that the χ_{ij} are the ith coordinates of the x_j on the alternative frame obtained from the original frame through the change represented by $\underset{\sim}{\xi}$.

$\uparrow_0(\underset{\sim}{y},\eta)$ There exists a unique $\underset{\sim}{\upsilon}$ satisfying (3) such that the η_k are the intensities at the y_k on the alternative scale obtained from the original scale through the change represented by $\underset{\sim}{\upsilon}$.

$\downarrow(\underset{\sim}{x},\chi)$ $\downarrow_0(x,\chi)$ and the $\underset{\sim}{\xi}$ in question satisfies (2).

$\uparrow(y,\eta)$ $\uparrow_0(\bar{y},\eta)$ and the $\underset{\sim}{\upsilon}$ in question satisfies (4).

$\langle z,\ \zeta,\ \underset{\sim}{x}\ \chi\rangle'_i$ $\downarrow_0(\underset{\sim}{x},\chi)$ and ζ is the ith coordinate of z on the alternative frame obtained from the original frame through the change represented by the $\underset{\sim}{\xi}$ in question.

$|z,\ \zeta,\ \underset{\sim}{y},\ \eta|'$ $\uparrow_0(\underset{\sim}{y},\eta)$ and ζ is the intensity at z on the alternative scale obtained from the original scale through the change represented by the $\underset{\sim}{\upsilon}$ in question.

Let $\mathcal{L}'$ have the following primitives:

$$<, \oplus, \otimes, \in, \lhd, \downarrow, \uparrow, \langle\ \rangle'_i, |\ |'$$

For each sentence $\mathcal{P}$ of $\mathcal{L}$, if $\langle\ \rangle'_i$ and $|\ |'$ do not occur in $\mathcal{P}$, let $\mathcal{P}' = \mathcal{P}$. Otherwise, let $\mathcal{P}''(\underset{\sim}{x},\chi,\underset{\sim}{y},\eta)$ be the result of substituting throughout $\langle \ldots, \underset{\sim}{x}, \chi\rangle'_i$ and $|\ldots, \underset{\sim}{y}, \eta|'$ for $\langle \ldots \rangle$ and $|\ldots|$ let $\mathcal{P}'$ be the following:

$$\forall\underset{\sim}{x}\forall\chi\forall\underset{\sim}{y}\forall\eta(\ \downarrow(\underset{\sim}{x},\chi)\ \wedge\ \uparrow(y,\eta)\ \to\ \mathcal{P}''(\underset{\sim}{x},\chi,\underset{\sim}{y},\eta'))$$

Let $\mathcal{A}'$ have as postulates the $\mathcal{P}'$ for $\mathcal{P}$ a postulate of $\mathcal{A}$ plus the following:

A7''. $\exists\chi\exists\underset{\sim}{\chi}\ \downarrow(\underset{\sim}{x},\chi)$
A8''. $\exists\underset{\sim}{y}\exists\eta\ \uparrow(\underset{\sim}{y},\eta)$

Then I1–I4 can be proved.

Denumericalizing Ontology

Informally the goal of the present section and the strategy for achieving it may be described as follows: Call a formula *nonnumerical,* if no number- or set-variables occur free in it. The goal is to produce a language $\mathscr{L}'^*$ with only point- and region-variables and a theory $\mathscr{A}'^*$ such that

N1. The primitives of $\mathscr{L}'^*$ are definable in $\mathscr{L}'$ and are nonnumerical.

N2. For every nonnumerical formula of $\mathscr{L}'$, there exists a formula of $\mathscr{L}'^*$ such that the equivalence of the two formula is deducible in $\mathscr{A}'$.

N3. The postulates of $\mathscr{A}'^*$ are deducible in $\mathscr{A}'$.

N4. Any sentence of $\mathscr{L}'^*$ that is deducible in $\mathscr{A}'$ is deducible in $\mathscr{A}'^*$.

Thus, $\mathscr{L}'^*$ and $\mathscr{A}'^*$ are to capture the nonnumerical content of $\mathscr{L}'$ and $\mathscr{A}'$.

The strategy is the trivial one of coding numbers and sets by points and regions. Any triple of points (x_0, x_1, x) satisfying

$\Diamond(x_0, x_1, x)$ x_0, x_1 are distinct, and x_0, x_1, x are collinear

determines a unique real number ξ, satisfying

$[x_0, x_1, x, \xi]$ ξ is the ratio of the distance between x_0 and x to that between x_0 and x_1.

(Here *sign* is determined by *orientation:* The sign of ξ is positive or negative according as x_1 and x lie on the same or opposite side of x_0.) Every real number is determined by such a triple of points, and two such triples (x_0, x_1, x) and (y_0, y_1, y) determine the same real number if and only if they satisfy the following:

$x_0, x_1, x \sim y_0, y_1, y$ The ratio of the distance between x_0 and x to that between x_0 and x_1 equals the ratio of the distance between y_0 and y to that between y_0 and y_1.

On the other hand, in the traditional symbolism of *proportionality:*

$x_0 x : x_0 x_1 :: y_0 y : y_0 y_1.$

If this is understood as implying or presupposing $\Diamond(x_0, x_1, x)$ and $\Diamond(y_0, y_1, y)$, then $\Diamond$ is definable in terms of $\sim$:

$\Diamond(x_0, x_1, x) \leftrightarrow (x_0, x_1, x \sim x_0, x_1, x).$

Formally the following are expressible by invariant, nonnumerical formula of $\mathscr{L}$, hence, by nonnumerical formulas of $\mathscr{L}'$:

$[x_0, x_1, x, \xi]$ For each i, the ith coordinate of x equals the ith coordinate of x_0 plus ξ times the ith coordinate of x_1.

$x_0, x_1, x \sim y_0, y_1, y$ $\exists\xi\exists\upsilon([x_0, x_1, x, \xi] \land [y_0, y_1, y, \upsilon]) \land \forall\xi\forall\upsilon([x_0, x_1, x, \xi] \land [y_0, y_1, y, \upsilon] \rightarrow \xi = \upsilon).$

$[[x_0,x_1,X,\Xi]]$ $\forall x \lhd X \exists \xi \in \Xi \; ([x_0,x_1,x,\xi]) \; \forall \xi \in \Xi \exists x \lhd X([x_0,x_1,x,\xi]).$

$x_0,x_1,X \approx y_0,y_1,Y$ $\exists \Xi \exists Y([[x_0,x_1,X,\Xi]] \quad \wedge \quad [[y_0,y_1,Y,Y]]) \quad \wedge$
     $\forall \Xi \forall Y([[x_0,x_1,X,\Xi]] \wedge [[y_0,y_1,Y,Y]] \rightarrow \Xi = Y).$

$x_0,x_1,x <^* y_0,y_1,y$ $\exists \xi \exists v([x_0,x_1,x,\xi] \wedge [y_0,y_1,y,v]) \wedge \forall \xi \forall v([x_0,x_1,x,\xi] \wedge$
     $[y_0,y_1,y,v] \rightarrow \xi < v).$

$x_0,x_1,x \in^* y_0,y_1,Y$ $\exists \xi \exists Y([x_0,x_1,x,\xi] \wedge [[y_0,y_1,Y,Y]]) \wedge \forall \xi \forall Y([x_0,x_1,x,\xi] \wedge$
     $[[y_0,y_1,Y,Y]] \rightarrow \xi \in Y).$

Similarly we have \$* for every other primitive \$ of $\mathscr{L}'$.

Let $\mathscr{L}'*$ have the following primitives:

$$\sim, \; \approx, \; <^*, \; \oplus^*, \; \otimes^*, \; \in^*, \; \lhd, \; \downarrow^*, \; \uparrow^*, \; \langle \; \rangle_i'^*, \; |\;|'^*$$

For each formula $\mathscr{P}$ of $\mathscr{L}'$, if no number- or set-variables occur free or bound in $\mathscr{P}$, let $\mathscr{P}* = \mathscr{P}$. Otherwise associate with each such variable ξ or Ξ distinct variables x_0,x_1,x or x_0,x_1,X not already occurring in $\mathscr{P}$, and let $\mathscr{P}*$ be the result of substituting throughout as follows:

For: Put:

$\forall \xi$ $\forall x_0 \forall x_1 \forall x \; (\; (x_0,x_1,x \sim x_0,x_1,x) \rightarrow \ldots)$

$\exists \xi$ $\exists x_0 \exists x_1 \exists x \; (\; (x_0,x_1,x \sim x_0,x_1,x) \wedge \ldots)$

$\forall \Xi$ $\forall x_0 \forall x_1 \forall X \; (\; (x_0,x_1,X \approx x_0,x_1,X) \rightarrow \ldots)$

$\exists \Xi$ $\exists x_0 \exists x_1 \exists X \; (\; (x_0,x_1,X \approx x_0,x_1,X) \wedge \ldots)$

$\xi = v$ $x_0,x_1,x \sim y_0,y_1,y$

$\Xi = Y$ $x_0,x_1,X \approx y_0,y_1,Y$

$\xi < v$ $x_0,x_1,x <^* y_0,y_1,y$

$\xi \in \Xi$ $x_0,x_1,x \in^* y_0,y_1,Y$

and similarly for other primitives \$ of $\mathscr{L}'$. Let $\mathscr{A}'*$ have as postulates:

A0*. $\mathscr{P}*$ for $\mathscr{P}$ a (logical) identity postulate of $\mathscr{L}'$

plus $\mathscr{P}*$ for $\mathscr{P}$ a (nonlogical) postulate of $\mathscr{A}'$. Then N1–N4 can be proved.

Synthetic Physics By Means of Geometric Algebra

The goal of the present section is to produce a language and a theory with a more attractively natural list of primitives and postulates.

The following are expressible by invariant, nonnumerical formulas of $\mathscr{L}$ hence by nonnumerical formulas of $\mathscr{L}'$, hence by formulas of $\mathscr{L}'$:

Bxyz   *y* lies between *x* and *z*.

Cxyrs   *x* and *y* and *r* and *s* are simultaneous, and the distance between *x* and *y* equals that between *r* and *s*.

Dxyzrst   The ratio of the difference in intensity between *x* and *z* to that between *x* and y equals the ratio of the distance between r and t to that between r and s.

Exy   The intensity at x is less than that at y.

Let $\mathcal{L}'_{\mathcal{Z}}{}^{\#}$ have as primitives the following:

$B, C, D, E, \lhd$

(Here, C,E are appropriate to the nonrelativistic, interval-type case; in other cases, other primitives would be used.) Using (slight extensions of well-known) results in geometric algebra, it can be proved that the primitives of $\mathcal{L}'^{*\#}$ are definable from the primitives of $\mathcal{L}'^{*}$ and conversely, in the converse direction proceeding as follows:

Use:	To Define:
B	$\sim, <^{*}, \oplus^{*}, \otimes^{*}, \langle \; \rangle_i{}'^{*}$
$B,\lhd$	$\approx, \in^{*}$
B,C	$\downarrow^{*}$
B,D	$||'^{*}$
B,D,E	$\uparrow^{*}$

For each sentence $\mathcal{P}$ of $\mathcal{L}'^{*}$, let $\mathcal{P}^{\#}$ be the result of substituting throughout for the primitives of $\mathcal{L}'^{*}$ their definitions in terms of the primitives of $\mathcal{L}'^{*\#}$. Let $\mathcal{A}'^{*\#}$ have the following postulates:

S1. *Basic Space-Time or Point-Order Axioms:* The points under B form a *four-dimensional affine space.*

S2. *Region-Extensionality Axiom:* A5.

S3. *Region-Comprehension Scheme:* A6.

S4. *Region-Completeness Axiom:* Every region contained in an interval is contained in a minimal interval.

S5. *Further Space-Time Axioms:* In the nonrelativistic case, simultaneity is a relation of equivalence, and the points equivalent to any given point under B,C form a *three-dimensional Euclidean space.*

S6. *Basic Intensity Axioms:* Trivial axioms, the same for all theories in the present format, about D.

S7. *Further Intensity Axioms:* Trivial axioms, differing in the interval-type case from the ratio-type case but the same for all theories in the interval-type case, about E.

S8. *Special Axioms:* A9$'^{*\#}$.

Using (slight extensions of well-known) results on geometric algebra, it can be proved that, for any sentence $\mathcal{P}$ of $\mathcal{L}'^{*}$, $\mathcal{P}$ is deducible in $\mathcal{A}'^{*}$ if and only if $\mathcal{P}^{\#}$

is deducible in $\mathcal{A}'*\#$; in deducing $\mathcal{P}\#$ for $\mathcal{P}$, a postulate of $\mathcal{A}'*$ from the postulates of $\mathcal{A}'*\#$ proceeding as follows:

Use:	To Deduce:
S1	$A0*\#$, $A1*\#$, $A7'*\#$
S1,S2	$A2*\#$
S1,S3	$A3*\#$
S1,S4	$A4*\#$
S1,S5	$A7''*\#$
S1,S6	$A8'*\#$
S1,S6,S7	$A8''*\#$

In the literature of geometric algebra, the correspondence between affine space axioms and ordered field axioms is worked out in great detail (e.g., Desargues' Theorem corresponds to the distributive law).

$\mathcal{L}'*\#$ and $\mathcal{A}'*\#$ provide a formalization (in elementary logic) of a synthetic alternative to the original analytic physical theory formalized as in $\mathcal{L}$ and $\mathcal{A}$.

Why Non-Elementary Logic Is Not Needed

There are two quite distinct ways in which one might suspect that auxiliary apparatus beyond the primitives of $\mathcal{L}'*\#$ and postulates of $\mathcal{A}'*\#$ would be needed in synthetic physics.

On the one hand, one might suspect that some such auxiliary apparatus would be needed at some stage for the sake of the transformation of analytic into synthetic physics. One might suspect that, without it, the definition of some notion or the deduction of some result could not be carried out (contrary to what has been asserted in the previous sections). Such suspicions might be suggested by reading Frege (1960, pp. 25–26), who wrote:

> Newton proposes to understand by number not so much a set of units as the relation in the abstract between any given magnitude and another magnitude of the same kind taken as unity. It may be granted that this is an apt description of number in the wider sense, in which it includes also fractions and irrational numbers; but it presupposes the concepts of magnitude and of relation in respect of magnitude. This should presumably mean that a definition of number in the narrower sense, or cardinal Number, will still be needed; for Euclid, in order to define the identity of two ratios between lengths, makes use of the concept of equimultiples, and equimultiples bring us back once again to numerical identity.

One might suspect that, in order to define notions pertaining to "identity of ratios" (like $\sim$ and D above) from attractively natural primitives, the notion of "equimultiples," or auxiliary apparatus in terms of which that notion can be defined (such as Frege's classes or concepts, or Field's nonelementary logical primitives) would be needed. Indeed Field invoked his auxiliary apparatus in just such a connection. Moreover, the invocation of some such auxiliary apparatus seems unavoidable, *if one follows Euclid (who follows Eudoxus) in the treatment of identity of ratios.*[9]

However, one need not follow Eudoxus (as Hilbert in effect does not). As for $\sim$, it can be defined in elementary logic from the notions of *collinearity, parallelism,* and *intersection,* which (as Field in effect noted) can be defined in elementary logic from the attractively natural primitive B. On one such definition, the general case is merely a combination of various special cases, each of which is readily understood on drawing a figure. For example, if $x_0 = y_0$ but is not collinear with x_1 and y_1, then $x_0,x_1,x \sim y_0,y_1,y$, if and only if the lines through x_1 and y_1 and through x and y are parallel; whereas, if the lines through x_0 and x_1 and through y_0 and y_1 are parallel, then $x_0,x_1,x \sim y_0,y_1,y$, if and only if the lines through x_0 and y_0, through x_1 and y_1, and through x and y intersect in a common point.

As for D, because it seems sufficiently attractively natural itself, the simplest procedure (although not the only possible procedure) is to admit it as a primitive. It expresses an idealization of what is established in the course of operationally determining the measure of the intensity of a scalar field using an instrument. For example, in determining the *Celsius temperature* of a sample using a *mercury thermometer*, what is established is roughly that $Dxyzrst$ holds, where the following hold:

r is at the 0° mark on the thermometer.

s is at the 100° mark on the thermometer.

t is at the top of the column of mercury.

x is in a sample of freezing water.

y is in a sample of boiling water.

z is at the bottom of the thermometer, in the sample where Celsius temperature is being determined.

So much for suspicions of the first kind.

On the other hand, one might suspect that some such auxiliary apparatus

---

[9]Field followed Eudoxus in defining $<_{st,Scal}$ in terms of his primitive S–Cong in his book (chapter 8, Part B, pp. 64–67). In the notation of the present chapter, this amounts roughly to defining D above in terms of:

Fxyrs   The difference in intensity between x and y equals that between r and s.

He used both his (finite) cardinality-comparison quantifiers and also a continuity axiom. The latter is needed, the former are not.

would be needed for its own sake in analytic physics, and would need to be preserved in transforming analytic physics into synthetic physics. One might suspect that, without it, $\mathscr{L}$ and $\mathscr{A}$ would be inadequate for the formalization of preformal analytic physics (contrary to what has been asserted in the first section). Such suspicions might also be suggested by reading Frege, who continued with the following:

> However, let it be, as it may be, the case that identity of ratios between lengths can in fact be defined without any reference to the concept of number. Even so, we should still remain in doubt as to how the number defined geometrically in this way is related to the number of ordinary life, which would then be entirely cut off from science. . . . [T]he question arises whether arithmetic itself can make do with a geometrical concept of number, when we think of some of the notions that occur in it, such as the Number of roots of an equation. . . . On the other hand, the number which gives the answer to the question *How many?* can answer among other things how many units are contained in a length.

Indeed, in analytic physics, one needs to be able to *count,* to answer "how many" points, regions, numbers, or sets satisfy some given condition.

However, notions and results pertaining to arithmetic and counting, to natural numbers (nonnegative integers, finite cardinals) can be developed in $\mathscr{L}$ and $\mathscr{A}$ without auxiliary apparatus using coding. Such use of coding might be illegitimate, if the goal were the Fregean one of providing an exegesis or explication of "the number of ordinary life." However, the Fieldian goal is a different one. In outline, one procedure for developing arithmetic and counting is as follows:

First, the usual definition of ξ is a natural number, namely ξ belongs to every set containing zero and closed under adding one can readily be formalized. Next, using it, notions and results pertaining to the *decimal expansion* of real numbers can be formalized. These include notions and results pertaining to the usual coding of ordered pairs of real numbers by real numbers, which involves *shuffling*. For example, if the following:

$$\xi = 3.14159\ldots$$
$$\upsilon = 2.71828\ldots,$$

then (ξ,υ) is coded by

$$\zeta = 32.1741185298.\ldots$$

A function from real numbers to sets of real numbers can be coded by the set of ordered pairs (ξ,υ), with υ an element of the value of the function for argument ξ; thus, such functions can now be coded by sets of real numbers. Thus, the usual definition as follows:

There exist exactly ξ-many Ξ such that $\mathscr{L}(\Xi)$.

Namely ξ is a natural number, and there exists a bijective function from the natural numbers less than ξ to the Ξ such that $\mathscr{L}(\Xi)$ can be formalized using this coding. Notions and results pertaining to the counting of sets can be formalized. Counting of numbers can be treated similarly (or reduced to counting of singleton sets). Finally, using the coordinate representation of points by ordered quadruples of real numbers and the coding of ordered quadruple real numbers by real numbers, counting of points and regions can be reduced to counting of numbers and sets. Field's quantifiers can be defined and, thus, are not needed as primitives. So much for suspicions of the second kind.

NOMINALIST REALISM

The label *realism* is one that is often used in connection with disagreements like that between Field and Quine. Unfortunately it is also one that has been used in many different senses in traditional and recent philosophy. Precedents could be cited for attaching it to any one of a large number of theses, each susceptible to any one of a large number of interpretations. Towards sorting out some of these senses, it may be well to begin with a quotation from the *Pragmatism* of William James, which Morris Kline (1985) commented on.[10] It describes an attitude towards the theories then current held by many from the time of Plato to the time of Newton:

> When the first mathematical, logical and natural uniformities, the first *laws,* were discovered, men were so carried away by the clearness, beauty and simplification that resulted that they believed themselves to have deciphered authentically the external thoughts of the Almighty. His mind also thundered and reverberated in syllogisms. He also thought in conic sections, squares and roots and ratios, and geometrized like Euclid. He made Kepler's laws for the planets to follow; he made velocity increase proportionally to the time in falling bodies; . . . and when we rediscover any one of these wondrous institutions, we seize his mind in its very literal intention.

The attitude thus described may be summarized as follows:

(0) Current theory is an image in the human mind of the creative design in the Divine Mind.

Historically (0) seems to have been held in conjunction with most or all of the following:

(1) The world is a projection of the creative design in the Divine Mind.

(2) Current theory is a reflection in the human mind of the world.

(3) One is justified in believing a theory, if and only if (or if and only if one is

---

[10]Chapter XII contains many quotations from many authors, all in a similar vein, with references and commentary.

justified in believing that) it is a reflection in the human mind of the world.

(4) One is justified in believing current theory.

Logically (1) and (2) together imply (0); whereas, given (3), (2) and (4) imply each other. On one interpretation, namely on an interpretation of the metaphor of reflection emphasizing the *causal* connection between any element of the image inside the mirror and the corresponding element of the scene outside the mirror, (3) implies the following:

(5) One is justified in believing a theory involving the hypothesis that objects of a given sort exist, only if the presence of that hypothesis in the theory is caused by the presence of objects of that given in the world.

Field and Quine agreed in roughly identifying *nominalism* with the denial and *antinominalism* with the affirmation of the following:

(6) (One is justified in believing (theories involving the hypothesis) that) numbers, functions, and sets exist.[11]

Field is a nominalist, Quine an antinominalist. To see the pertinence of (0)–(5) to their disagreement over (6), note that they seem to agree as follows:

(A) Current theory involves the hypothesis that numbers, functions, and sets exist.
(B) Numbers, functions, and sets are not *physical* and do not *physically* cause belief (in theories involving the hypothesis) that they exist.
(C) *No* objects *aphysically* cause *any* beliefs.

Field, unlike some nominalists, rejected *reinterpretations* of current theory denying (A).[12] Quine, unlike some antinominalists, would view as *confused* anyone who denied (B) and took numbers to be physical (or for that matter, mental), and as *superstitious* anyone who denied (C) and took beliefs to be effects of ectophysical, hyperphysical, or paraphysical causes, or of extrasensory, suprasensory, or praetersensory perceptions. Now given (A), (4) implies (6); whereas, given (B) and (C), (5) implies not-(6).

---

[11]Both Field and Quine tended to "ascend" from questions of the status of numbers, functions, and sets to questions of the status of theories—hence, the parenthetical clauses. Field tended to write of "belief," Quine of "assertion;" but the possibility of *insincerity* or assertion-without-belief did not seem to be an issue between them.

[12]See his (unfavorable) remarks on Charles Chihara's strategy of reinterpretation in several passages (listed in the index) in his book.

Quine roughly identified *realism* with the affirmation and *antirealism* with the denial of (3). Quine is an antirealist. He wrote (1963, pp. 78–79):

> The fundamental-sounding philosophical question, How much of our science is merely contributed by language and how much is a genuine reflection of reality? is perhaps a spurious question which itself arises wholly from a certain particular type of language. Certainly we are in a predicament if we try to answer the question; for to answer the question we must talk about the world as well as about language, and to talk about the world we must already impose upon the world some conceptual scheme peculiar to our own special language. . . . We can improve our conceptual scheme, our philosophy, bit by bit while continuing to depend on it for support; but we cannot detach ourselves from it and compare it objectively with an unconceptualized reality. Hence it is meaningless, I suggest, to inquire into the absolute correctness of a conceptual scheme as a mirror of reality. Our standard for appraising basic changes of conceptual scheme must be, not a realistic standard of correspondence to reality, but a pragmatic standard. Concepts are language, and the purpose of concepts and of language is efficacy in communication and in prediction. Such is the ultimate duty of language, science, and philosophy, and it is in relation to that duty that a conceptual scheme has finally to be appraised.

Indeed Quine's antinominalism is a *consequence* of his antirealism. He recognized that current theory, involving the hypothesis that numbers, functions and sets exist, is extremely efficacious; and it is because he recognized no criterion as more important for science than that of efficacy in communication and prediction, and recognized no criteria exterior, superior, or ulterior to those of science, that he viewed belief in the existence of numbers, functions, and sets as justified.

I suggest that similarly Field's nominalism may be a consequence of realism. (Realism in Quine's sense; that is, in Field's own usage, *realism* amounts to little more than *antinominalism,* and *antirealism* to little more than *nominalism.*) In a recent paper, Field described what he took to be "probably the main ground for suspicion" about numbers, functions, and sets:[13]

> According to the Platonist picture, the truth-values of our mathematical assertions depend on facts involving Platonic entities that reside in a realm outside of space-time. There are no causal connections between the entities in the Platonic realm and ourselves; how then can we know what is going on in that realm? . . . It seems as if to answer these questions one is going to have to postulate some *aphysical connection,* some *mysterious mental grasping,* between ourselves and the elements of this Platonic realm.

Changing rhetorical questions to forthright denials and suppressing the term of abuse "Platonic" and the technical jargon "truth conditions," this seems to

---

[13]I am indebted to Field for providing me with a copy of this paper prior to publication. I am informed that it has subsequently appeared (1983).

amount to an argument from overt premises, like (B) and (C) to a conclusion like not-(6). Such an argument requires a covert premise, like the causal interpretation (5) of the realist criterion (3) for justification of belief. Presumably, for Field, both conclusion and covert premise would carry a proviso: One is not justified in believing certain theories *unless* no suitable alternative theories can be produced. Producing such suitable alternative theories is for Field the *main* part of the argument for not-(6).

In a footnote to the quoted passage, Field cited a well-known paper of Paul Benacerraf. Benacerraf propounded (without pretending to be able to resolve) the following dilemma: There seem to be initially plausible arguments *both* for the *negative* conclusion that we *cannot* have knowledge of numbers *and also* for the *positive* conclusion that we *do* have knowledge of numbers. Field in effect paraphrased the argument for the negative horn of Benacerraf's dilemma. In his paper, Benacerraf (1983) described this argument as resting on a *causal* criterion for knowledge, and, writing with Hilary Putnam in the editorial introduction to the new edition of their well-known anthology (Benacerraf & Putnam, 1983), Benacerraf described much opposition to Quine as resting on *realist* assumptions.[14] What I am suggesting is that the causal criterion is itself a realist assumption and that Field is one of the opponents of Quine whose opposition rests on realist assumptions.

The disagreement between Quine's overt antirealism and what seems to be Field's covert realism is broad. It arises not only in philosophy of mathematics but also in philosophy of semantics, where the Quinean *disquotational* theory of truth stands opposed to the Fieldian *reductionist* theory of truth.[15] The disagree-

---

[14]In the editorial introduction, one finds:

> But why should the simplest . . . theory . . . have any tendency to be *true?* Quine, good pragmatist that he is, tends to pooh-pooh such questions; but more realistically minded philosophers are sure to be troubled. (p 35)

> The question "Why should one believe that there is a preestablished harmony between our feelings of simplicity . . . and *truth?*" . . . assumes a "realist" notion of truth. (p. 37)

On Quine's *disquotational* theory of truth, belief in the hypothesis that a theory is true is not importantly different from belief in the theory itself and is justified by pragmatic criteria of efficacy, including simplicity.

[15]See Field (1972). The literature to which this paper has given rise cannot be adequately summarized here. Roughly Field viewed the presence of the phrase "is true" in current language as illegitimate pending the production of a reductive definition that would show, say, an utterance or inscription of "white" being true of snow in English to amount to air or ink, snow, and the nervous tissue of English-speakers being *physically related* in some special way. Roughly Quine (1963) denied that the function of the phrase is to reflect any physical or aphysical relation among any physical or aphysical objects in the extralinguistic world; rather the function of the phrase is the intralinguistic one of disquotation, which contributes to efficacy in communication and, thus, justifies the presence of the phrase in current language. The disagreement between Quine and Field over "is true" seems to me *exactly* analogous to their disagreement over "two."

ment between Quinean antirealism and what seems to be Fieldian realism is also deep. Quineans reject the goal of reflection not merely as *unimportant* in comparison to the goal of efficacy but rather as *unintelligible*.

In his book, Field advocated achieving economy or parsimony in ontology and ideology through extravagance and prodigality in logic. To Quineans, the suggestion that theory would better reflect the world, if its ontology and ideology where deflated and its logic inflated, is *unintelligible*. For Quineans, the very distinction ontology/ideology/logic is merely a "recapitulation" of the distinction noun/verb/sentence, which is only a feature of the "philology" of a particular, special kind of language and not something imposed on us by the extralinguistic world.

Quine's favorite example of a language lacking noun phrases (including pronouns or variables) and, hence, presumably lacking ontology, is *predicate-functor* language. Quine has told us that "variables [can be] explained away," and that "to be is to be the value of a variable." Hence, presumably *being* can be explained away; having this sort of ontology rather than that sort of ontology cannot be something imposed on us by the extralinguistic world, because *having an ontology at all* is not something so imposed.)

I suggest that the disagreement between Quine and Field is so broad and so deep that it cannot be settled by any mere technical trick—not even by one that out-Newtons Newton.

ACKNOWLEDGMENTS

Over the past several years, through the kindness of several hosts, I have had the opportunity of presenting several versions of several sections of the present paper under several titles to several audiences, and have benefited much from the ensuing discussion. Among the many persons to whom I have thus become indebted, C. Wade Savage and Michael Kremer merit special mention as having inspired (or provoked) the inclusion of the final two sections of this chapter.

For my understanding of most of the issues surrounding the work of Hartry Field I am indebted to Saul Kripke—so much so that I have omitted discussion of many of these issues, considering that they should best be left to Kripke himself, whose long-awaited commentary on Field's work I hope will soon be forthcoming.

REFERENCES

Benacerraf, P. (1983). Mathematical truth. Reprinted in (Benacerraf & Putnam, pp. 403–420.

Benacerraf, P., & Putnam, H. (Eds.). (1983). *Philosophy of mathematics* (2nd ed.). Cambridge: Cambridge University Press.

Burgess, J. P. (1983). Why I am not a nominalist. *Notre Dame Journal of Formal Logic, 24,* 93–105.

Burgess, J. P. (1984). Synthetic mechanics. *Journal of Philosophical Logic, 13,* 379–395.

Field, H. (1972). Tarski's theory of truth. *J. Phil., 69,* 347–375.

Field, H. (1980). *Science without numbers.* Princeton: Princeton University Press.

Field, H. (1983). Realism and anti-realism about mathematics. *Philosophical Topics, 13,* 45–69.

Frege, G. (1960). *Foundations of arithmetic.* (J. L. Austin, Trans.) New York: Harper & Row.

Kline, M. (1985). *Mathematics and the search for knowledge.* Oxford: Oxford University Press.

Quine, W. V. O. (1963). Identity, ostension, and hypostasis. Reprinted in *From a logical point of view* (2nd ed.). New York: Harper & Row.

8 Quantitative Nonnumerical Relations in Science: Eudoxus, Newton, and Maxwell

Arnold Koslow
Brooklyn College and the Graduate School, C.U.N.Y.

In an earlier study,[1] I tried to draw the distinction between quantitative and qualitative concepts without reference to or reliance upon numbers, concatenation operations, or ordering relations. Why should one try to do this? There were two very simple needs. The first was the obvious one that would occur to anyone who surveyed the older literature. Certain accounts of scientific method, and at least one influential movement in the theory of measurement, used the quantitative–qualitative distinction freely. Wouldn't it be nice to have a clear and relatively simple characterization of the distinction? The classic studies of Hempel and Oppenheim (1936), Hempel (1952), and Carnap (1966) provided examples of classificatory, comparative, and quantitative notions. However, there was no account of the distinctions that made it evident that we had been given contrasting classes, where the three types of relations were mutually exclusive and belonged to a restricted but coherent group of relations. It seemed to me to be a small but worthwhile task to draw the distinctions so that these kinds of relations contrasted with each other. The second need was for a characterization of quantitativeness that was independent of numerical assignments. If it was required of all quantitative concepts that they be expressed with the aid of real-valued functions, then one would have to say that the Greeks had no quantitative account of the ratio of magnitudes; for they had no concept of the reals. It would be absurd to think of the Greeks as lacking a quantitative notion of ratios.[2] In fact Eudoxus developed a theory of a four-place relation $R(x,y,z,w)$: the ratio of x to y

---

[1]A. Koslow, "Quantity and quality: Some aspects of measurement."

[2]This point was forcefully made and cogently stated by E. Adams in "The aim and purpose of measurement."

is the same as the ratio of z to w, where the variables x,y,z, and w range over magnitudes. As we shall see, the relation R is a quantitative relation and non-numerical, although it takes a good part of Eudoxus' theory to show that the relation has these features.

There are other historical examples of deliberation over whether a concept is quantitative although nonnumerical. Newton was embroiled in a rather complicated argument with R. Cotes over the concept of one body's having the same quantity of matter (mass) as another, and Maxwell was probably the first to argue that the notion of "same temperature as" was quantitative. All three cases were discussed without appeal to numbers; all involved issues over quantitativeness. There has to be a way of making sense of these deliberations. However, there is no way of understanding how those issues were resolved by Eudoxus, Maxwell, and Newton, if the only way to understand the concept of quantitativeness requires mappings into the reals.

There were various ancillary theses connected with the division of relations into classificatory, comparative, and quantitative. Carnap suggested that the historical record revealed a predominant use of the quantitative over the comparative, and the comparative over the classificatory, as science became more successful. Further, he suggested that there was an increase in epistemological objectivity as one passed from classificatory to the other kinds of concepts. Whatever one thinks of these claims (and I do not think that any of them are unqualifiedly correct), it still seems important to have an understanding of the distinction between those concepts that are quantitative and those that are qualitative.[3]

The other source we referred to can be traced to the development of a representational theory of measurement, comprehensively studied in Krantz, Luce, Suppes, and Tversky (1971). It was sometimes argued that the goal of a theory of measurement is to show how one can pass from the qualitative to the quantitative. Thus, Suppes (1957, pp. 265–266) wrote the following:

> The primary aim of the theory of measurement, for instance, is to show in a precise fashion how to pass from qualitative observations ("this rod is longer than that one", "the left pan of the balance is higher than than the right one") to the quantitative assertions needed in empirical science ("the length of this rod is 7.2 centimeters," "the mass of this chemical sample is 5.4 grams"). In other words, the theory of measurement should provide an exact analysis of how we may infer quantitative assertions from fundamentally qualitative observations.

Indeed, in Scott and Suppes' (1958) classic paper, the reason given for using extensional structures—sets together with relations on them of various ranks—is that each of these various relations R^n is supposed to represent a complete set of

---

[3]The program for showing that significant parts of physical theories can be formulated using only qualitative relations stands Carnap's view on its head.

"yes" or "no" answers to a question asked of every n-termed sequence of objects of the set. This is suppose to convey the idea that it is mainly qualitative empirical data that are under consideration. Not only the data but the axioms of the theory employed are supposed to be qualitative as well. All the more reason then for understanding the difference. We think that the distinction is important despite the fact that the goals for a theory of measurement—whether those set by Hempel and Carnap, or those set by the representational view—are not convincing. The idea of Hempel and Carnap was that there was a special problem about quantitative or metric concepts: How are they "introduced" into science? However, it has now been acknowledged that the problem, posed this way, is badly framed. There is no problem of introducing quantitative terms—no more than there is a problem of how theoretical terms get "introduced" (cf. Putnam, 1962, and Hempel, 1970). This particular goal for quantitative terms presupposes that there is a problem when there is none. On the other hand, the goal sometimes associated with the representational theory of measurement is not persuasive as a general goal. Is it always plausible to think that, by proving a representation theorem, we have shown how to pass from the qualitative to the quantitative?

It seems critical for this task that what we use is a theory that is qualitative. Otherwise there is no passage from the qualitative. However, if our proposed characterization of quantitative relations is correct, then there already are a host of relations and assertions in the theory that will count as quantitative. For example, if the theory has a concatenation operation *, and a two-place relation "xLy" (x is at least as long as y), then any assertion such as $[(x* \ldots *x)L(y* \ldots *y) \& (y* \ldots *y)L(x* \ldots *x)]$ for n xs and m ys (i.e., n xs are exactly as long as m ys) expresses a quantitative relation. Along the same lines, the statement that $x = (y*z)$ or that $[xL(y*z) \& (y*z)Lx]$ (i.e., that x is the concatenation of y with z, or that x is exactly as long as the concatenation of y with z), counts as an example of a three-place quantitative relation. If the language used to study the quantitativeness of a notion already has quantitative resources in it, then there is no problem in passing from the qualitative to the quantitative for such a theory; we are already there.

There is an additional problem with taking the passage from the qualitative to the quantitative as a general goal. For some concepts, it is a plausible one; for others, it is not. Thus, Suppes (1956) argued persuasively as follows:

> Because of the many controversies concerning the nature of probability and its measurement, those most concerned with the general foundations of decision theory have abstained from using any unanalyzed numerical probabilities, and have insisted that quantitative probabilities be inferred from a pattern of qualitative decisions. (p. 88)

Here we have a good example of why a definite restriction to the qualitative is reasonable. Quantitative assertions using the concept of utility and subjective probability are in contention, and the restriction to qualitative patterns represents a minimal, uncontested ground. Carried through, the program would be a real advance, which cuts through and indeed settles a scientific controversy. However, the relevance of these considerations in the case of, say, length or mass, seems remote. Suppose that we paraphrased the previous quotation, using "length" or "mass" rather than "probability":

> Because of the many controversies concerning the nature of length [mass] and its measurement, those most concerned with the general foundations of geometry [mechanics] have abstained from using any unanalyzed numerical lengths [masses], and have insisted that quantitative lengths [masses] be inferred from a pattern of qualitative information.

The plausibility of such a goal for length or mass, in contrast with utility or subjective probability, is extremely low. What are the many controversies about the nature of length (or mass) and their measurement that would render a qualitative theory of those quantities a significant scientific contribution or would encourage us to think that we had cut through those controversies by arguing from an uncontested middle ground?

Of course there have been controversies about the nature and measurement of both length and mass. The history of science is filled with controversies over the nature and measurability of mass: the efforts of Descartes to frame an adequate concept of mass; the extended discussion between Newton and R. Cotes that concerned the variety of concepts that Newton used, and the need to square those concepts with the idea that inertia is a measure of the mass of a body; the controversies raised by the proponents of the electromagnetic world-view over the nature of "mechanical" mass; the differences between relativistic and classical concepts of mass, to mention just a few landmarks. However, the history of science, in my opinion, discloses no case when these issues were resolved by finding a middle ground that was qualitative. For example, I have not found in Mach's writings any attempt to introduce a qualitative ordering of bodies. Instead he introduced a number of quantitative empirical laws involving the notion of "mutually induced accelerations," which he thought sufficient to characterize the masses (or mass-ratios) of bodies under consideration.

There have also been some controversies over the nature and measurement of length, area, volume, and angle. However, the ancient struggles to provide a coherent theory of proportion—the comparison or "ratio" of magnitudes—when they might be incommensurable, or the nineteenth and twentieth century controversies over a host of different measures for geometrical and set-theoretical entities—the Riemannian, Borel, and Lebesgue integrals, for example, or debates over the projective account of "metric" concepts—in none of these cases does it seem that the issues were settled or that the controversies were cut through by an appeal to purely qualitative theories.

The goal of passing from the qualitative to the quantitative seem to be well-motivated for concepts like utility and subjective probability, and fails to be well-motivated for concepts like length or mass. Despite these reservations, there is no doubt about the power, fertility, and intellectually exciting character of the particular theories that have emerged within the representational theory of measurement. The difficulties in formulating goals for a theory of measurement may be due to the fact that there are many goals—mathematical ones, those that concern faithfulness to scientific practice, those that concern the inclusion of sophisticated scientific concepts such as relativistic momentum among the measureable. No one goal seems to cover all these concerns—but then, why should it? The present-day theory of measurement may be at least at that level of complexity, where asking for its goals may produce the same problem we encounter when we ask, if we were to ask, for the goals of physics, chemistry, or mathematics. Nevertheless the difference between qualitative and quantitative concepts remains an important one, whatever problems there may be in describing appropriate goals.

The task is to distinguish between quantitative and qualitative relations. It is not our aim to reduce the former to the latter or to systematically replace quantitative relations by qualitative ones. It is not essential to quantitative relations that they be numerical. Some are, and some are not. The conditions for a relation to be quantitative have to do with the way that the relation interacts with a partition of its domain (and, as we shall see, there is only one partition with respect to which a relation can be quantitative, if there are any at all). There are many relations that count as quantitative but not numerical—as we shall see below. Of course there are many numerical relations that are quantitative, although not all of them are. If this is correct, then certain problems do not seem to be well-formed. For example, it seems that many advocates of the representational theory of measurement believe that it is possible to give a qualitative characterization of physical laws (in order, for example, with the aid of numerical representation theorems, to prove dimensional invariance). Although many laws are formulated numerically, it is thought that such equations are only a "shorthand of what is really a complex set of possible qualitative observations." (Krantz et al., 1971, p. 504) It is hard to see any grounds for pursuing a program of exhibiting physical laws as compendia of qualitative observations. Sometimes the program looks a bit like a refurbished restatement of Machian epistemology, according to which laws are also thought to be summaries of experimental results, provided we thought that the experimental results were qualitative. However, there seems no reason to think that this is generally true. D. Scott and P. Suppes (1958) seem to have thought of a complete set of "yes"–"no" answers recorded by using some n–place relations as counting as qualitative. However, if that is the way things go, then there is a conflict with the present proposal that some relations are already quantitative. In that case, the empirical relational systems as used by the representational school may not be inherently qualitative structures. The distinction that is drawn with the aid of empirical relational systems is not one between qualitative and quantitative structures. Rather it is, I think, a distinction between numerical and nonnumerical structures. If I am correct, the use of empirical relational structures by the representational school has nothing to do with qualitative versus quantitative. Some quantitative relations are numerical; others are not. Furthermore, some qualitative relations are numerical; some are not. Similarly H. Field's (1980) recent attempt to provide an account of scientific theories that meets nominalist standards is not about the replacement of quantitative relations and laws by nonquantitative or qualitative counterparts. It is, only if certain quantitative relations and laws are described with the aid of numbers, functions, sets or other abstract entities, that they become the target of Field's nominalistic program. However, if I am correct, there are many quantitative relations that are not numerical. There is, therefore, nothing in Field's nominalistic program that calls for the replacement of these quantitative terms. On the other hand, there are qualitative relations that are numerical and would have to be replaced in order to meet the Field conditions. Field's program is, therefore, not to be thought of as requiring the replacement or reduction of quantitative relations and laws by qualitative counterparts. In fact many of the relations that Field used in his account, certainly the congruence relations that he employed, count as quantitative on my account. Consequently I do not think of Field's program as an attack on the use of quantitative relations in science.

Emil Artin's generalized discussion (1957) of Descartes' Coordination Problem showed how the points of various geometries can be characterized by using coordinates from various associated mathematical fields, in such a way that the characteristic relations in each geometry are associated with characteristic algebraic conditions in the associated field. However, even in the special case when the associated field is that of the real numbers and points get "represented" by n–tuples of real numbers, it would be a mistake to think that the geometries in question are purely qualitative theories that are shown to have quantitative representations in the reals. For the geometries in question are certainly not purely qualitative; there are many relations in them that count as quantitative (although of course nonnumerical). Thus, although there are discussions in the literature that look as if they concern the reduction of the quantitative to the qualitative or conversely, I think that, in each case, it is another distinction that is under investigation. In the case of Field's Program, it is the distinction between expressions that are nominalistically acceptable and those that are not; in the case of Artin's problem, the distinction concerns the connection between geometric and algebraic theories and their respective relations.

Our task, therefore, is to distinguish between quantitative and qualitative relations. They are, as we shall see, disjoint types of relations. However, from that fact, it does not follow that one type is or ought to be, reducible, definable, or replaceable by the other.

CLASSIFICATORY, COMPARATIVE, AND QUANTITATIVE RELATIONS

The basic idea is to begin with a family of relations on a nonempty set S and to distinguish between those that are classificatory, comparative, and quantitative. The initial qualification is that relations are not described as of one kind or another simpliciter but as comparative or quantitative, or classificatory, relative to some partition of the domain S.

Let S be any nonempty set (the domain). An *equivalence relation* on S is any binary relation on S that is reflexive, symmetric, and transitive. A *partition M* on S is any set of subsets of S (not containing the empty set) such that every member of S is a member of exactly one member of M. To each equivalence relation E, there is a corresponding partition M_E—for any equivalence relation E and any a in S, let $E_a = \{y | y$ is in S and $E(a,y)\}$. Let M_E be the set of all subsets of S of the form E_a. It is a partition of S. If M is a partition of S, then let E_M be the binary relation on S such that, for any a and b in S, $E_M(a,b)$, if and only if a and b belong to the same member of M. E_M is an equivalence relation on S.

Let $EQ(S)$ be the set of all equivalence relations on S and $Part(S)$ be the set of all partitions on S. There is a partial order definable for each of these sets: For any two equivalence relations E and E^*, let the order be given by the subset relation, and for any two partitions P and P*, we shall say that P is a refinement of P^* ($P \leq P^*$), if and only if every member of P is a subset of some member of P^*. There is an order-preserving isomorphism of $EQ(S)$ and $Part(S)$—let ϕ be the mapping that assigns to any equivalence relation E the partition M_E. ϕ is easily seen to be one-to-one, and it is onto, because, for any M in $Part(S)$, $\phi(E_M)$ = M. Moreover, it is easy to check that, for any equivalence relations E and E^* of EQ, $E \subseteq E^*$, if and only if $M_E \leq M_{E^*}$). Given the isomorphism, we shall sometimes describe the relativization of the various relations either with respect to equivalence relations or to their associated partitions.

The set $EQ(S)$ of all equivalence relations on S has a decent mathematical structure—it is a complete lattice. The definition of the meet is obviously given by set intersection; the join operation on EQ is nicely defined by Gratzer (1979).

Let R^n be any n–place relation on S. We think of it either as a function mapping S^n (the n–fold Cartesian product of S with itself) to the set $\{t,f\}$ or equivalently as a subset of S^n.

We shall need the notion of a congruence relation in the characterization of all three kinds of relations. Let E be any equivalence relation on S. Extend E to an equivalence relation on S^n as follows: If p is any member of S^n, then, for any i, $1 \leq i \leq n$, let p_i be the ith component of p (the ith member of the n–tuple p). For any p and p^* in S^n, we shall say that $E(p,p^*)$, if and only if $E(p_i,p^*_i)$, for all i. We shall say that an equivalence relation E is a *congruence* of the relation R^n, if and only if the following:

(C) For any p and p^* in S^n, if $E(p,p^*)$, then $R^n(p)$ if and only if
$R^n(p^*)$.

—where we write "$R^n(p)$" for "$R^n(p_1, \ldots, p_n)$". The set of congruences of R^n (on S) also form a complete lattice (Gratzer, 1979, chapter 1, Section 10; Cohn, 1965,).

All three types of relation, classificatory, comparative, and quantitative (on S), will be thought of as relativized to equivalence relations (or their associated partitions), which are also congruences of the relation under study.

Classificatory Relations

Let S be any nonempty set, and E an equivalence relation on S. We shall say that an n–place relation R^n on S is *classificatory with respect to* E, if and only if the following:

1. E is a congruence of R^n.
2. There is a set $A = \{a_1, \ldots, a_m\}$ of m distinct members of S, no two of which are equivalent under E, such that, for any p in S^n, if $R^n(p)$, then, for any i ($1 \le i \le n$), there is a j ($1 \le j \le m$) such that $E(p_i, a_j)$.
3. For any p in S^n, if $R^n(p)$, then no two components of P are equivalent (under E).

Two comments are in order. In the older literature, classificatory terms were exemplified by monadic predicates, sorting out elements of a certain kind within a domain. "Red," "Square," and so on were the usual examples. There was, as far as I can determine, nothing especially interesting to say about classificatory terms. They were used to highlight the comparative and quantitative terms as the kind of terms that had greater scientific utility. It was noted that classificatory terms could be refined, but, on the whole, there was nothing special that could be said about them beyond what one could say generally about predication and its problems. As far as I can see, the scheme just described generalizes the earlier notion to include a simultaneous sorting of the members of the domain into several disjoint types. However, it is an understatement to say that examples of scientific use of such relations are hard to come by. Its present use is to provide a contrast with the comparative and quantitative relations, but, aside from its being an appropriate generalization of one member of the older trilogy, it hasn't any scientific or philosophical interest to speak of. One should also mention that the notion of a classificatory term was generalized in another direction by Hempel and Oppenheim (1936). Instead of using one monadic predicate, they considered using several predicates. Thus, one might use the characteristics of having mathematical ability, having physical dexterity, and being emotionally stable, to classify people of some population. A loose analogy was suggested with the idea that, just as a point may be located by reference to several different dimensions, so too objects could be thought of as located in a multidimensional space. Some examples were provided from psychology, but this type of generalization, to my mind, has had no scientifically interesting examples that would make the notion worth studying in any depth.

It should be noted that, given this notion of a classificatory relation, it is possible that a relation can be classificatory with respect to different equivalence relations. For example, if the domain S consisted of objects that were either red or green, with examples of the shades (light red, dark red, light green, dark green), then the relation $R(x,y)$ (either x is red, and y is green, or x is green, and y is red) is easily seen to be classificatory with respect to the equivalence E (same color) as well as the different equivalence E^* (same shade of color). E^* is a refinement of E, and the set A required by the definition would be different (for E, let A be a set of two members, one of which is red, the other green; for E^*, let A^* be a set of four members that are light red, dark red, light green, and dark green). As we shall see below, this is in parity with the case of comparative relations for which it always holds that, if a relation is comparative with respect to an equivalence E, it is also comparative with respect to any equivalence E^* that refines (is a subset of) E. Furthermore, both classificatory and comparative relations differ from quantitative relations; the latter can be quantitative with respect to only one equivalence relation.

Comparative Relations

Let R^n be a n–place relation on a nonempty set S, and let E be an equivalence relation on S. We shall say that R^n is *comparative* with respect to E, if and only if the following conditions are satisfied. We first consider the case when $n = 2$.

1. E is a congruence of R^2.
2. For any a and b in S, either $R^2(a,b)$ or $R^2(b,a)$ (or both).
3. R^2 is transitive.

Now consider the general case. We shall say that $(R^n)^*$ is a (two-place) specialization of R^n, if and only if there is some p_0 of S^n and some i and j, where $i \neq j$, and $1 \leq i,j \leq n$ such that, for any p in S^n, $(R^n)^*(p) = R^n(p^*)$, where, for any p in S^n, P^* differs at most from p_0 on the ith and jth components, and p^* agrees with p on the ith and jth components. The (two-place) specialization of R^n induces a binary relation IR on S according to which, for any a and b in S, $IR(a,b)$, if and only if $(R^n)^*(p)$, where the ith and jth components of p are a and b respectively, and any component k of p, other than the ith and jth, is just the kth component of p_0. Finally we shall say that R^n is *comparative with respect to the equivalence relation* E, if and only if there is a (two-place) specialization of R^n

that induces a binary relation on S that is comparative (as in the case previous, for $n = 2$).

It is worth noting some elementary observations:

1. If R^n is comparative with respect to an equivalence relation E, then it is also comparative with respect to any equivalence relation E^* that refines E (the partition M_{E_*} that is associated with E^* is a refinement of the partition M_E associated with E). Thus, in particular, if a relation is comparative with respect to any partition, it is also comparative with respect to the discrete partition on S (the members of the partition consist of sets having exactly one member of S). Consequently, if R is comparative with respect to a nondiscrete partition, there are at least two partitions with respect to which it is comparative.

2. No relation R^n is both classificatory and comparative. Consider the case where $n = 2$. If R^2 is classificatory with respect to E, then, for any p in S^2, if $R^2(p)$, then p_1 and p_2 are not equivalent (under E). R^2 is comparative; thus, it is reflexive (by the second condition on comparatives). However, that is impossible.[4]

3. As we noted, the congruences of a relation form a complete lattice. It is possible to use the comparative to identify the maximal congruence. In the case of a two-place comparative, the maximal congruence with respect to which it is comparative is easily seen to be $E(a,b)$: $[R^2(a,b)$ & $R^2(b,a)]$.[5]

Quantitative Relations

Let R^n be a n–place relation on a nonempty set S, and E an equivalence relation on S. For any p and p^* of S^n, and any i ($1 \leq i \leq n$), we shall say that $i(p,p^*)$ holds, if and only if p and p^* differ at most on their ith components. We shall say that R^n is *quantitative with respect to E*, if and only if the following:

1. E is a congruence of R^n.
2. For any p and p^* in S^n, and any i ($1 \leq i \leq n$), if $R^n(p)$, and $R^n(p^*)$, and $i(p,p^*)$, then $E(p_i,p^*_i)$.

---

[4]The case for $n \neq 2$ is proved similarly by noting that any (two-place) specialization of R^n will be reflexive in the ith and jth places of the specialization.

[5]The case for a comparative R^n (with respect to E), of greater than two places is complicated by the fact that there may be several two-place specializations available. Each of those induces a binary relation (say IR_i) on S that is comparative with respect to the congruence relation given by the symmetrization $[IR_i(a,b)$ & $IR_i(b,a)]$, which contains E. The maximal congruence with respect to which R^n is comparative is also a congruence of all the induced binary relations IR_i. The join of all these congruences exists, but it is difficult to obtain a clear connection between it and the maximal congruence of R^n. (If the join of all the maximal congruences of all IR_i is a congruence of R^n, then the two are identical.)

This says that, if two n–tuples of objects of S both belong to R^n, and they differ at most in their ith component, then those ith components belong to the same member of the partition. Quantitative relations are, in this intuitive sense, "tight."

We shall say that a n–place relation Rn on S satisfies the *covering condition*, if and only if, for any member a of S, there is some p in S^n such that $R^n(p)$ holds, and a is the ith component of p, $a = p_i$, for some i ($1 \leq i \leq n$).

The following are easily seen:

1. If R^n is quantitative with respect to the equivalence relation E (on S) and satisfies the covering condition, then E is the only equivalence relation with respect to which R^n is quantitative. For suppose that R^n is quantitative with respect to E and E^*. Let a and b be any members of S such that $E^*(a,b)$. By the covering condition, there is some p in S^n such that $R^n(p)$, and a is the (say) ith component of p. Let p^* be the same as p except for having b as its ith component; then $i(p^*,p)$. E^* is a congruence of R^n, and $R^n(p)$; thus, it follows that $R^n(p^*)$. Therefore, by the second condition on quantitative relations, $E(p_i, p^*_i)$. That is, $E(a,b)$. Thus, for any a and b in S, if $E^*(a,b)$, then $E(a,b)$. The converse is proved similarly. So E and E^* are coextensional.

2. If R^n is quantitative with respect to a partition that has at least two members (there are at least two members of S that are not equivalent), then it cannot be comparative with respect to any partition. This is easiest to see in the binary case. For any a and b in S, either $R(a,b)$ or $R(b,a)$, because R is comparative. If $R(a,b)$, then, because $R(a,a)$, and R is quantitative, it follows that $E(a,b)$ (similarly if $R(b,a)$ holds). So every b in S is in the same equivalence class as a. This contradicts the condition that the partition has at least two members.[6]

Although quantitative relations can be numerical, then need not be.[7] The

---

[6]The case for n greater than 2 is essentially the same. Take any (two-place) specialization of R^n. Suppose that it is the ith and jth places that have not been fixed. Then for any a and b in S, either $(R^n)^*(p)$ or $(R^n)^*(p\hat{\ })$, where the ith component of p is a, the jth component is b, and the ith component of $p\hat{\ }$ is b, and its jth component is a, and all the other components are the respective ones from p_0 used to obtain the specialization. Since the (two-place) specialization is comparative, we have $(R^n)^*(p')$ where the ith and jth components of p' are both a, and the kth component (k different from i and from j) is the kth component of p_0. Moreover, because any two-place specialization of a quantitative relation is quantitative, it follows that a and b are equivalent (under E), for any a and b in S. This contradicts the assumption that the partition has at least two members.

[7]Even if a relation R is quantitative and nonnumerical, there still will be cases where R can be represented homomorphically by an appropriate relation defined over a numerical relational system. Such representation theorems are proved in Koslow (1982). However, the fact that a relation R can be represented numerically is not what makes it quantitative; certain ordering relations can be represented in numerical extensional systems.

focus for the remainder of this study will be on three examples of such quantitative but nonnumerical relations that seem to be of the same type but each having a distinct nontrivial scientific interest: (a) sameness of ratio (Eudoxus), (b) sameness of temperature (Maxwell), and (c) sameness of mass (Newton). These are very simple examples as far as quantitative relations go, but their simplicity belies the strategic roles they have played and their conceptual subtlety. There are many other examples of nonnumerical quantitative relations. For example, in empirical relational systems that have some comparative binary relation xLy and some concatenation operation $*$, then the relations $[xLy \text{ \& } yLx]$ (x is exactly as long as y); $[xL(y*y) \text{ \& } (y*y)Lx]$; ($x$ is exactly twice as long as y); $[xL(y*z) \text{ \& } (y*z)Lx]$ (x is exactly as long as the concatenation of y with z) are all quantitative relations with respect to the partition M, where each M_i consists of exactly those elements x,y such that $[xLy \text{ \& } yLx]$. In Euclidean geometry, the relations $P(A,B,C)$ (A, B, and C are the consecutive sides of a right triangle with hypotenuse C), $T_\Delta(A,B,C)$ (A,B, and C are the consecutive sides of a triangle that is congruent to the triangle Δ), and $S_\Delta(A,B,C)$ (A, B, and C are the consecutive sides of a triangle that is similar to the triangle Δ) are all quantitative and non-numerical with respect to the partition of the set S of all line segments with respect to the relation of congruence. In set theory, the relation of a set X being in one-to-one correspondance with the power set $P(Y)$ of the set Y, and the relation by which a set Z is in one-to-one correspondance with the union of two disjoint sets X and Y, are quantitative and nonnumerical relations, where the relevant equivalence relation holds between only those sets that are in one-to-one correspondance with each other. These are all quantitative nonnumerical relations, some patently empirical, others more mathematical in content. There are of course numerical relations that are not quantitative such as the relation of being greater than (on say the reals). The moral is that there is only a partial overlap between quantitative and numerical relations. Being numerical is neither necessary nor sufficient for being quantitative.

EUDOXUS

Let us turn first to Eudoxus' theory of proportionality of magnitudes.[8] There is an interesting problem over how "magnitudes" were understood by Euclid and Eudoxus. Are they the lines, plane figures, solids, and angles (as well as other, nongeometric objects), or are they as I. Mueller (1983) suggested, abstractions from geometric objects: lengths (of lines), areas (of plane figures), volumes (of solids), and whatever the property is in the case of angles? Either view has its problems, exegetical as well as substantive. It might seem plausible to think of lengths, areas, and volumes as features, attributes, or properties of things rather

---

[8]I am indebted here to I. Mueller's exceptional study (1983), especially chapter 3.

than the things themselves. If that is so, then it is hard to understand what could be meant by Euclid's assumption, for example, that magnitudes have parts (Mueller, 1983, p. 123). It does seem easier to think of magnitudes as objects, abstracted in such a way that only geometric properties serve to individuate them—provided that we have a grasp of what it is to be a geometric property.

However "magnitude" is understood, there is no question that, for Eudoxus, the ratio of two magnitudes is not a magnitude. Consequently the sameness of two ratios is not settled by the sameness or difference of magnitudes. In effect Eudoxus developed a theory of a four-place relation $R(x,y,z,w)$ with x, y, z, and w ranging over magnitudes. It was thought of as expressing the relation that the ratio of x to y is the same as the ratio of z to w and was defined this way. $R(x,y,z,w)$, if and only if (for every m and n): (i) $(mx > ny \rightarrow mz > nw)$, and (ii) $(mx \simeq ny \rightarrow mz \simeq nw)$, and (iii) $(mx < ny \rightarrow mz < nw)$. The use of terms that refer to natural numbers is, as Mueller noted, an expository device used by Mueller but not by Euclid. Euclid assumed that there are magnitudes that are multiples of others, and, as Mueller observed, Euclid consistently used the relation "x is the same multiple of y as z is of w" (Mueller, 1983, p. 121). Thus, there is, in Euclid's account, no essential reference to numbers.[9]

Eudoxus' explanation of the sameness of ratios does not presuppose that there is any object or magnitude that is the ratio of two magnitudes. There is an explanation that he offered of the idea that x and y have a ratio that is expressed by saying that some multiple of x exceeds y and some multiple of y exceeds x (Mueller, 1983, p. 144)

We have then a four-place relation R, defined over magnitudes or objects abstracted or individuated in some special way, and the question is whether it is quantitative, for it is not numerical.[10] It is fairly straightforward to check that R is quantitative with respect to the equivalence relation $\simeq$. The first condition to be checked is that $\simeq$ is a congruence of R. Consider one case: If $x \simeq x^*$, and $R(x,y,z,w)$, then $R(x^*,y,z,w)$. This holds, because $mx > ny \rightarrow mz > nw$, and $mx^* \simeq mx$. Therefore, $mx^* > ny \rightarrow mz > nw$. Thus, clause (i) of the definition of R holds—similarly for clauses (ii) and (iii). Consequently $R(x^*,y,z,w)$. Similar remarks hold for y and y^*. The case for $z \simeq z^*$ and for $w \simeq w^*$ requires a slight modification in the original definition of R. Instead of using conditionals, the revision uses biconditionals. This makes no difference to the Eudoxian theory of proportion, because that theory also requires that $R(x,y,z,w) \rightarrow R(z,w,x,y)$ for all x,y,z, and w.

---

[9]Cf. Mueller's discussion of the constructivity of Euclid's notion of the multiplication of magnitudes (p. 121 et seq.). It is possible to express the multiplication of magnitudes geometrically. cf. D. Hilbert (1968) for the case of multiplication of line segments in a purely geometrical way, without the use of terms that refer to or range over numbers.

[10]We take for granted that the point of studying such a relation is the construction of a general theory of proportionality of magnitudes that covers incommensurable as well as commensurable magnitudes.

In order for R to count as quantitative, it only remains to check that the second condition holds: Let p and p^* be any quadruples of magnitudes. If $R(p)$ and $R(p^*)$ where p and p^* differ only in the first component (say x is the first component of p, and x^* the first of p^*), then $x \simeq x^*$—similarly for the other components. Suppose, for example, that $R(x,y,z,w)$ and $R(x^*,y,z,w)$. Then, by (i), for all m and n, $(mx > ny \leftrightarrow mz > nw)$, and $(mx^* > ny \leftrightarrow mz > nw)$. Consequently $(mx > ny \leftrightarrow mx^* > ny)$, for all multiples (mx), (mx^*), and (ny) of x, x^*, and y respectively. Therefore, $x > y \leftrightarrow x^* > y$. By clauses (ii) and (iii) of the definition of R, it follows that $x \simeq y \leftrightarrow x^* \simeq y$, and $x < y \leftrightarrow x^* < y$. Thus, from the definition of R, we have $R(x,y,x^*,y)$. However, it is also a feature of Eudoxus' theory that, if $R(x,z,y,z)$, then $x \simeq y$. In particular then, $x \simeq x^*$. Similar arguments hold for $R(x,y,z,w)$ & $R(x,y^*,z,w)$, implying that $y \simeq y^*$ (as well as the cases for z and z^* and w and w^*). Thus, $R(x,y,z,w)$ is a quantitative relation on the set of magnitudes, with respect to the equivalence relation.[11]

Our aim here was the limited one of showing that a relation central to Eudoxus' theory of proportions is quantitative and not numerical. We have taken it for granted that Eudoxus' theory is a landmark in the history of mathematics. However, one should not think of its influence as limited to the mathematical. The influence upon Newton was a powerful one (McGuire & Tamny, 1983), and no less a physicist than C. G. Stokes was concerned about the use of proportions and incommensurables in his definition of mass, and explored the connection between the algebraic (numerical) and the Euclidean (Eudoxian) theory of proportions.[12]

MAXWELL

The second example of a scientifically significant quantitative relation we wish to consider is the notion of one body's having the same temperature as another. In the second chapter of his *Theory of heat, thermometry, or the theory of temperature* (1871), Maxwell defined the temperature of a body as a (thermal) state of the body related to its power to communicate heat to other bodies. If two bodies are thermally connected, and one gains and the other loses heat, then the one that "gives out" heat is said to have the higher temperature. The corollary he drew is that, when two bodies are "in thermal contact," and neither loses nor gains heat, then they have the same temperature. These remarks are followed by

---

[11] $R(x,y,z,w)$ is a condition for sameness of ratios. It is quantitative, as the previous argument shows. There are other relations that figure in the full theory of proportions, such as $G(x,y,z,w)$: the ratio of x to y is greater than the ratio of z to w (for some multiple mx of x, and ny of y, $mx > ny$, but not $(mz > nw)$. G is easily seen to be comparative.

[12] These interesting but undated studies can be found in Stokes' collected papers, Cambridge University Library. The definition of mass is given in PA1091 (Definition of Mass, Third Law of Motion), and PA1071 (Definition of Proportion in Euclid & Algebra).

what Maxwell called the *Law of Equal Temperatures:* Bodies whose temperatures are equal to that of the same body have themselves equal temperatures.

The law of equal temperatures (LET) might appear to be a special case of the Euclidean claim that things equal to the same thing are equal to each other. Maxwell, however, was quite explicit on the matter. The law is not a truism, not a special case of the Euclidean dictum, and, we might add, not a theorem of the theory of identity. The truth that, if A and C are in thermal equilibrium, and B and C are in thermal equilibrium, then so too are A and B, is nothing less, he said, than "the foundation of the whole science of thermometry (Maxwell, 1871, p. 33).

It is remarkable that Maxwell stressed that LET was not a logical truth but a law that is the basis for all of thermometry. It is a law that supports the simplest use of thermometers: If a piece of iron is plunged into water and found to be in thermal equilibrium with it, and then, without altering its temperature, it is plunged into oil and is in thermal equilibrium with it, then if the oil and water were in thermal contact, they would also be in thermal equilibrium. As for the "foundational" claim—I believe that it just comes to this: If LET were not true, then the use of thermometers would be very limited. We would have no basis for thinking that two bodies that have the same temperature as the thermometer also have the same temperature. We would be in a situation comparable to relating things by sameness of color; where it is not generally true that two things having the same color as a third, have the same color as each other. However, Maxwell, as well as Mach, thought that LET was true and had empirical content. At the very least, it was not regarded as a logical truism.[13]

Now it follows from the Law of Equal Temperatures that the relation $E(A,B)$ (A has the same temperature as B, or A and B are in thermal equilibrium upon thermal contact) is a quantitative relation. The reason is that, because E is symmetric (from its characterization: upon thermal contact, neither of A and B gives up heat to the other), then given LET, E is also transitive. To see that E is quantitative, a partition is needed. For each body A, let E_A be $\{C \mid E(A,C)\}$. The collection of sets of the form E_A for all A in S is a partition of S, and E is clearly

---

[13]Notice that, if temperature were thought of as a function mapping bodies to the reals, then LET would be a consequence of the theory of identity. For A and B would have the same temperature, if and only if $T(A) = T(B)$, and it is a consequence then that, if $T(A) = T(B)$, and $T(A) = T(C)$, then $T(B) = T(C)$. This construal of temperature is incompatible with Maxwell's view of the nontriviality of LET. It is worth noting that Mach, in his *Theory of heat,* which appeared after Maxwell's (1871) work, agreed with the thermal example and had earlier (1868) already considered a *Zeroth* style law for mass in "Über die Definitionen der Masse," *Reportorium für physikalische Technik*, Bd IV, 1868, 355 et seq., and in *History and root of the principle of the conservation of energy* (trans. and annotated by P. E. B. Jourdain, Open Court, Chicago, 1911, p. 83), he wrote that "Only experience can teach us that two bodies which behave to a third as equal masses will also behave to one another as equal masses." A similar moral can be drawn from the Law of Equal Masses (LEM), as one might call it: If it is not a theorem of the theory of identity, then mass cannot be construed as a function from bodies (say) to the reals. Otherwise LEM is just a special case of a theorem of the identity relation.

quantitative with respect to that partition. Of course, if it were assumed that E is an equivalence relation, the matter of its being quantitative would be obvious.

Thus, the relation "A has the same temperature as B" is a quantitative relation, and it is the Law of Equal Temperatures, or as it is currently known, the Zeroth Law of Thermodynamics, that insures that the relation is quantitative. We also think that $E(A,B)$ and the Law of Equal Temperatures are nonnumerical—at least in the accounts provided by Maxwell and Mach (1868, 1911), as well as Helmholtz (1977). For it is clear that, even if a thermometer is used to determine that two bodies are in thermal equilibrium, neither one gaining nor losing heat, it is only the mark on the thermometer, not its particular value that is used to determine whether $E(A,B)$ holds. It comes as no surprise that, in Maxwell's orderly exposition of the subject, that it is only after the discussion of the Law of Equal Temperatures that there is an account of the different kinds of thermometers and the construction of scales. None of the latter is needed to express and to determine the truth of LET. Thus, although it is a simple quantitative relation, $E(A,B)$ is nonnumerical and has a significant role to play in the expression of the Zeroth Law of Thermodynamics.

The law itself is rather striking. It does look, at first sight, to be like a truism, deserving passing attention at most. However, one can understand why Mach might have called special attention to the law that bodies that behave to a third as equal masses will also behave that way to each other. On his account of mass, the claim is far from obvious. For he characterized the mass-ratio m_{ij} of two bodies i and j, as the negative inverse ratio of their accelerations, ϕ_{ij}/ϕ_{ji}, which, under certain circumstances, the bodies induce in each other (ϕ_{ij} is the acceleration that the ith body induces on the jth, and Mach required that $m_{ij}m_{jk} = m_{jk}$, or that $\phi_{ij}\phi_{jk}\phi_{ik} = \phi_{ji}\phi_{kj}\phi_{ki}$.[14] However, this relation among induced accelerations is hardly obvious, although it yields the law of equal masses. Thus, on Mach's construal of relative masses, the law of equal masses is not transparently true. However, Maxwell seems to have been unaware of Mach's early discussion of this law (1868), and there is no mention of it in the appropriate place in his *Matter and motion* (1924).[15]

Why did Maxwell isolate LET as especially significant? Unfortunately there

---

[14]For a fuller discussion, cf. Koslow (1968) and the literature cited there.

[15]A question has been raised by an anonymous referee, whether J. Black (1803) has priority over Maxwell and Mach for the recognition of the law of equal temperatures (*Lectures on the elements of chemistry*, 1803). Mach seems not to have thought so, because no credit is given to him despite Mach's extensive citation of Black's work. The relevant passage is reprinted in Magie's *Sourcebook of physics* (Harvard), in which Black wrote: "All bodies communicating freely with each other, and exposed to no inequality of external action, acquire the same temperature, as indicated by a thermometer. All acquire the same temperature as the surrounding medium." At best this seems to be a special case of LET, when all the bodies are simultaneously in thermal equilibrium. LET permits the ascription of the same temperature to bodies, although they are not in thermal equilibrium with each other. The passage could also be read less generously as indicating only that bodies (under certain conditions) that are in thermal equilibrium, have the same temperature.

are no hints in *The theory of heat* itself. There is an original draft of the work, but the second chapter, curiously enough, is missing from it.[16] In October of 1878, the last year of his life, Maxwell lectured on thermodynamics. Those lectures might have shed some light on the matter. There is a bound volume of notes taken by A. Fleming, who, when he presented them to the Cavendish Laboratory some fifty two years later, said that he "took careful notes and wrote them out with some additions after each lecture. . . ." However, Fleming has to be mistaken. The presented volume cannot be a record of Maxwell's last thoughts about the theory of heat.[17]

Why did Maxwell single out LET? What called it to his attention? Speculation here has to be brief; the facts are few and indecisive at best. It is possible that Maxwell, as well as Mach and Helmholtz, knew of other relations for which a *Zeroth*-style law failed, and this might have raised the question of when such a type of law holds. For example, when $R(A,B)$ is the relation of just matching in color, a "Law of Equal Colors" fails. It is hard to think that Maxwell was not aware of such examples, because he knew Helmholtz's *Physiological optics;* he carried out experiments on the eye's sensitivity to light; he probably knew of Fechner's work; and, in some of his scientific studies on colors, Maxwell used the distinction between optical and chromatic similarity, which is related to threshold phenomena. However, this is speculative. He made no reference, as far as I am aware, to the failure of a *Zeroth* style law for the chromatic matching of colors.

We shall have to reserve for another occasion, the seminal way in which Helmholtz thought about these issues.[18] He thought of the cases of sameness of temperature, of mass, and other quantities, as special cases of a more general relation of "alikeness." Alikeness relations are denoted by " $=$," and Helmholtz required that, for any alikeness relation, if $A = B$, and $A = C$, then $B = C$. There are two features of his account that are worth special notice. The first is connected with some issues of realism. There is an ambiguity in Helmholtz's description of the alikeness relation. On the one hand, " $A = B$" is supposed to be a

---

[16]Through the tenth edition (1894) with additions by Rayleigh, the relevant sections on the Law of Equal Temperatures remains the same as in the first edition. The draft manuscript is in Add.7655/IV,1 (Box 2), and contains only the Preface, parts of chapters 3–8, 18, and 22. One suggestion has been that the relevant chapters were used for other writing or scrap. So far there is no trace of those missing pages.

[17]Fleming's remarks occur in *J. C. Maxwell, A commemoration volume, 1831–1931,* Cambridge Press, 1931, and the bound volume is Add.8082 (Cambridge University Library). Unfortunately the reader should be advised that these notes turn out to be a verbatim copy of large sections of a book by R. E. Baynes, who wrote a more mathematical supplement for his students at Oxford, based upon the fourth edition of Maxwell's work. He sent a copy of it to Maxwell on 27 June, 1878. Why Fleming copied Baynes' book, commas and all, is puzzling. One can only hope that the lecture notes still exist somewhere.

[18]They can be found in "Numbering and measuring" and "The facts of perception", in Helmholtz (1921, 1977).

relation among physical objects or magnitudes. So one thinks of the special cases of "$A = B$" when A and B are bodies that are in thermal equilibrium or have equal mass. On the other hand, Helmholtz sometimes described the alikeness relations as holding between properties or attributes of objects. The view he held, although I cannot argue the case here, is that a specific alikeness relation R holds between A and B, and there are certain attributes of A and B that cause or issue in A's being related to B by R. There is no guarantee that there will be such an attribute, and it seems to me that what is needed to express this idea is a family of attributes. However, it is evident that Helmholtz thought that such attributes and their causal role are a part of the story about alikeness relations. Although Helmholtz referred to attributes, he also thought of the relevant attributes as capacities of the objects for producing the effect of being alike. It is not clear whether it has to be properties, or whether it could be certain states of these objects that result in their being alike. Clearly Maxwell thought of temperature as a state "with reference to" a power to communicate heat to other bodies. It seems that something causal is being suggested for the outcome of A and B as being alike (if they are alike). One of the reasons for going causal is that, if it should turn out that, whenever A and B are alike (with respect to some relation R), they are also alike by some other relation S, then it is the attribute that resulted in A and B as being alike (by R) that also causes them to be alike (by S). At least that seems to be the program in which attributes are supposed to have a special role. Briefly if, whenever objects (or properties) are alike by one relation, they are also alike by another relation, then the explanation will appeal to attributes that caused the first kind of outcome. Although states of objects might do as well, Helmholtz called attention to the kind of simple problem for which realism suggests the kind of solution that he thought was needed: a causal one, or at the very least, a kind of empirical dependency.[19]

Helmholtz was also explicit about the Zero-type laws for alikeness relations. Roughly speaking, for each alikeness relation R, we have the corresponding Zeroth Law: (Z_R); If $R(A,B)$, and $R(A,C)$, then $R(B,C)$. Each (Z_R) has empirical content. However, Helmholtz also remarked that, if (Z_R) were false, then R would not be an alikeness relation. Thus, he thought that the schema (Z_R) had no objective content but was a necessary condition for being an alikeness relation. However, the particular instances of (Z_R) are supposed to have empirical content. Helmholtz's account of the measurement of (say) length requires that the relation

---

[19]Thus, it is a mistake to say, as did P. Hertz in his admirable notes to the Helmholtz article on measurement and numbering, that Russell and Frege showed how there is always such a property underlying any alikeness relation. If "alikeness" is an equivalence relation, Hertz noted that there always is a property P such that, if A and B both have P, then they will be related by the equivalence and conversely. Even if we granted these observations of Hertz, they still miss Helmholtz's point. Although A and B will be alike, if and only if they both have the property P, Helmholtz wanted a property P that causally results in A and B being alike. The Russell–Frege construction would be a logically sufficient but not necessarily a causal condition for A and B being alike.

"A has the same length as B" is an alikeness relation; thus, it follows that, if the Zeroth law of lengths (Z_L) were false, then, according to his theory, length would not be measurable. Consequently the Zeroth law becomes crucial on Helmholtz's theory of measurement.[20]

NEWTON AND THE SAMENESS OF MASS

The third example of a nonnumerical quantitative relation belongs to a little-known episode that occurred between the publication of the first and the second editions of Newton's (1687/1713) *Principia*. The problem was raised by Roger Cotes, the editor of the second edition, in correspondence. What made it a serious rather than a minor problem for Newton was the combination of asser-tions of the first edition against the background of thoughts that Newton held ever since his undergraduate days at Cambridge, and had expressed in unpublished studies and notes.

In the Third Corollary to Proposition Six of the Third Book of the *Principia* (first edition), Newton asserted that not all spaces are equally full (of matter) or that there is a vacuum. The target was of course Descartes, and the argument seemed simple: If all spaces are equally full of matter, then any two spaces of equal volume are completely filled. Consequently they have the same quantity of matter. However, Newton thought that, by his experiments with pendulums, he had shown that the weight of a body is proportional to its quantity of matter. Consequently any two spaces of equal volume have the same weight. Now any sphere, of gold or any other substance, will displace a volume of air that thas the same volume as the sphere. So the weight of any body is the same as the (same) volume of air that it displaces. However, by Archimedes' law (the buoyant force on a body in a fluid is equal to the weight of the fluid that the body displaces), there will not be any net force on a body, because its weight and the buoyant force are equal. Thus, no body will descend in air. Now that is patently false. The conclusion that Newton wished to draw was that the first assumption was false: Not all spaces are equally full; there is a vacuum.

Cotes had no objection to the conclusion. However, he did raise serious questions about the argument that Newton used. It seemed to Cotes that the relation of having the same quantity of matter was used ambiguously by Newton. One way of smoothing over the ambiguity required an assumption about pri-migenial particles for which there was no evidence. Even worse, as Cotes

---

[20]Despite the many references to Helmholtz in the literature of the representation theory of measurement, Helmholtz's theory differs in several key ways: the mathematical analog used is not the Dedekind–Peano version of arithmetic but Grassmann's, and there are no ordering relations assumed. On the contrary, special ordering relations are introduced by Helmholtz using a whole–part relation on the objects.

stressed, Newton (1952/1704) was already on record (in the *Optics*) as considering the possible falsity of that assumption. In the end, Newton conceded the point, and instead of the categorical conclusion he had in the first edition—that there was a vacuum—he now settled for a conditional conclusion: There is a vacuum, *if* all the solid particles of all bodies have the same density (and cannot be rarefied without pores). There was a struggle in the correspondence over the relation of sameness of quantity of matter that is worth reviewing briefly.

Let us denote, by "$M(A,B)$," the condition that body A has the same quantity of matter as body B. There is no question that both Newton and Cotes understood the condition $M(A,B)$ to be a quantitative relation. The difficulty, as Cotes saw it, arose, because Newton linked $M(A,B)$ to two other quantitative relations: $I(A,B)$ (A and B have the same inertia); and $V(A,B)$ (the volume that body A completely fills is the same as the volume that body B completely fills). The argument for a vacuum would then look like this:

1. $M(A,B)$, if and only if $V(A,B)$, and
2. $M(A,B)$, if and only if $I(A,B)$. Consequently
3. $V(A,B)$, if and only if $I(A,B)$. The volumes that the bodies A and B can completely fill are the same, if and only if their inertias are the same.

Newton then used the results of his pendulum experiments, according to which the weight of a body is proportional to its inertia. Consequently $W(A,B)$, if and only if $I(A,B)$. Therefore, $V(A,B)$, if and only if $W(A,B)$. It is at this stage that Newton considers any body A that completely fills a volume (i.e., pulverize it, or condense it until it cannot be condensed further, or "discount" the pores). That volume is the same as the volume of air that it displaces. Consequently the body and the air that it displaces have the same weight. However, by Archimedes' law, the net force on the body is then zero. Consequently a body will not descend in air, and Newton added, that goes for any body. Thus, Descartes was wrong. For, if one assumed that all spaces are equally filled with matter, then (1) holds. For, if A and B have equal volumes, then they have the same quantity of matter, because all volumes are completely filled with matter according to Descartes. This way of connecting (1) with Descartes is plausible given the Cartesian identification of extension (volume) with matter. On that view, any two bodies are completely filled with one kind of matter (there is only one kind of matter for Descartes, although there are different kinds of bodies) so that any two equal volumes have to contain the same quantity of matter.

Cotes thought that there was a difficulty with (3). Why should one think that two globes A and B of equal volume that are completely filled with matter will have the same inertia? The quantity of matter might be different. Is it impossible, he asked Newton, that God could give them different inertia?[21] Cotes continued

---

[21]Letter of Cotes to Newton, Feb. 16, 17$\frac{12}{13}$, in Hall and Tilling (1975),

with a diagnosis: The notion of quantity of matter does double duty in (1) and (2). The second assertion was, he thought, what Newton meant all along. Thus, he pressed Newton not to think of the quantity of matter as proportional to the space that the body can perfectly fill without void interstices.

Newton's reply is a defense of the original argument: "This happens only if the quantity of matter is proportional to its gravity, and in addition matter is impenetrable, so that matter always has the same density in completely filled spaces."[22] Thus, Newton seems to have thought that, from the proportionality of the quantity of matter to weight (this would be shown by Proposition 6, Book III, whose Third Corollary was under discussion), and the impenetrability of matter, it followed that matter in completely filled spaces always has the same density.

However, Cotes remained unconvinced. He repeated his view that Newton always estimated the quantity of matter by inertia, and that the objection had not not been obviated. He then suggests this as a possible emendation: "This holds only if the magnitude (bulk) or extension of matter in completely filled spaces is always proportional to the quantity of matter and to the force of inertia, and also thus to gravity: For by this proposition [Theorem VI, Book III] it is shown that the force of inertia and the quantity of matter are proportional to gravity."[23]

The effect of Cotes' suggestion is to isolate the claim that $M(A,B)$, if and only if $V(A,B)$, and to render the conclusion that there is a vacuum as conditional upon it. He ignored Newton's attempt to rest the conclusion on the impenetrability of matter. In his response,[24] Newton said that he will prevent the cavils (sic) of those who think that there are two kinds of matter. He then spelled out in greater detail just how the impenetrability of matter leads to the conclusion that poreless bodies of the same volume will have the same quantity of matter. The idea is that, once the pores of a body are contracted, the solid (primigenial) bodies in it will all abut on each other (by their impenetrability), and the body so reduced completely fills its space. Newton then thought that, if the volumes of two such bodies are equal, then so too are their quantities of matter. That is, $M(A,B)$, if and only if $V(A,B)$. However, such a deduction requires that the densities of all the solid particles are the same (and nonzero). This is the point that Cotes pressed in his reply.[25] He informed Newton that he was still not satisfied on this issue— unless Newton was prepared to make the argument for the existence of a vacuum conditional upon this: that the primigenial particles, out of which the world is

---

[22]cf. Cotes to Newton, Feb. 23, 17$\frac{11}{12}$, ibid., in which Cotes quotes Newton's response to his opening objection: "Hoc ita se habebit si modo materia sit gravitati suae proportionalis & insuper impenetrabilis adeoq: ejusdem semper densitatis in spatii plenus."

[23]"Hoc ita se habebit si modo magnitudo vel extensio materiae in spatiis plenis, sit semper proportionalis materiae quantitati & vi Inertiae atq: adeo si gravitatis: nam per hanc Propositionem constitit quod vis inertiae & quantitas materiae sit ut ejusdem gravitas." Parenthetical reference added.

[24]Newton to Cotes, Feb. 26 17$\frac{11}{12}$, ibid.

[25]Cotes to Newton, Feb. 28, 17$\frac{11}{12}$, ibid.

supposedly constituted, are all equally dense. However, he pointed out, this is an assumption that has no known support. For, he said, he did not see how it can be proved a priori or inferred from experiments. We are back again to what Newton had earlier described as the cavils of those who think that there might be two sorts of matter. So a concession has to be added, according to Cotes; there is no known support for it. Moreover, Cotes added, things may be worse: Newton seems to have thought that the denial was possible (*Optics,* Query 31).[26]

The result of this series of proposals and counterproposals is Newton's conditional assertion of the existence of a vacuum: "*If* all the solid particles of all bodies are of the same density, and cannot be rarefied without pores, then a void, space, or vacuum must be granted. By bodies of the same density, I mean those whose inertias are in the proportion of their bulks" [emphasis added]. (1947, p. 414)

The issue is now resolved with an emended Corollary 3 and an added Corollary 4, by reverting to a conditional proof of the existence of a vacuum. The additional condition requires that matter is impenetrable and that the solid particles of all bodies have the same density. However, the explanation is added, as we have seen, that bodies have the same density, if and only if the ratio of their inertias to their volumes is the same. That, Newton said, is what sameness of density means. It is this particular explanation of density that recalls the thorny issues that have been raised, from Mach onward, about the circularity of Newton's definition of mass. "Mass,"it is said, is defined with the aid of density, but "density" is defined with the aid of "mass." However, I think that, strictly speaking, there is no circularity. In the first "Definition" of *Principia,* the one concerned with mass or the quantity of matter, (1) a "measure" is given for the quantity of matter, using density and volume. (2) In the addendum (Corollary 4) of the second edition, the sameness of density is explained using inertia and volume. It would be a mistake to think that (1) provides a definition of a previously unexplained term, "quantity of matter." The concept of the quantity of matter was one that was familiar to Descartes, Newton, and their contemporaries. I do not think it is a case of defining an unfamiliar phrase; it is more a matter of stating a truth about something familiar. Even familiar terms, however, can be defined, but I think that Newton believed that there was no difference between himself and Descartes over the extension of the relation "$M(A,B)$." For Newton's argument against Descartes begins with the observation that two bodies that completely fill spaces of the same volume have the same quantity of matter. The argument would be completely off the mark, if there were disagreement over this initial assumption. Newton seems to have thought of quantity of matter in such a way that the argument will hold against Descartes' view of matter as completely filling any space. If this is correct, then it would explain

---

[26]Newton did not think that it was a contradiction to think otherwise. That is the point of his remarks about the possibility of particles having different density, forces, and different laws of nature.

why he did not define the quantity of matter of a body as its inertia, despite Cotes' pressure in that direction. It is evident that that would have begged the issue against Descartes, because Descartes would not have allowed quantity of matter to be defined as anything other than a geometric notion such as the content or volume of the appropriate region of space. Inertia was clearly not a geometric concept (as they thought of such concepts), and it would have been patent to all that inertia would not have been countenanced as belonging to physical theory by Descartes or any of his strict followers. However, Newton did think of the inertia of a body as a *measure* of its quantity of matter. The use of the concept of inertia points to a deep difference between Newton and Descartes over what concepts may be employed in physical explanations, but it is not a difference over how quantity of matter was understood.

What seems to be involved in Newton's argument for the vacuum can be thought of as the use of a term such as "$M(A,B)$" used in two claims that connect that notion with (1) equal volumes of bodies A and B that completely fill their spaces, and (2) equal inertias of A and B. (1) and (2) are both taken as "measures" of the same quantity of matter, and having it both ways, was, as Cotes clearly saw, not justifiable on any grounds that Newton had yet provided.

There is another way, other than definitional, of thinking of the two measures that Newton wished to retain. The notion $M(A,B)$ is a quantitative relation on bodies that completely fill their spaces or for which interstitial pores are discounted. On our account of quantitative relations, some partition is needed. If the collection of bodies that completely fill their spaces is partitioned by the equivalence relation $V(A,B)$, let that partition be denoted by M_V. Then it is easy to see that, if $M(A,A)$ holds for all A, then, for all A and B, $M(A,B)$, if and only if $V(A,B)$, if and only if the relation $M(A,B)$ is quantitative with respect to the partition M_v. Thus, the requirement that "same quantity of matter" be quantitative with respect to the partition induced by sameness of volume leads to the conclusion that, for all A and B, $M(A,B)$, if and only if $V(A,B)$—the first premise of Newton's original argument for the vacuum. This biconditional is not a definition by contemporary standards, and it is not clear that it would be a definition by eighteenth century standards. Those standards are probably closer to the ones found in Euclid than they are to those of present logical theory. In any case, the biconditional between sameness of mass and sameness of volume is the one that Newton attributed to Descartes, and, if Cotes had not made things difficult to do so, Newton would have adopted it for the Primigenial particles of bodies and ultimately for all bodies that are rendered poreless.

Similar remarks hold for the relation between mass and inertia. Newton did think that inertia was a measure of the quantity of matter of a body. However, there is no evidence that he thought of this as a matter of definition. Suppose now that the set of bodies is partitioned by the equivalence relation $I(A,B)$, and let M_I denote the corresponding partition. Then we have the result that, if $M(A,A)$ holds for all A, then the relation $M(A,B)$ is quantitative with respect to the partition M_I, if and only if, for all A and B, $M(A,B)$, if and only if $I(A,B)$. This is the second premise of Newton's original argument for the existence of a vacuum. On this nondefinitional reconstruction, we can say that Newton wished to assert that $M(A,B)$ was quantitative with respect to the relation of sameness of volume and also quantitative with respect to the relation of sameness of inertia. According to this gloss, to say that inertia is a measure of the quantity of matter is to say that the relation "A has the same quantity of matter as B" is quantitative with respect to the partition induced by the relation of having the same inertia. Although the claims that the relation $M(A,B)$ is quantitative with respect to M_V and that $M(A,B)$ is quantitative with respect to M_I are weaker than their corresponding definitional counterparts, Newton's argument against Descartes still goes through, if it is assumed, as he did, that M is quantitative with respect to each of the partitions M_V and M_I. For, in that case, we know that M can be quantitative with respect to only one partition, if it is quantitative with respect to any. Consequently, if M is quantitative with respect to M_V as well as M_I, it follows that, for all A and B, $I(A,B)$, if and only if $V(A,B)$. This is the third step of Newton's original argument for the vacuum. Furthermore, from here onward, the original Newtonian argument can be resumed by using the pendulum experiments to support the connection between sameness of inertia and sameness of weight. Cotes' objection, on this reconstruction, is that Newton had all along assumed that $M(A,B)$ is quantitative with respect to M_I and that, in his discussion of the existence of the vacuum, Newton also seems to have assumed that M is also quantitative with respect to M_V. However, there are no known grounds, either a priori or empirical, to show that $M(A,B)$ is quantitative with respect to the partition M_V.

The question "What is the measure of the quantity of matter?" is not, we have suggested, the question of how quantity of matter is to be defined. It is the question of what partition it is, with respect to which the relation "A and B have the same quantity of matter" is quantitative. On the definitional view, the conflict between Newton and Cotes resembles some of the difficulties familiar from the work of Carnap, in which two stipulations or definitions of the meaning of a term yield an empirical consequence (in this case, that bodies have the same inertia, if and only if they have the same volume). On our reconstruction using quantitativeness with respect to a partition, the partitions with respect to which a relation is quantitative have to be coextensional, and that would, in Newton's argument, force sameness of inertia to be coextensional with sameness of volume (for bodies that are poreless).

There is a further question about $M(A,B)$, whose resolution is far from clear. We have seen how the quantitativeness of $M(A,B)$ figured in a significant way in the discussion of whether there is a vacuum. That it was quantitative was clear; less clear was the appropriate partition. What we have called the choice of a partition is what Newton refered to as an empirical measure or an estimate of the sameness of the quantity of matter. The best known discussion of Newton about empirical estimates or measures of certain quantities occurs in his discussions of relative space and time in the *Principia*. In those passages, he said that, because the parts of space and time are not sensible, we need to have sensible measures of them. These are the relational notions he mentioned, such as hours, days, months, and years used to estimate or measure absolute duration. Similar remarks hold for places of absolute space. We think that there is a parity of matter with space and time in the *Principia*. The quantity of matter, no less than regions of absolute space and durations of absolute time, also fail to be sensible quantities and require sensible, empirical measures as well. Much of the dispute between Cotes and Newton centers around the several measures that Newton employed in his argument against Descartes' plenum. Newton thought that the volume of bodies without pores was a natural measure of their quantity of matter. Anyone who thought differently was described as someone who was caviling. Certainly the objection by Cotes seems to have caught Newton short, but there is no mistaking the determination with which Newton persisted in his view. In fact there is reason to believe that, ever since his undergraduate days, he believed it possible that bodies might just be "determined quantities of extension which omnipresent God endows with certain conditions."[27] That would certainly make it plausible that the quantities of matter of poreless bodies is just the volume or extent of some region of space. The comparison of the mass of two (poreless) bodies would be a comparison of the associated regions of space. Although it was speculation on Newton's part that bodies be thought of in this way, it was a central part of his early unpublished attack on Descartes' physics, and it seems clear that he thought that it was true. He certainly needed no reminder from Cotes, although he did receive one, that although the masses of bodies were to each other as their volumes, it was still a question of evidence that was needed. Otherwise its use would have violated the canons of scientific reasoning that Newton used to distinguish his own scientific work from that of Descartes and others. The picture that results is one in which nonsensible quantities have their sensible measures. However, in the case of mass or quantity of matter, just as in the case of absolute space and time, the measures were neither a definition nor a replacement for what they measured. What they measured in the case of the quantity of matter seems to have been a completely filled part of space.

ACKNOWLEDGMENTS

This research was supported by a grant from the CUNY Research Foundation.

---

[27]cf. Newton's "De Gravitatione et Aequipondio Fluidorum" which contains this suggestion about bodies being at any time some region of space that God focuses upon and makes the apparent source of various sensible effects upon us. The text and a translation can be found in Hall and Hall (1962, p.140).

REFERENCES

Adams, E. W. (1966). On the nature and purpose of measurement. *Technical Report No. 4*. University of Oregon.

Artin, E. (1957). *Geometric algebra*, New York: Interscience.

Black, J. (1803). *Lectures on the Elements of Chemistry*, Longman & Rees. London.

Carnap, R. (1966). *Philosophical foundations of physics* (M. Gardner, Ed.). New York: Basic Books.

Cohn, R. M. (1965). *Universal algebra*. New York: Harper & Row.

Field, H. (1980). *Science without numbers*. Princeton: Princeton University Press.

Gratzer, G. (1979). *Universal algebra* (2nd ed.). New York: Springer-Verlag.

Hall, A. R., & Hall, R. B. (1962). *Unpublished scientific papers of Isaac Newton*. Cambridge: Cambridge University Press.

Hall, A. R., & Tilling, L. (1975). *The correspondence of Isaac Newton, Volume V, 1709–1713*. Cambridge: Cambridge University Press (Published for the Royal Society).

von Helmholtz, H. (1977a). Numbering and measuring from an epistemological viewpoint. In R. S. Cohen & Y. Elkana (Eds.), *Hermann von Helmholtz: Epistemological writings* (pp. 72–114). Dordrecht: Reidel.

von Helmholtz, H. (1977b). The facts in perception, in R. S. Cohen & Y. Elkana (Eds.), *Hermann von Helmholtz: Epistemological Writings* (pp. 115–185). Dordrecht: Reidel.

Hempel, C. G. (1952). *Fundamentals of concept formation in empirical science*, International Encyclopedia of Unified Science, Vol. II, No. 7. Chicago: Chicago University Press.

Hempel, C. G. (1970). On the standard conception of scientific theories. *Minnesota studies in the philosophy of science* (M. Radner & S. Winokur Eds.). Minneapolis: Minnesota University Press.

Hempel, C. G., & Oppenheim, P. (1936). *Der Typus Begriff im Licht der Neuen Logik*. Leiden: A. W. Sijthoff.

Hilbert, D. (1968). *Grundlagen der Geometrie*, (mit Supplementen von Dr. P. Bernays. 10-th ed., B. G. Teubner, Stuttgart.

Koslow, A. (1968). Mach's concept of mass: Program and definition. *Synthese, 18*, 216–233.

Koslow, A. (1982). Quantity and quality: Some aspects of measurement. *PSA 1982, 1*, 183–198.

Krantz, D. H., Luce, R. D., Suppes, P., & Tversky, A. (1971). *Foundations of measurement*. New York: Academic Press.

Mach, E. (1868). "Über die Definitionen der Masse," in *Reportorium für physikalische Technik*, Bd IV, 355 et seq.

Mach, E. (1911). *History and Root of the Principle of the Conservation of Energy* (trans. & annotated by P. E. B. Jourdain, Open Court, Chicago Original German 1872.

Magie, W. F. *A sourcebook in physics*. Harvard University Press.

Maxwell, J. C. C. (1871). *Theory of heat*, London: Longmans.

Maxwell, J. C. C. (1924). *Matter and Motion*, reprinted with notes and appendices by J. Larmor, Dover. New York. Original ed 1877.

Maxwell, J. C. C. (1931). *J. C. Maxwell, A commemoration Volume, 1831–1931*. Cambridge Press. Cambridge. (Also Add. 8082 Cambridge University Library)

McGuire, J. E., & Tamny, M. (1983). *Certain philosophical questions, Newton's trinity notebook*. Cambridge University Press. Cambridge

Mueller, I. (1983). *Philosophy of mathematics and deductive structure in Euclid's Elements*. M.I.T. Cambridge Mass.

Newton, I. (1952). *Optics* (1st ed. 1704), Foreword by A. Einstein, and Introduction by Sir E. Whittaker. Preface by I. B. Cohen Dover, New York (Based on the Fourth Edition, 1730).

Newton, I. (1972). *Philosophiae naturalis principia mathematica, The third edition (1726) with variant readings.* Assembled and Edited by A. Koyré and I. B. Cohen, with the Assistance of A. Whitman. Two Volumes, Harvard University Press. Cambridge.

Newton, I. (1947). *Sir Isaac Newton's Mathematical Principles of Natural Philosophy and His System of the World.* trans: A. Motte, and edited by F. Cajori, University of California Press. Berkeley.

Putnam, H. (1962). What theories are not. reprinted in Putnam, *Mathematics Matter, and Method,* V.1, Cambridge University Press, New York.

Scott, D., & Suppes, P. (1958). Foundational aspects of theories of measurement. *The Journal of Symbolic Logic,* 23, 113–128 and reprinted in Suppes, *Studies in the Methodology and Foundations of Science. Selected Writings from 1951 to 1969),* (1969) Reidel, Dordrecht.

Stokes, C. G. Collected Papers, Cambridge University Library, PA1091 and PA1071.

Suppes, P. (1956). The role of subjective probability and utility in decision making. in *Proceedings of the Third Berkeley Symposium on Mathematical Statistics and Probability, 1954–1955,* 61–73 and reprinted in Suppes (1969).

Suppes, P. (1957). *Introduction to Logic,* Van Nostrand. Princeton N.J.

9 Conventionalism in Measurement Theory

Brian Ellis
La Trobe University, Bundoora, Australia

The conventionalist program of analysis and rational reconstruction of science was seriously undermined by the movements toward epistemological holism and scientific realism in the 1960s, and very little work is now being done in this tradition. The holists argued that the distinctions required for the program could not be made satisfactorily; the realists claimed that the accepted laws and theories of science should be interpreted, more or less as they are, as literally true statements about the world and, hence, that rational reconstruction is unnecessary. However, I am convinced that something important was lost in this process, and I want to argue for a new program, which preserves what is good in the old one but does not depend on the usual conventionalist distinctions and is compatible with a sophisticated form of scientific realism.

Let me indulge in some personal history. When I wrote *Basic concepts of measurement* (1966) (hereafter *BCM*), I was still very much influenced by the conventionalist writings of some of the early positivists, particularly Mach, Poincaré, and Reichenbach. I found their works on classical mechanics, geometry, heat theory, space and time, and many other subjects exciting. They brought out various more or less hidden assumptions of the theories they investigated and classified them as empirical facts or conventions. Like the early positivists, I thought this was an important thing to do, because it indicated where we had degrees of freedom, if they should be needed, in reconstructing or improving our theories and where they were fixed by the empirical data. However, I thought it was always important to know just what would be involved in changing any of these conventions, for, like Poincaré, I did not believe they were arbitrary. Therefore, as I saw it, it was an integral part of the conventionalist program to discover what reasons, if any, there may be for adopting some conventions rather

167

than others. I thought this was one of the more valuable things a philosopher of science could do.

Like many other philosophers at the time, I accepted a version of the analytic/synthetic distinction. Analytic propositions, like "A bachelor is an unmarried man," I should have said are true simply in virtue of the meanings of words. As such, they are conventional but trivial and uninteresting. Of much greater interest, I thought, were the hidden conventions of scientific theories and practices, which could not be discovered just by linguistic analysis. These conventions, I supposed, reflected decisions, often unconscious, to accept certain propositions, although they were neither semantically nor empirically warranted, because it was useful (for the theory or practice) to do so. These propositions were not analytic, as I understood analyticity, because they were not true simply in virtue of the meanings of words. Nor were they straightforwardly empirical, because they could not be inductively supported and could be refuted (or made no longer useful to accept) only by replacing the theory or changing the practice to which they belonged.

The analytic/synthetic distinction was strongly criticised by W. V. O. Quine and others in the 1950s, but philosophers of science were slow to see this criticism as casting doubt on their own distinction between empirical and conventional propositions. Adolf Grünbaum (1968, p. 4) for example, argued that ". . . whatever the merits of the repudiation of the analytic–synthetic dichotomy and the antithesis between theoretical and observation terms, it is grievously incorrect and obfuscating to deny as well the distinction between factual and conventional ingredients of sophisticated space-time theories in physics." He thought, as most of us did, that the analytic/synthetic distinction was only concerned with the meanings of words and could safely be abandoned. The conventions of interest to philosophers of science were not regarded as analytic propositions. They were not just trivial semantic conventions but conventions that had a substantial role in structuring our theories. Nevertheless the epistemological holism advocated by Quine gained ground in the 1960s through the writings of I. Lakatos, T. S. Kuhn, and P. K. Feyerabend who attacked the foundationalist epistemologies of the empiricists, and in doing so, they seriously undermined the empirical/conventional distinction that the conventionalists required for their program.

At the same time, J. J. C. Smart, D. M. Armstrong, and others were developing strong arguments for scientific realism, which was anticonventionalist for a different reason. The holists did not think the distinction could be made satisfactorily; the scientific realists wanted to interpret the laws and theories of science as literally true generalised descriptions of reality. For example, they wanted *a much more literal* interpretation of statements of the results of measurements and, hence, of quantitative laws, than I was prepared to give. Thus, if one quantity is proportional to another or to the square root of another, in certain circumstances, then their view was that these relationships must hold between the categorical bases of the quantities concerned, *independently of how we might measure these quantities*. Consequently, if we measure the quantities *correctly* in these circumstances, our measurements should reflect the underlying relationships of proportionality. If they do not, then we are not using the correct scales. On the view I took in *BCM*, there are no true or correct scales for the measurement of quantities—only more or less useful ones, resulting in more or less simple mathematical expressions for the laws of nature.

Since that time, I have also come to think there is no very useful distinction to be drawn between what is conventional and what is not.[1] At the extremes, there are trivial semantic conventions, and there are empirical facts, and the distinction between them is easy enough to make. However, most of the interesting propositions of science are not clearly either facts or conventions. If we say these propositions are true by definition, and so conventional, then we are forced to say that other propositions, which are just as plausibly conventional, are empirical or factual.[2] So the distinction often seems to be forced and arbitrary. Moreover, the distinction, when made in this way, has no epistemological force. A proposition, arbitrarily declared to be true by definition, is as much open to revision in the light of experience as any proposition that must consequentially be declared to be empirical or factual.

I am also much more of a scientific realist than I was when I wrote *BCM*. I now hold that a satisfactory ontology for science must include a categorical basis for the quantitative relationships we are able to observe. However, the question of what sort of categorical basis for quantities we need to assume is an important one for scientific realists to face up to, and very few have done so.[3] In *BCM*, I identified quantities with objective linear orders, saying that a quantity exists, if and only if such an order exists. Thus, I claimed that quantities are essentially *relations* and denied that they are *properties* (which come in degrees or have magnitudes) that an object considered in isolation might possess. Our knowledge of quantities, I thought, was basically just knowledge of quantitative relationships, and I supposed that these relationships, or some of them at least, had *primary ontological status* (i.e., were not reducible to or dependent upon any intrinsic properties of the objects they related). Some such account as this seemed to be required anyway for *distance* and *time-interval*. I held that a similar account was required for other quantities.

Whereas I still have some sympathy with my earlier position on this, because

---

[1]The clearest statement of my rejection of the distinction is to be found in Ellis (1971, pp. 177–203).

[2]I use these terms here and throughout this essay as though they were interchangeable, although I do not think they are. I do so, because the empiricists whose views I am trying to recapture made no distinction between facts and empirical facts.

[3]The most notable exceptions are Henry C. Byerly and Vincent A. Lazara in their excellent paper, "Realist Foundations of Measurement," (1973), pp. 10–28. More recently, there have been excellent papers on the topic published by C. Swoyer, and by J. Bigelow and R. Pargetter.

it provides a nicely unified theory of quantities, I no longer think that the account, which is appropriate for distance and time-interval, can be generalised in this way. I now think we need an ontology that includes *both* primitive quantitative properties (upon which some quantitative relationships depend) *and* some primitive quantitative relationships, such as the spatiotemporal ones.

Between them, these two movements—epistemological holism and scientific realism—virtually demolished the conventionalist program of analysis. I think this is a pity. I do so, despite the fact that I agree with both the holists and the scientific realists on most of the important issues. I agree with the holists, for example, that it is useless to try to classify all of the propositions of science as empirical or conventional as the early positivists hoped to do, and I agree with Byerly and Lazara that my neo-operationist account of the meaning of law statements will not do. Nevertheless it remains of interest to know why we accept the propositions we do and what would be involved in rejecting any that we could reject. For these are just the sorts of *case studies* in the theory of knowledge that should be the foundation for any general epistemology of science.

In what follows, I shall:

1. Argue for a modified program of analysis and rational reconstruction of science that retains what is valuable in the original conventionalist program, without commitment to any particular epistemology or ontology.

2. Try to say what kind of theory of quantities a scientific realist should be committed to. I shall focus particularly on the theory of dimensions and the expression of quantitative laws, for this is where the conventionalist theory of measurement has been most fruitful, and the new program of analysis and rational reconstruction I wish to advocate can be best illustrated. It also raises all of the important questions concerning the nature of quantities I wish to discuss.

THE CONVENTIONALIST PROGRAM

The aims of the conventionalist program of analysis were as follows:

1. To provide a clear theoretical framework for discussion of the area to be studied by explicating the concepts we normally work with, introducing new concepts and distinctions where necessary.

2. To discover and distinguish between the empirical presuppositions and unexamined conventions that underlie our theories and practices in the area.

3. To find out the extent to which the choices we have effectively made in adopting these conventions depend on or are constrained by empirical facts, theories, considerations of convenience, formal simplicity, and so on, and to what extent their adoption appears to be arbitrary.

4. To reconstruct rationally the theory or practice that is the subject of this analysis.

I am convinced that these aims, or something like them, are still worth pursuing, although the distinctions they require seem muddier now than they once did.

UNITS, DIMENSIONS, AND SCALE SYSTEMS

The value of conventionalist analysis may be illustrated by the theory of units and dimensions developed in *BCM*. For it explained clearly, as had not, I think, been done before, the scope and limitations of dimensional analysis, and how and why it was successful to the extent it was. It exposed the nonsense that people used to go with about dimensionless quantities, and it showed how, by changing our conventions concerning the expression of quantitative laws, the power of dimensional analysis can be increased. The theory, therefore, has demonstrated its practical utility.

The intuitive idea of a unit of a quantity q is that it is the $q$ness of a given, or well-defined, object that serves as a standard for the measurement of q, (on a scale that assigns the number 1 to this object). However, in *BCM*, I argued that the conception of a quantity that is implicit in this way of thinking about units is unacceptable. If a is greater in q than b, this is not because a has more $q$ness than b, I should have said. For $q$ness is not like a substance of which one may have more or less; rather, like position or velocity, it is purely relational, and if a has a certain degree of $q$ness, this is only because it occupies a certain position in the order of q, which it does by virtue of the q–relationships it bears to other things (e.g., to b). For these (and other) reasons, I took the view that unit names should never be regarded as the names of any specific amounts or intensities of the quantities they measure (which the standards used might be supposed to possess intrinsically). Rather *unit names should always be regarded as the names of scales*.

On the account that was once standard and is still widely accepted, quantities have dimensions that are either simple or complex. A simple dimension is that of *one of the basic physical quantities in terms of which all other physical quantities are ultimately definable*. A complex dimension, or dimensional formula, is a product of powers of the simple or basic dimensions that reflects the way in which the quantity that has this dimension has been defined in terms of the basic quantities.[4]

---

[4]This is the kind of view taken by G. Burniston Brown, for example, in "A new treatment of the theory of dimensions," (1941) pp. 418–431, and by W. E. Duncanson, "The dimensions of physical quantities," (1941), pp. 432–448.

However, I think this account of dimensions is quite unsatisfactory, as those who have tried to work with it have found. They did not know how to pick out the basic quantities, even in mechanics, and they were still more confused when it came to assigning dimensions to the quantities involved in heat theory and electrodynamics.[5] They did not know how to deal with so-called dimensionless quantities, like angle, or mechanical advantage, which were alike in being dimensionless but obviously very unlike conceptually. Measures of such quantities were said to be "pure numbers." Moreover, it was hard to explain, on the standard theory, why dimensional formulae should always be products of powers, or how and why dimensional analysis could be so useful. Finally the standard account obscured some important conventions concerning the construction of scale systems and the expression of quantitative laws.

According to the theory developed in *BCM, dimensions should properly be identified with classes of similar scales* (where two scales are said to be similar, iff measurements on these scales are uniformly related by similarity transformations, that is, transformations of the form $y = mx$, where m is a constant). The common dimension of length, for example, is the class of scales similar to the metre scale. It includes the foot and fathom scales, but it does not include the various diagonal scales described in the chapter of *BCM* on fundamental measurement or any other members of the power group that do not belong to the similarity class. The ordinary dimension of force is the class of scales similar to the newton scale. It includes the dyne and pound weight scales, but it does not include any scales that are not related to these by similarity transformations.

The so-called *basic quantities* are just those measured on independent scales that are used to the define various *systems of scales of measurement* (e.g., the MKS and FPS systems). The systems so defined may be said to be *centered* on these scales. However, apart from the fact that these quantities normally have a fairly central role in physical theory, there is nothing very special about them. We could use more or less highly centered scale systems, if we wished, or choose to center them on scales for the measurement of different quantities. A *scale system* is a set of interrelated dependent and independent scales. The dependent scales are either: (a) scales that we have made dependent on other scales by definition (e.g., our fundamental scales for the measurement of area and volume), or (b) derivative scales for the measurement of various quantities defined by the values of system-dependent constants in quantitative laws. A system-dependent constant is one that is characteristic of a system, or a system at a time, but that may vary from system to system or with time. Elasticity, density, and refractivity are quantities typically measured on derivative scales. In general, the complex unit

---

[5]For example, Burniston Brown believed that two basic dimensions (of length and time) were enough for the whole of physical theory, but Duncanson thought we needed a dimension of charge as well. However, neither system is useful. The reductions in the number of basic dimensions required are achieved at the cost of the information contained in the dimensional formulae for other quantities.

names given to dependent scales simply indicate how they depend on the independent scales of the system. *The fact that we center our scale systems as we do on some independent scales for the measurement of a few basic quantities reflects an important convention in the practice of measurement. It is also conventional that we center them on scales for the measurement of these particular quantities.*

A quantitative law relates the idealised results of measurements of different quantities on various scales. Now there are many ways in which such a law might be expressed, depending on the classes of scales for which we wish it to be valid. For example, we could express any quantitative law so that it is valid for scales *linearly* related to the usual scales for the measurement of some or all of the quantities involved. The gas law, for example, could be expressed as: $pV = R(aT + b)$, where a and b are scale dependent constants. (For the Celsius Scale, $a = 1$ and $b = 273$. For the Fahrenheit Scale, $a = 5/9$ and $b = 255$.)

In practice, however, we use a much more conservative form of expression. *We always express quantitative laws either: (a) with respect to particular scales for the measurement of some or all of the quantities involved, so that the law is valid for just these scales; or (b) with respect to classes of similar scales for the measurement of some or all of the quantities involved, so that the law is valid for all scales in these classes.* Thus, the laws of mechanics are normally expressed with respect to classes of similar scales for the measurement of all of the quantities involved and with reference to a scale system that is centered on independent scales for mass, length, and time-interval.

On the other hand, laws involving the so-called "dimensionless" quantities, like angle, and quantities measured independently on associative scales, like temperature, are always expressed with respect to *particular* scales (e.g., the radian or the Absolute scale). *The so-called dimensionless quantities are not, however, dimensionless;* they are just quantities measured on scales that are defined in ways which make them independent of the scale system. However, there is no good reason why we should not, and very good reason why we should, express laws involving angle with respect to the class of scales similar to the radian scale R and adopt the *MKSR,* or a similar scale system, for mechanical measurement. For the power of dimensional analysis would demonstrably be increased, if we were to adopt such a system.[6] Likewise, the convention that we should always express our temperature laws with respect to a particular temperature scale has no rational basis. On the contrary, there are very good reasons for expressing laws involving temperature with respect to the class of scales similar to the Absolute scale.

The theory of dimensions developed in *BCM* was surely an advance on previous theories of dimensions. Yet the theory was arrived at by following the original conventionalist program of analysis and rational reconstruction as it

---

[6]See *BCM,* pp. 145–151 for a demonstration of this.

applied to the practice of expressing quantitative laws. Therefore, whatever the merits of the theoretical underpinning of this program, there must be something to be said in its favor. It would be regrettable, if the arguments against conventionalism should prevent this sort of thing being done in future.

HOLISTIC OBJECTIONS TO CONVENTIONALISM

Holism in epistemology is the view that our knowledge consists of a theoretically and conceptually integrated system of items of knowledge. These items are assumed to have no identity independent of the system to which they belong, because of the pervasive influence of theoretical interpretations on both language and belief. In addition, epistemological holists typically hold the following theses, or variants of them:

1. There are no basic items of knowledge or belief that could serve as a foundation for knowledge.
2. There is no theory-neutral observation language; all observation reports are theory-laden.
3. An observationally acquired belief that is incompatible with our theoretical expectations may cause us to modify our belief system, but any belief can be defended, if we are prepared to make drastic enough revisions elsewhere in the system.
4. Normally many different theories are involved in testing a given hypothesis, and if the hypothesis is refuted, it is only because we prefer to abandon it rather than any of these other theories.

Epistemological holism is not strictly incompatible with an empirical/ conventional distinction. Indeed the Duhemian thesis, (4), specifically allows that some hypotheses may be maintained indefinitely as conventions, whatever the empirical evidence may be. However, it does suggest that the body of science may contain a range of more or less provisionally accepted propositions—some that might be given up quite readily and others (like the propositions of arithmetic perhaps) that we should probably retain in any circumstances. It also suggests that propositions accepted as conventions may be more or less arbitrary, depending on how they relate to other beliefs in the system. A convention that has been adopted for good theoretical reasons is not an arbitrary convention. Nor is it arbitrary, if it could not be abandoned without seriously complicating our theories. Conventions may, thus, be constrained by theoretical considerations. However, our theories in turn are constrained by empirical evidence. Therefore, the acceptability or otherwise of a convention may ultimately depend on such evidence. We should not, therefore, expect to be able to draw a clear distinction between what is empirical and what is conventional. On the contrary, epistemological holism suggests that the propositions of science should be interrelated in a wide variety of ways and that it is, or should be, one of the tasks of epistemology to map the interconnections between them.

REALIST OBJECTIONS TO CONVENTIONALISM

According to the dominant strain of scientific realism, it is most rational to believe that the world is literally more or less how our best scientific theories say it is. However, this runs counter to the main tradition of conventionalism, which regards the ontological claims of current science with a great deal of scepticism. Conventionalists would argue that what is needed is a *critical* approach to the claims of science—one that demands empirical justifications for these claims—if science is to be rid of the relics of past metaphysics. Thus, realists tend to regard conventionalists as sceptics, and conventionalists typically think of realists as naive. Both attitudes are well justified. What is needed for the new program I wish to advocate is a sophisticated form of scientific realism—one that takes the ontological claims of science seriously but is not above questioning the ontological status of entities postulated in scientific theories.

The main argument for scientific realism is an argument from the best explanation. Scientific realists make the reasonable assumption that the best explanations we have of why things behave as they do are the accepted scientific ones. These explanations normally purport to refer to theoretical entities of some kinds. Therefore, they argue, it is at least the case that the world behaves *as if* things of these kinds existed. Yet the best explanation of why this should be so is that things like these *really do* exist. Therefore, it is most reasonable to believe in the existence of the sorts of theoretical entities postulated in the best scientific theories.

However, the main argument for scientific realism does not apply to such theoretical entities as points in space or space-time that are not postulated as having causal roles. For it cannot be said of these entities that the world behaves as if they existed. Moreover, it clearly does not apply to the theoretical entities occurring in constructive explanations of the kind discussed by Nancy Cartwright (1983). For such entities are idealised objects to which real things are at best only approximations, and there is no reason whatever to believe in them—again because they are not postulated as causes. As I see it, the main argument for scientific realism is an argument from known effects to postulated causes in the best causal process explanation. As such, it is a good argument, but it is not a good argument for the existence of theoretical entities occurring in other kinds of theories or explanations.

On the other hand, the main argument for scientific realism is *prima facie* a good argument for the existence of many kinds of entities besides particles, fields, and other things that have mass or energy. It seems, for example, to be a good argument for the existence of the *properties* of these things, the *spatiotemporal relationships* between them, the *fundamental forces* (conceived as basic kinds of causal interactions) to which they are subject and the *events* to which they give rise.[7]

For it is certainly true to say that the world behaves (is) as if these properties, relationships, forces, and events existed (occurred), and surely the best explanation for this is that they really do exist (occur).

Now the most striking thing about the fundamental properties of nature is that they are nearly all quantitative. That is, they come in degrees. Therefore, any adequate ontology for science must recognise the fundamental existence of quantitative universals (i.e., universals like mass, charge, spin, colour, flavour, strangeness, and so on) that may be variously instantiated. I do not know how to develop such a theory, but somehow we must try to explain what two things that differ in mass, for example, have in common, as well as what differentiates them, and the same sort of account will be needed for all of the other fundamental quantities.

In *BCM,* I construed all quantities on the model of spatiotemporal relationships, which I did not think and still do not think could be explained as relationships between any intrinsic properties of the objects or events they relate. Thus, I would have denied that the charge on an electron is an intrinsic property of the particle, just as I would have denied that its position is intrinsic to it. Rather I would have drawn the explicit analogy with position in space and said that the electron has the charge it has *in virtue of its electromagnetic relationships to other things* (cf. the electron has the position it has in virtue of how it is related spatially to other things).

I no longer think that this account is tenable. For the best explanation of the fixedness and stability of the properties of the fundamental particles is just that these properties are intrinsic to them. The fact that all electrons have the same charge, mass, spin, and so on is best explained by supposing that these properties are all intrinsic to electrons. It is not well explained by the hypothesis that they all happen to bear the same electromagnetic, dynamic, and so on relationships to other things. For why should they do so, if these properties are not intrinsically but extrinsically determined? The case is different with spatiotemporal relationships. There is no such stability in the positions of things that would be explained by the supposition that their positions are intrinsic. The main argument for scientific realism, thus, comes out decisively in favor of the existence of some intrinsic quantitative properties.

---

[7]This range of possibilities is discussed fully in a paper being written concurrently with this entitled "The ontology of scientific realism." The paper is to appear in a volume of essays edited by Philip Pettit and Richard Sylvan, and dedicated to J. J. C. Smart on the occasion of his retirement from the Chair of Philosophy at the Australian National University.

I do not know of any satisfactory theory of quantitative properties and relationships. My own theory that quantitative properties always supervene on quantitative relationships, in the sort of way that spatiotemporal position supervenes on spatiotemporal relationships, will not do for the reasons given. On the other hand, D. M. Armstrong's theory, that quantitative relationships always supervene on quantitative properties, does not account adequately for the continuum of spatiotemporal relationships. For we should at least need to have a non-denumerable infinity of points, each with their own, intrinsic locations in space-time, to ground such a continuum of relationships.

What is needed is a general, ontologically sound theory of quantitative properties and relationships that we can use to say what sorts of quantities exist in nature, what their properties are, and how they may be related to each other in lawlike or accidental ways. However, even when we have such a theory, there is still the problem of what degrees of freedom we have in metrising these relationships and what grounds there may be for choosing one metrical system rather than another. To answer these questions, we will have to engage in a new program of analysis and rational reconstruction, not so very different from the kind undertaken in *BCM*.

THE NEW PROGRAM OF ANALYSIS AND RATIONAL RECONSTRUCTION

The following issues are important ones that are independent of the global aims of conventionalist analysis:

1. There are many presuppositions of scientific theories and practices, which have no empirical justification, and so are conventional in the traditional sense, and it is not without interest to find out what they are, why they should be accepted (if indeed they should be), what other conventions might replace them, and at what cost or benefit.

2. There are many empirical presuppositions of science that have never in fact been tested, either because they have not been recognised as presuppositions or have been taken for granted, or because the technology does not exist to test them. These too should be stated, tested if possible, and the possibilities of other assumptions should be explored.

3. There are many propositions that are arguably either empirical or conventional, depending on your theory of empirical justification. For these, it probably does not matter much how you classify them. If you say they are conventions, then they will not be considered to be *arbitrary* conventions but ones adopted for good pragmatic reasons. If you say they are empirical, then it will be because you think that these *very same reasons* are empirically (as opposed to pragmatically) justifying. In either case, we should seek to be clear what

the reasons are and whether they are sufficient to justify accepting these propositions rather than others.

As an example of the first kind of case, consider the conventions governing the construction and centering of scale systems. First, it is conventional that we should choose to center our scale systems for mechanical measurement around scales for mass, length, and time-interval. I suppose the practice derives from the seventeenth century mechanistic world view, according to which the universe consists of matter in motion. Obviously this implies that mass, length, and time-interval are in some sense primary quantities (cf. also the seventeenth century distinction between primary and secondary qualities). However, this would not be a good rationale for centering our scale systems for mechanical measurement on just these quantities, even if the seventeenth century world view were still tenable. For what is important in making this choice is what information it enables us to include (about the forms of the most fundamental laws of mechanics) in the complex unit names for indirectly measured quantities and constants. Systems centered only on scales of mass, length, and time-interval are demonstrably not optimal as systems for mechanical measurement.

Second, it is a matter of convention—one that has no rational justification—that we should express quantitative laws with respect to *classes of similar scales* for the measurement of some quantities and with respect to *particular* scales for the measurement of others. For example, mechanical laws are normally expressed dimensionally (i.e., with respect to classes of similar scales for *all* of the quantities involved), but laws involving angle, temperature, and electrical resistance are usually *not* expressed dimensionally, but with *specific* reference to the Radian, Absolute, or Ohm scales for these quantities. Rationally, however, these laws should also be expressed dimensionally, for then we should be able to use dimensional analysis more widely to discover the forms of derivative laws involving these quantities.

The most famous example of an empirical presupposition that was not recognised as such, and was consequently unquestioned by the scientific community, is probably that of the absoluteness of time. Before 1905, it had been almost universally assumed that times and time-intervals are the same for all frames of reference, so that time could be represented by a single variable. In his 1905 paper, Einstein abandoned this assumption, which, until then, had not been generally recognised even to be an assumption, and took the radical step of allowing that the times of events, and the time-intervals between them, might be different for different observers. Indeed he allowed that events that are simultaneous in one system might not be simultaneous in another. It may be doubted whether this was an *empirical* presupposition of classical physics; however, whatever its standing, it was unquestioned and, as it turned out, unwarranted.

The program of analysis and rational reconstruction I now wish to advocate would try to avoid disputes about the status of those propositions whose epistemic justification is in question, because such disputes detract from the program's main purposes. The question whether there is a clear or useful distinction to be drawn between what is empirical and what is conventional in science is no doubt an important one. However, the process of analysis and reconstruction I propose may be carried out whatever view one takes on this, and the results obtained will not be affected. If a proposition is rejected, it does not matter, for our purposes, whether the reasons for rejecting it are judged to be empirical, pragmatic, or a complex of both kinds of reasons. What matters is whether they are *good* reasons.

The main purposes of the new program of analysis and rational reconstruction are as follow:

1. To explicate the basic concepts of the various theories and practices of science.

2. To specify adequate boundary conditions for these theories and practices. In the case of a theory, a clear statement of the aims of the theory (e.g., to construct a theory of such and such a kind, compatible with such and such facts to explain the following data) is required. In the case of a practice, such as measurement or taxonomy, we need to know what its purposes are and how it seeks to achieve them.

3. To determine what further assumptions or choices must minimally be made to justify our current theories and practices, given these explications and specifications.

4. To consider what reasons there may be for making these assumptions or choices rather than others.

5. To work out in detail the consequences of making other assumptions or choices, where the reasons for making the usual ones do not appear to be strong.

6. To advocate changes to our theories or practices, where it can be shown that other assumptions or choices are preferable to the usual ones.

The new program retains what was important in the old conventionalist one, but strips it of its verificationist and empiricist assumptions. It is not suggested that it is always possible to draw a clear distinction between empirical and conventional elements in scientific theories. The purposes of the analyses required have nothing to do with the empiricist objective of trying to specify the empirical contents of the laws and theories of science. The new program is indeed compatible with epistemological holism and, therefore, with the view that this empiricist objective cannot even in principle be achieved.

The program is also compatible with a sophisticated scientific realism that does not always take the ontological claims of science at face value. A naive scientific realism that does do so is untenable anyway and is not warranted by the main argument for realism about theoretical entities. For this argument has force, only if the theoretical entities concerned are among postulated causes of the events explained by the theory. Even then we should not automatically assume that the entities referred to exist. Newton, for example, distinguished absolute space and time from relative spaces and times, and referred his laws of motion to this absolute framework. There can be no doubt that his explanations of the phenomena of motion were the best then available. However, it was not irrational for philosophers then, or since, to challenge Newton's ontology. If the ontological claims of science are justified, then let us see the arguments for them rather than appeal to authority.

REFERENCES

Brown, G. B. (1941). A new treatment of the theory of dimensions. *Proc. Amer. Phys. Soc., 53,* 418–431.

Byerly, H. C., & Lazara, V. A. (1973). Realist foundations of measurement. *Phil. of Science, 40,* 10–28.

Cartwright, N. (1983). *How the laws of physics lie.* Oxford: Oxford University Press.

Duncanson, W. E. (1941). The dimensions of physical quantities. *Proc. Amer. Phys. Soc., 53,* 432–448.

Ellis, B. (1966). *Basic concepts of measurement.* Cambridge: Cambridge University Press.

Ellis, B. (1971). On conventionality and simultaneity—a reply. *Austral. J. Phil., 49,* 177–203.

Grünbaum, A. (1968). *Geometry and chronometry in philosophical perspective.* Minneapolis: University of Minnesota Press.

Pettit, P., & Sylvan, R. (forthcoming).

10 Are There Objective Grounds for Measurement Procedures?

Karel Berka
Czechoslovak Academy of Sciences, Prague

TOWARDS A PHILOSOPHY OF MEASUREMENT

History of science testifies to the growth of measurement procedures in various branches of science and technology. This tendency was expressed by the well-known dictum of Galileo: "To measure what is measurable and to try to render measurable what is not so as yet." It was further strengthened by the development of natural science, especially physics, and during the second half of this century extended to behavioral and social sciences as well.

The common practice of utilizing measurement procedures as widely as possible, even beyond their justifiable range, is closely connected with extensions of mathematical concepts and methods in social practice, and is one important aspect of contemporary mathematization. One can, therefore, assume that measurement theory and philosophy of measurement, which until recently were elaborated only very partially, will undergo a development similar to mathematical metatheory and philosophy of mathematics. What I have in mind is the transition from Hilbert's program of formalization to Tarski's emphasis on semantics, and from semantics to Quine's ontological commitment implied by the adopted language of mathematics.

Naturally this is only a very broad analogy. What is relevant for present purposes is the overt tendency for certain philosophical or metaphysical assumptions to express themselves in measurement theory, although often in positivist terminology. This tendency can be roughly characterized by the change from the position advocated in 1966 by B. Ellis (1966 p. 3) who based his "consistent positivist account of the nature of measurement" on the thesis "that certain metaphysical presuppositions, made by positivists and nonpositivists alike, have played havoc with our understanding of many of the basic concepts of measurement, and concealed the existence of certain more or less arbitrary conventions"—to the modification of his view, as presented in this volume.

In pointing to the increased interest in philosophical analyses of measurement, I cannot neglect mentioning the previous, rather methodologically oriented approaches: homocentric operationalism as represented by H. Dingle (1950), methodological operationalism as advocated by P. W. Bridgman (1959), instrumentalism, conventionalism, and the formalism closely connected with a model platonism (Radnitzky, 1973, p. 40). The realistic conception of Byerly and Lazara (1973), which stresses the importance of philosophical foundations in measurement theory for the elucidation of its basic concepts and procedures, represents the starting point for a new systematic philosophy of measurement.

The variety of partial or more complex approaches to philosophical foundations of measurement reflect the perennial struggle between materialism and idealism in history of philosophical thought, and could easily induce scientists to adopt a neutral standpoint toward philosophical problems of measurement, of course without intending to follow the positivists in this regard. It is clear that, when deciding whether this or that philosophical position is correct and appropriate for solving basic problems of some scientific theory, one cannot proceed with the precision and strength available in logical or mathematical proofs. What is feasible, however, is to adopt the method of Aristotle, who, in his first philosophy, supported the fundamental principles of cognition and knowledge by pointing out the absurd consequences that would follow, if they were violated.

MATERIALISTIC VERSUS IDEALISTIC FOUNDATIONS OF MEASUREMENT THEORY

In the present chapter, I shall defend an ontologically committed conception of measurement, in agreement with the materialistic solution of the fundamental philosophical question of whether matter is prior to mind. The fruitfulness of this materialistic position will be demonstrated by an analysis of various controversial topics in measurement theory.

The advocated standpoint has the following basic components:[1]

1. Measurement is ontologically committed (i.e., rooted in and, hence, grounded by objective reality).

2. Magnitudes are historically and theoretically determined reflections of quantitative aspects of objectively existing entities and not merely the outcome of metricization or measuring procedures.

---

[1]See (Berka, 1983, p. 206).

3. The object of measurement exists prior to metricization or measuring procedures.

4. In agreement with the historical determination of every phenomenon, a transfer of methods from one universe of discourse into another one is adequate only on the objective condition that certain structural similarities hold between the domains in question.

In its accentuation of the ontological grounding of measurement, the materialistic standpoint clearly opposes various shades of positivism, logical positivism, and postpositivism. Presupposing a dialectical unity of qualitative and quantitative aspects of measured entities, it aims toward a unification of the empirical operations used in measuring procedures and the conceptual operations utilized in metricization. Such an approach may overcome the one-sidedness of both operationalism and formalism, which in fact represent the Charybdis and Scylla of contemporary philosophy of measurement.

The materialistic standpoint differs from the idealistic one in several respects. The most important respect, which will be unacceptable to many measurement theorists, is its ontological grounding. The view that measurement is ontologically grounded has direct consequences for the scope of measurement. Opposing thinkers will simply "reject the view that quantities have a kind of primary ontological status", (Ellis, 1968, p. 38), because they are well aware that, by admitting such a view, the range of measurability cannot be conventionally extended. The ontological status of magnitudes determines objectively the possibility of measurement and at the same time narrows the concept of measurement into an objectively restricted frame.

This consequence of course vitiates the attempt of many proponents of extraphysical measurement to apply measurement in various fields of behavioral and social sciences, and even in humanities. Having in mind "the dignity implied by the term measurement" (Stevens, 1960, p. 45), they strive to achieve a very broad conception of measurement. This goal requires also a very vague definition of measurement, according to which measurement is defined as "the assignment of numerals according to rule," or more explicitly as the "assignment of numerals to things so as to represent facts and conventions about them" (Stevens, 1960, pp. 145, 148).[2]

What follows from this viewpoint? We can, according to some rule, assign numerals to practically everything so as to create a nominal scale; thus, the range of measurement is not objectively limited. This boundless extension of measurement is supported by the fact that, for a nominal assignment of numerals, it is very easy to formulate some rule, for example, "Do not assign the same numeral

---

[2]These definitions have their origin in Campbell's (1957, p. 267) following definition: "Measurement is the assignment of numerals to represent properties;" but Campbell used the term "numeral" in a different sense.

to different classes or different numerals to the same class" (Stevens, 1960, p. 145). Such assignment fulfills the requirement of operationalism according to which measurement is concerned only with operations.

This conception together with its consequences contradicts the materialistic, foundational view of measurement. If we are to conclude that the object of measurement exists independently and prior to measuring procedures, we have to refute the view that measurement is just created by these procedures. The theoretical reproduction of quantitative aspects of objectively existing entities requires the assignment of numbers and not the assignment of numerals, which, in the criticized conception, are merely labels, names of numbers. The results so far attained by measurement procedures in social practice yield sufficient evidence that the broad conception is incorrect and misleading. The value of measurement consists in its ability to generate numerical data that help us to formulate numerical laws or to test empirical hypotheses.

It has to be further pointed out that operationalism ignores the fact that every empirical operation, if it has to convey theoretically relevant results, presupposes various hypotheses that depend on the objective nature of the measured entities. That a magnitude cannot be measured by a single operational procedure in the whole range of its occurrence is again objectively determined by the specificity of nature. This variability of measurement procedures is of course also dependent on the attained level of our theoretical knowledge. These circumstances, not the measuring operations or the nature of the measuring instruments, primarily determine the process of measurement. I need not mention that the construction of measuring instruments is based on numerical and empirical laws as well as on theoretical considerations, again a fact that operationalism does not take into account. Every change in the theoretical level modifies the operations used. The differentiation of operational procedures when measuring some magnitude under different conditions and in various ranges (e.g., when measuring length in very short and very far distances, on Earth or in the Universe) is objectively determined and has important methodological features that are closely connected not only with the theoretical framework of a given scientific branch but also with broader philosophical conceptions. This does not, however, imply fragmentation of magnitudes into various observationally reproducible instances. If it is possible, when measuring some magnitude, to obtain approximately identical numerical values by different operations, this outcome testifies to the fruitfulness of these operations and enables us to make the numerical results more precise but does not support the operationalist standpoint. The selection of operations is not primarily a matter of some pragmatic advantage but a result of theoretical insight and substantive adequacy rooted in the nature of the object of measurement.

A quite different standpoint, which, however, has very similar consequences, is defended by adherents of formalism. In their attempt to develop a theory of measurement, they concentrate their investigations on purely formal problems. On the formalist conception, the ultimate goal is the proof of two theorems, axiomatically deduced:[3] a representation theorem and a uniqueness theorem. They assume that the conditions of metricization[4]—in the weaker case, only those of topologization—are sufficient to constitute special magnitudes of various kinds of nonextensive measurement.

Before analysing this formal standpoint, let me note that axiomatization in logic or mathematics serves the goal of deductive systematization of some theory previously studied only intuitively, together with the clarification of the deductive and definitional structure of the theory in question. An axiomatic system in this case contains, besides axioms, primitive terms, inference rules and definitions, and a very large subset of theorems.

Such axiomatic systems can be found in works dealing with the systematization of extensive magnitudes, where various axiomatizations are isomorphic with axiomatic systems elaborated in arithmetics. As an example, consider the axiomatic systems of O. Hölder (1901) or E. V. Huntington (1902), which are explicitly related to mathematics.

Axiomatizations in the field of nonextensive magnitudes or measurements in behavioral and social sciences as developed by adherents of the formal approach are different. Axiomatic systems of intensive magnitudes (e.g., expected utility) or of various kinds of measurement (e.g., difference measurement, bisection measurement, or conjoint measurement) are not intended to reveal the structural features of some theory. They have been explicitly elaborated for one reason: to deduce the representation theorem and the uniqueness theorem.

Both theorems describe the metricization conditions for some nonextensive magnitude and a corresponding measurement scale whose numerical values are expected to be obtained. The real reason why axiomatization is so widely utilized in measurement theory of intensive magnitudes flows from a desire to justify the concept of measurement by formal means in a very broad sense and to overcome the well-known difficulties of behavioral and social measurement.

Against this specific, axiomatic approach, several objections can be raised. Many of these have been made by M. Allais (1953) in connection with axiomatized expected utility theory.

It is not difficult to show that the axioms are provided neither with a sufficient syntactical and semantical justification nor with a convincing empirical interpretation that would serve as a basis for actual measurements. One should recall the discussions concerning the relationship of structural and behavioral axioms, and the attempts to prove the empirical nature of the strong independence axiom of P. A. Samuelson (1952, p. 672) and the sure-thing principle of L. J. Savage (1954, pp. 21ff).

Another objection is based on the argument of conceptual economy. It seems rather "expensive" to use a very complicated, formal procedure with the humble

---

[3]See (Krantz, Luce, Suppes, & Tversky, 1971).
[4]See (Hempel, 1952).

result of deducing only two theorems. However, what is more, the whole, deductive chain leading to them is burdened with serious doubts whether the deduction is correct from the logical or methodological point of view. The empirical relational systems are assumed to be logically prior to the numerical ones; therefore, the axioms cannot refer to numerical expressions. Nonetheless the theorems deduced from these nonnumerical axioms deal with numerical expressions. Both horns of the dilemma resulting from this situation are apparent: Either the representation theorem is not solely deduced from the axioms, or the axioms contain, at least implicitly, numerical connotations. If the derivation of the basic theorems is not exclusively determined by the axioms, then it is incorrect from the logical point of view. If some numerical assumptions are implicitly contained in the axioms, then the deduction is invalid for methodological reasons.

It is further questionable whether the deduction of both theorems, if one concedes their validity from the logical and methodological points of view, can be considered as a sufficient grounding of the measurability of some nonextensive magnitude. The theoretical conditions under which a magnitude can be measured do not yet guarantee its measurability by empirical procedures. The construction of a mathematical model must be tested in practice. Such a test requires a significant empirical interpretation of its concepts and a feasible operationalization of the metricization conditions.

Another critical remark amounts to the following argument. In order to check the theoretical appropriateness and the practical relevance of both basic theorems, one does not need to construct an axiomatic system at all. Instead of this approach (which is difficult, due to lack of justification for the choice of the primitive notions and axioms), it suffices to substitute the axiomatic justification of the representation theorem by an immediate formulation of correspondence rules holding between the empirical and numerical characteristics of both relational systems, whereas the uniqueness theorem can be supplanted by the property of invariance of a scale with regard to its admissible transformations. This direct procedure is very simple and plausible. An empirical interpretation and operational verification of the conditions required to obtain numerical results, by measuring some intensive magnitude, will immediately show whether or in what sense it is correct to assume that these conditions obtain.

Neither operationalism nor the formal approach recognize that measurement is ontologically committed and that this objective determination constitutes the foundation of its conceptual and theoretical framework. Seen from this point of view, it is obvious that the assignment of numbers to empirical entities—in agreement with the conditions of metricization—is appropriate, only if (and because) these entities have some quantitative aspects.

The thesis that ontological assumptions are necessary preconditions for measurability neither implies nor requires an unmediated, direct relationship. We can significantly assign numbers to empirical entities also in a mediated way (as, e.g., in the case of associative measurement). However, a purely qualitative aspect of empirical entities that cannot be related somehow to a quantitative aspect cannot be measured in the strict sense of the term. Without such a relation, the assignment of numbers would not be adequate; it would neither reflect the degree nor the size of the quantitative aspects in question.

The core of the materialistic position is that objective reasons make it impossible to change the ontological status of a property by metricization or measuring operations. The assignment of numbers cannot be understood in the sense of reductionism, for one cannot reduce qualities to quantities by measurement procedures. Neither conventions nor postulates can, thus, replace the constraint of what is objectively measurable and what is not.

The thesis of the ontological dependency of measurement procedures of course cannot be absolutized, because measurement is also historically determined by the evolution of social practice, by the growth of knowledge. The dialectics of the process of cognition include the active role of man, the socially conditioned reflection of his activities, in the given case those of various measurement procedures and measurement conceptions. It would be a mistake, or rather a concession to mechanistic or vulgar materialism, to deny the influence of man's activities when constructing and using diverse measurement procedure or the relative impact of measuring instruments and techniques on measuring operations and their results. From the standpoint of dialectical and historical materialism, the thesis of the priority of the ontological status of magnitudes yields a theoretically adequate and methodologically fruitful conception of measurement only when it is connected with the thesis of the historically determined nature of this method.

SOME SPECIAL PROBLEMS OF MEASUREMENT

I will now consider the implications of the materialistic conception of measurement for various miscellaneous topics in measurement theory.

The distinction between fundamental and derived measurement, and between fundamental and derived magnitudes, is acknowledged by all measurement theorists. However, its elucidation is—in regard to the ontological and antiontological standpoints in the philosophical foundations of measurement—a matter of dispute. The dispute arises from the view of operationalism that magnitudes depend on measuring operations described in a purely phenomenological manner. According to operationalism, if one succeeds in constructing some measuring instrument by means of which a derived magnitude can be directly measured, then the derived magnitudes changes into a fundamental one. (E.g., the density of a liquid is considered as a derived magnitude, if its numerical values are obtained by calculation from the numerical values of volume and mass, but, if measured directly by some instrument—for example, a hydrometer—it will be considered a fundamental magnitude.) Thus, every change in instrumental techniques modifies the division between basic and nonbasic magnitudes. However, these modifications are determined only operationally, not objectively.

A similar problem arises with regard to temperature measurement on Stevens' theory of scales. If we measure temperature by using a scale with an arbitrary zero, as is the case of Reaumur or Celsius scales, it will be considered, by antiontological measurement theorists, as a magnitude measurable by means of an interval scale. However, when utilizing the Kelvin scale, which employs an absolute zero, temperature has to be classified as a magnitude measurable by means of a ratio scale. The difference between these types of scales is often related to the difference between nonextensive and extensive magnitudes, or between nonadditive and additive ones. In consequence, Stevens' view implies that a magnitude can be both extensive and nonextensive.

The nonontological conceptions have unpleasant consequences, and they lead to a serious discrepancy between the theoretical framework of physics and dimensional analysis. By adopting the materialistic standpoint, these difficulties can easily be avoided. The decision, whether a magnitude belongs in the class of fundamental or derived magnitudes, has its objective grounds. The class of magnitudes that are fundamentally measured in the known system of physics and, hence, conceived as fundamental is determined by the structure and evolution of objective reality and its theoretical reflection by man. The distinction between fundamental and derived magnitudes, although it can per analogiam be explicated by the function of primitive and defined concepts of some axiomatic system, is neither conventional nor arbitrary. From the materialistic point of view, length is a fundamental magnitude for reasons stemming from the nature of objective reality, whereas density will remain a derived magnitude, even if it can be measured fundamentally.

Operational criteria violate fundamental measurement. Every magnitude (e.g., length), which, for ontological reasons, is the most basic fundamental magnitude, presupposes the possibility of assigning numerical values from the domain of real numbers. However, only rational numbers are attainable by actual measurement procedures. The set of empirically measured values of a magnitude is practically finite but theoretically infinite. Numerical laws of physics require values from the set of real numbers, which is infinite; therefore, these laws cannot rest on operationalist methods. A very simple example supports this criticism: From the operationalistic point of view, the length of the hypotenuse of a square whose side is equal to 1 meter cannot be determined. The use of operational procedures will have fruitful results only if there are objective conditions that are connected on one side with the nature of the measured entities independently (whether we have or have not constructed for them some measuring operation) and, on the other side, with calculations based on theoretical considerations. Without an objectively determined and theory-laden interpretation of the results obtained by measurement procedures, no scale value is actually significant.

Another problem of extraphysical measurement, whether based on Stevens' theory of scales, Hempel's conception of metricization, or the axiomatic deduction of representation and the uniqueness theorems, arises in connection with the ontological dependency or independency of concepts used when describing the nature of the empirical relational system. It is assumed that this empirical system is the starting point of the construction of scales of measurement, metricization or axiomatic deductions. In fact, however, the empirical nature of its basic concepts and operations is only pretended. This becomes obvious when we take into account the concept of equality as used in Stevens' conception. One cannot maintain that "nominal scales . . . are merely scales for the measurement of identity and difference" (Ellis, 1968, p. 42), because identity is without any doubt just a purely logical concept. Similarly such operations as "determination of equality of ratios" (Stevens, 1960, p. 143); "forming the center of gravity" (Neumann & Morgenstern, 1953, p. 21) (or, to use verbal equivalents, "combination of alternatives," "combined options," "mixed prospects"), which have to be performed on elements of the empirical relational system, cannot be understood *in pleno sensu* as empirical operations. These seemingly empirical concepts and operations are in reality quasiempirical counterparts of numerical concepts and operations.

Another characteristic example of this problem is the search for some adequate empirical counterpart of the numerical operation of addition implied by the requirements of extensive measurement. There are great obstacles to finding some appropriate equivalent in the outer world to the concatenation operation, even in the measurement of length; thus, various suggestions have been made to replace or narrow these requirements. In J. Pfanzagl (1959, p. 284), additivity is replaced by a metric connection concerning the distance holding between scale numbers, which makes a regular division of scale intervals possible. However, this conception lacks an objectively justified background in those cases where there does not exist a really empirical equivalent to the numerical addition. Even if one acknowledges that the metric connection is theoretically and methodologically acceptable, it is weaker than the usual additivity condition of extensive measurement. Even the additivity condition is dropped in the case of non-extensive measurement, and empirical interpretation is required only for fundamentally measured magnitudes. Other magnitudes that are measured by derived or associative measurement procedures can be measured in the strict sense of this term (i.e., as instances of extensive measurement), if they are connected by theoretical, numerical, or empirical laws with fundamentally measured magnitudes. (This conception, which is illustrated by the measurement of temperature, has to be accepted.)

Setting aside the just-mentioned difficulties of extraphysical measurement, the advantage of the reversed order between the empirical and numerical relational systems is quite clear. It is well known under what conditions the assignment of numbers can be considered with full right as an instance of measurement; therefore, the proponents of the very broad measurement conception are striving to find for the relevant numerical concepts and operations some counterparts with a more or less plausible empirical interpretation. An overt admission of this intention in the case of utility, the measurement of which has become the standard model of extraphysical measurement, appears in the initial specification of expected utility theory by J. Neumann and O. Morgenstern (1953) in the following words: "We have practically defined numerical utility as being the thing for which the calculus of mathematical expectation is legitimate" (p. 28).

This approach is in principle admissible, if the following conditions are fulfilled. First, when introducing an empirical interpretation for numerical concepts and operations, we have to be well aware of the difference between the idealized mathematical concept and its fuzzy counterparts in reality, and draw from this fact the necessary conclusions (e.g., in respect to the empirical unrealizability of the transitivity property). Second, if measurement has to fulfill its practical goals, the empirical interpretation has to be further complemented by operational realizations. Finally, if the interpretation is to be a truly empirical one, we have to check its ontological footing. This last step is often avoided for various reasons, chiefly because it is intuitively known but not taken into account that, in the given instance, no feasible empirical equivalent with an operational realization can be correlated with the relevant numerical concept or operation. For example, there is usually no feasible empirical operation of addition in such cases.

An "experimentum crucis" to defend my standpoint against the proponents of extraphysical measurement can be devised for the zero point (scale zero) or the origin of a scale, and the existence of the measurement unit.

When dealing with different kinds of temperature scales, an arbitrary or conventional scale zero of the Celsius, Reaumur, or Fahrenheit scales is confronted with the natural or absolute origin of the Kelvin scale of temperature. Without going into details,[5] I will only point out that the existence of an arbitrary origin of a scale cannot be considered as a confirmation of conventionalism in measurement theory. I do not deny that the scale zeros of temperature scales that admit "positive" and "negative" scales values are more conventional than the absolute zero of the Kelvin scale. However, in spite of this fact, and the term "arbitrary," these scale zeros are not arbitrarily stipulated but ontologically determined by dependency on objective laws of nature and are simultaneously influenced by social practice as well. The boiling and freezing points of water under constant conditions in respect to other factors (as, e.g., pressure of air) that determine the calibration of thermometers in general use are due to the construc-

---

[5]But see (Berka, 1983, pp. 87ff).

tion of such instruments, especially with regard to the thermometric substance represented by different scale numbers. This "convention" is evidently less arbitrary than it seems at first glance.

When analysing the question of measurement units, the conventions applied in selecting measurement units are also arbitrary only in a very limited sense. Their choice is historically determined and for this reason shows a considerable variability, but not arbitrariness, even when we take into account the variety of units that man has used in different epochs and countries for the measurement of length, mass, or volume. The choice of various units for the measurement of one and the same magnitude is never made without sufficient reason, at least from the standpoint of its originator. If the choice of units were really conventional, there would be no difficulty in introducing units for magnitudes assumed to be measurable in behavioral or social science. The lack of appropriate measurement units in this domain testifies convincingly that measurement units cannot be introduced arbitrarily. The existence of measurement units in physical measurement and the absence of them in most instances of extraphysical measurement must be considered the decisive argument against view that measurement units are conventional. This view has been adopted by adherents of the antiontological standpoint as rationalization for an unjustified extension of measurability. These facts concerning units are a clear confirmation of the objective nature of measurement procedures and of their ontological determination.

A CASE STUDY: EXPECTED UTILITY

The measurability of expected utility is commonly regarded as a model case of extraphysical measurement of intensive magnitudes. This justification is based, so to speak, on a relative proof, that is, on an analogy with temperature measurement.

Assuming the measurability of temperature by means of an interval scale, one attempts to show that the measurement of expected utility has the characteristic features of interval scales; namely (a) a constant unit of measurement, (b) an arbitrary scale zero, and (c) invariance of scale form under any linear transformation.

This analogy, as I shall now briefly indicate, does not serve its purpose, because neither of the three conditions is satisfied. The proponents of the view that utility is measurable at least on an interval scale have not succeeded in producing a unit of measurement nor even an acceptable pseudounit. Some authors have introduced, as a unit, the utile, however, without sufficient reasons for this choice and without an explication or empirical reproducibilty. The proposal of S. S. Stevens (1959, p. 55) to define one utile as the utility of one U.S. dollar is absurd. To refute this view, it suffices to point out that this proposal contradicts Bernoulli's conception of the "moral" value of money as opposed to its "numerical" value. Other authors[6] try to find a way out by introducing arbitrary numbers without labeling them. If one employs this approach, one cannot avoid considering one of these arbitrarily chosen numbers as the unit of measurement and some other one as the origin of the scale. If there are no grounded reasons for these choices, why not take as a unit the number 3 or 121? The absurdity of this possible consequence is obvious. Neither will it help to follow the suggestion of E. W. Adams (1960, p. 183) to take, as a unit, the difference between 0 assigned to the least desirable alternative and 1 assigned to the most desirable one.

The arbitrariness of the zero of the utility scale cannot be understood in the same sense as the zero of temperature scales. For the origin of the utility scale— by contrast with that of the temperature scales—can be practically chosen without restriction, that of satisfying the ordinal property of expected utility, namely $u(x) < u(y)$. This restriction in fact allows an unlimited choice. It is curious that the proponents of the analogy of temperature and utility scales do not see that it already fails, simply because the scale zero of temperature measured on an interval scale does not represent the smallest value. By contrast, the zero of the utility scale is usually selected in a manner analogous to that for the zero of the Kelvin scale. Can we, therefore, conclude that utility is a magnitude measurable on a ratio scale? The standard numerical representation of the utility scale in its canonical form—for example, limiting the utility interval by the numerical interval [0,1], where the number 0 functions as an absolute zero—is in fact determined by the requirement of isomorphism between the quasinumerical utility interval and the numerical probability interval, or rather by their illegitimate identification. Both intervals differ of course in essential ways: the elements of the utility interval are formed by desirabilities of alternative events (prospects, options, etc.), whereas those of the probability interval are determined by probabilities of the occurrence of the alternative events in question.

The first two conditions are not satisfied; thus, eo ipso neither is the third one fulfilled. The linearity of utility and the linear transformation of interval scales differ. For utility scales, there is no significant interpretation of the transformation formula.

$$y = ax + b \quad a > 0$$

The transformation of two interval scales (e.g., represented by the Celsius and Fahrenheit scales) requires that the constants a and b have a semantically justified and operationally realizable sense: a indirectly designates the unit of measurement and b the scale zero. However, this requirement does not hold for utility scales.

---

[6]E.g., (Luce & Raiffa, 1957, p. 33).

CONCLUSION

The thesis that measurement has its objective grounds that cannot be neglected or arbitrarily surpassed supports a restricted concept of measurement. It will, therefore, disappoint all those who desire to extend measurement procedures to various branches of behavioral and social sciences in an extreme manner. This desire cannot be satisfied at any cost. There are objective limits for measurement procedures, as for other forms of mathematization. The utilization of measurement in physics cannot be taken as the paradigm for all sciences. It should not lead us to an uncritical standpoint that would ignore the ontological limitations and historical determination of measurement. If, in behavioral and social sciences, qualitative procedures predominate over quantitative ones, no derogatory evaluation of these disciplines is thereby implied. People are not rigid bodies. Hence, the analysis of their behavior cannot be made by procedures utilized in mechanics. Mathematical methods, including measurement, outside natural sciences will lead to fruitful outcomes, only if they are applied in accord with the regularities and evolution of objective reality and by means that are theoretically justified, empirically feasible, and developed, if not on materialistic foundations, at least on a realistic basis.

REFERENCES

Adams, E. W. (1960). Survey of Bernoullian utility theory. In H. Soloman (Ed.), *Mathematical thinking in the measurement of behavior* (pp. 151–268). Glencoe, IL: Free Press.

Allais, M. (1953). Le comportement de l'homme rationnel devant le risque: critique des postulates et axiomes de l'ecole americaine. *Econometrica, 21,* 503–546.

Berka, K. (1983). *Measurement: its concepts, theories and problems.* Dordrecht: Reidel.

Bridgman, P. W. (1959). *The way things are.* Cambridge, MA: Harvard University Press.

Byerly, H. C., & Lazara, V. A. (1973). Realist foundations of measurement. *Phil. Science, 40,* 10–28.

Campbell, N. (1957). *Foundations of science: The philosophy of theory and experiment.* New York: Dover. Original work published 1920

Dingle, H. A. (1950). Theory of measurement. *Brit. J. Phil. Science, 1,* 5–26.

Ellis, B. (1966). *Basic concepts of measurement.* Cambridge: Cambridge University Press.

Hempel, C. G. (1952). *Fundamentals of concept formation in empirical science.* International Encyclopedia of Unified Science, *II*(7). Chicago: University of Chicago Press.

Hölder, O. (1901). Die Axiome der Quantität und die Lehre vom Mass. *Berichte der Sächs. Ges. Wiss., Math.-Phys. Classe, 53,* 1–64.

Huntington, E. V. (1902). A complete set of postulates for the theory of absolute continuous magnitude. *Trans. Amer. Math. Soc. 3,* 264–279.

Krantz, D. H., Luce, R. D., Suppes, P., & Tversky, A. (1971). *Foundations of measurement* (vol. 1). New York: Academic Press.

Luce, R. D., & Raiffa, H. (1957). *Games and decisions: introduction and critical survey.* New York: Wiley.

Neumann, J. v., & Morgenstern, O. (1953). *Theory of games and economic behaviour* (3rd ed.). Princeton: Princeton University Press.

Pfanzagl, J. (1959). A general theory of measurement—application to utility. *Naval Research Logistics Quarterly, 6,* 283–294.

Radnitzky, G. (1973). Toward a theory of research which is neither logical reconstruction nor psychology or sociology of science. *Teorie a metoda* (Theory and method), *2,* 25–54.

Samuelson, P. A. (1952). Probability, utility and the independence axiom. *Econometrica, 20,* 670–678.

Savage, L. J. (1954). *The foundations of statistics.* New York: Wiley.

Stevens, S. S. (1959). Measurement, psychophysics, and utility. In C. W. Churchman & P. Ratoosh (Eds.), *Measurement: definitions and theories.* New York: Wiley.

Stevens, S. S. (1960). On the theory of scales of measurement. In A. Danto & S. Morgenbesser (Eds.), *Philosophy of science* (pp. 141–149). New York: Meridian.

11 Measurement from Empiricist and Realist Points of View

Zoltan Domotor
University of Pennsylvania

The term "measurement" conjures up many meanings. It suggests ways of assigning numbers to extents of quantities, types of interaction between physical systems and sensors, modes of detection, coding, transfer and storage of information, and much more.

In this chapter, I shall concentrate on certain obstructions to empiricist conceptions of measurement and on some realist ways of overcoming them. Furthermore, I will propose a framework for reasoning about measurement theories. The need for such a framework is prompted by the ever-increasing proliferation of representation results in axiomatic measurement theory and the desire for unification. Traditional epistemology holds that measurement is a fundamental means by which we come to know things. No details of this idea seem to be available even within the simplest instance of measurement theories; therefore, I will give an account of how measurement results affect the states of our knowledge.

My main task here is to bring the empiricist and realist viewpoints into sharper focus than customary by showing their specific consequences within the context of measurement theories. The position I will defend takes theoretical quantitative structures to be of primary empirical importance, whereas the spectrum of associated qualitative measurement structures is regarded as secondary. However, unlike some realists, including Friedman (1983), I perceive observable structures not as some sort of partial submodels of certain theoretical models but as appropriate quotient structures of these models, obtained by classifying away some of their theoretical aspects. The idea is that theoretical models are *projected* onto their observational structures, and being so, some features are understandably lost or forgotten. Formally this is the exact opposite of *injecting* or embedding observational structures into larger theoretical models, frequently criticized by the realists.

As in Domotor (1981), I continue to recognize the importance of quantitative representations of qualitative structures, but my conclusion will be that representation or injection of the qualitative into a quantitative is fully justified only when coupled with the dual procedure of projection.

In their attempts to understand how science works, some philosophers of science find it important and interesting to single out and contrast the *empiricist* and *realist* approaches to scientific theories. These approaches differ primarily over the attitude they take to the nature of theoretical terms and theoretical laws introduced by a scientific theory—in our case, quantities and their lawlike relationships. According to the empiricist approach, the fact that a theory happens to be presented within a language that is blessed with abstract theoretical terms does not mean that these terms are to be taken seriously. There is no reason to suppose that the world actually contains anything that corresponds to these special terms. The tasks that the theory has to perform do not in any way require such metaphysical commitments. Similar things are believed about the nature of theoretical laws. Laws are adequate to the extent that they respect the data and lead to good predictions, and the question of their global truth is not for science to answer.

To this, the realist objects on two counts. First, a theory is more than just an instrument for deriving predictions; it actually must satisfy our demand for explanation by telling us how and why things happen. However, for this purpose, the theory must be taken as something that aims at a *genuine* description of what actually goes on. Further, a theory's success in yielding predictions would itself be mysterious unless there was in fact some connection between the way the theory worked and the way reality is. Second, the practice of science shows that it is precisely by viewing theories realistically that science progresses. It is by thinking of theories as literal albeit perhaps approximate descriptions of what goes on that we are able to suggest good ways of extending or generalizing them and can see where they might require modification. To this, the empiricist responds by pointing out that realism principally expresses the overall goals of science rather than its actual structure. In addition, what the structure of science suggests is that there is no fixed ontology and everlasting semantics. Instead there are many alternative theoretical ontologies and interpretations, and, in some cases, there is a mathematical approach to how these ontologies are created and how interpretations are conceived.

Unfortunately, in view of their excessive generality and abstractness, these arguments have limited force in the delicate contexts of measurement.

Currently there are two basic approaches to measurement, which I shall call the *representational* approach and the *interactionist* approach.

In the representational approach, one deals with numerical (and possibly geometric) representations of certain qualitative empirical structures of measurable attributes. The underlying doctrine of these representations is a modern-day implementation of Ramsey's empiricist methodology. As is well-known among philosophers of science, for Ramsey (1950), every empirical theory comes in a bifurcated language. Observational facts and their phenomenological generalizations are stated in a *primary* language L_0, whereas the systematizing, theoretical aspects of these facts are expressed in a conceptually fancier *secondary* language L. Linkages between the primitives of these languages are made visible by suitable *correspondence* rules. What is important for us is that the empirical semantics of L_0 is quite different from that of L. Although the ontology and meaning of terms in the primary language are fully determined by the intended experimental procedures, the meaning of theoretical terms in the secondary language is widely open and the metaphysics of these terms is of secondary importance. Theoretical terms are conceptual analogs of fictional characters, and, as such, their job is not so much referring to reality as organizing and systematizing our theoretical reasoning about reality. Calling L a "secondary" language surely expresses this sort of semantic or metaphysical contempt.

Now how does a scientific theory $\mathbf{T}(L_0,L)$, erected over a disjoint pair of languages L_0 and L, manage to refer to reality? As Ramsey saw it, the theory succeeds in referring to reality precisely via its body $\mathbf{T}(L_0,L) \upharpoonright L_0$ of *observational* consequences, and, I would add, its class of validating models Mod $\mathbf{T}(L_0,L) \upharpoonright L_0$. Ramsey also noted that every observable prediction $P(L_0)$ made by the full theory $\mathbf{T}(L_0,L)$ can be made equally well, logically speaking, by the ontologically less demanding *Ramsey sentence* $\exists L\ \mathbf{T}(L_0,L)$ of the theory, obtained by second-order existentially quantifying away all primitives in L as they occur in the formulas of the theory:

$$\frac{\mathbf{T}(L_o,L) \vdash P(L_o)}{\therefore \exists L\,\mathbf{T}(L_o,L) \vdash P(L_o)}$$

However, there is more. The Ramsey sentence is first-order derivable within the observable component $\mathbf{T}(L_0,L) \upharpoonright L_0$ of the theory precisely when the models of this component coincide with the observational reducts of models of the full theory:

$$Mod(\mathbf{T}(L_0,L) \upharpoonright L_0) = (Mod\ \mathbf{T}(L_0,L)) \upharpoonright L_0.$$

When this high-flown logical terminology about the commutativity between models and languages is brought down to earth, it says that a Ramsey sentence is true precisely when the observational fragment of a model of the theory is extendable—by adding appropriate theoretical structure—to its full model. In other words, the L–terms are eliminable from $\mathbf{T}(L_0,L)$ precisely when the models of the observational component $\mathbf{T}(L_0,L) \upharpoonright L_0$ are extendible to appropriate models of $\mathbf{T}(L_0,L)$.

Applying this view to measurement, the Ramsey-style empiricist point is that a generic measurement theory is built over a pair of disjoint sets of qualitative/quantitative primitives, where only the qualitative part of the theory is of primary empirical importance. Quantitative terms play only a pragmatic role in that they aid the formulation of the theory as a whole and make it conceptually and calculationally manageable.

A representationalist research program, therefore, consists in axiomatic characterizations of the qualitative (observational) components of measurement theories, necessary and/or sufficient for proving the Ramsey sentences of these theories.

According to the interactionist approach, measurement is based on a physical interaction between a measuring instrument by which the measurement is carried out and a physical system on which the measurement is being done. At the end of the interaction, the instrument indicates its result of measurement (i.e., some fragment of information obtained by the instrument about the value of a measured attribute of the system).

The formal background for interactionist theories goes back to the classical distinction between *intensive* and *extensive* quantities. Quite specifically, with every ring R of measurable magnitudes (reals being the prime example) and a physical space X, there comes a ring R^X of intensive quantities on X with their possible magnitudes in R, defined by suitable (continuous, measurable) maps from X to R. The central features of intensive quantities, essential in dimensional analysis, are their multiplicativity and contravariance. Thus, in addition to being a linear space, the space R^X is actually a ring under pointwise multiplication

$$f \cdot g(x) = f(x) \cdot g(x)$$

for all x in X and $f \cdot g$ in R^X.

Furthermore, intensive quantities transform contravariantly in the sense that every map $h : X \to Y$ induces a ring homomorphism $R^h : R^Y \to R^X$ in the reversed direction, defined by the usual functional composition $R^h(f) = f \circ h$. Here and below the notation $h : X \to Y$ means that h is a function with domain X and codomain or range Y.

Dually with every ring R and a physical space X, there comes a module $R(X)$ of extensive quantities on X with their magnitudes in R, defined by measures on X. The fundamental characteristics of extensive quantities are their linearity or convexity (in the case of probabilities) and covariance. What this means is that $R(X)$ is a module over the ring R^X, and every map $h : X \to Y$ induces an unreversed module homomorphism $R(h) : R(X) \to R(Y)$, defined by the direct image formula

$$R(h)\mu(B) = \mu(h^{-1}(B))$$

for all measurable subsets B of space Y and measure μ in $R(X)$.

Now these dual pairs of spaces of intensive and extensive quantities are brought together by the fundamental bilinear inner product or evaluation map $\langle | \rangle : R^X \times R(X) \rightarrow R$, defined by the usual expectation integral

$$\langle f \mid \mu \rangle = \int_X f(x)\mu(dx),$$

and satisfying the principal substitution law $\langle f | R(h)\mu \rangle = \langle R^h(f) | \mu \rangle$. Finally Radon–Nikodym derivatives produce intensive quantities from pairs of extensive quantities (e.g., density from mass and volume), and, in general, the foregoing inner product generates extensive quantities from pairs of intensive/extensive quantities. By including tensor products of extensive and/or intensive quantities, representing empirical interactions, we obtain virtually every type of quantity used in natural science in general and in physics in particular.

According to the interactionist view, measurement is basically a species of physical interaction that is capable of empirical instantiation of the inner product defined previously. So a result of measurement is nothing more than the numerical value of some empirically realized inner product, involving the quantity measured and some other quantities, characterizing the state of the system and its form of interaction with the measuring instrument.

It is important to point out that the representational measurement theorists have not succeeded thus far in convincing the interactionists to go beyond the inner product conception of measurement. In my own view, this is precisely the place where many realists part company with the empiricists. Inner products lead to numbers in a nice way, so why go beyond?

It is high time we looked at some specific examples, discussed mainly from an empiricist point of view.

OBSTRUCTIONS TO EMPIRICIST INTERPRETATIONS OF MEASUREMENT

How is measurement possible? Empiricists of today hold that measurement hinges on the possibility of a quantitative *representation* of stereotype bodies of qualitative data regarding objects, events, and actions. The aim of measurement theory, therefore, is to discern and lay bare the species of those data structures that actually admit such representations.

The relevant formal methodology is *axiomatic*. Data structures are described in terms of mixtures of empirically testable and technically or normatively desirable axioms, and they are reasoned about *extensionally* in terms of suitable set-theoretic predicates, defined by the axioms, including "is an extensive measurement structure," "is an intensive measurement structure," "is an additive conjoint measurement structure," and many, more. The most important measurement-theoretic task is to find empirically adequate lists of axioms that guarantee the existence of desired quantitative representations and possibly characterize or cast light on the nature of their uniqueness.

I begin, as a way of entering the subject of this section, by characterizing a particular empiricist interpretation of measurement, which, although not representative of the more recent formulations of some writers, is, in my view, the most frequent form encountered in current textbooks and monographs, including Pfanzagl (1968), Krantz, Luce, Suppes, & Tversky (1971), Roberts (1979), and Narens (1985).

Throughout this chapter, I will illustrate the relevant measurement-theoretic concepts with simple examples drawn from the realm of measuring subjective probability. I dwell on these examples in order to emphasize the importance of representational measurement theory in the social sciences as opposed to natural science, where interactionist theories are important. Further, as Adams (chapter 4 in the present volume) shows this circle of examples is worth studying in detail, because it beautifully illustrates and motivates the methodological problems of axiomatic measurement. Finally examples will I hope help lessen the risk of becoming lost in an abyss of formal definitions so typical in modern measurement theory textbooks.

From a logical point of view, much of axiomatic representational measurement theory may be viewed as a series of instantiations of and variations on the following dual pair of Ramsey formulas:

Representation

$$\mathbf{M}(E,\rho) \text{ iff } \exists P[\mathbf{C}(E,\rho,P) \text{ \& } \mathbf{T}(E,P)]$$

Uniqueness

$$\mathbf{M}'(E,\rho) \text{ iff } \forall P[\mathbf{C}(E,\rho,P) \Rightarrow \mathbf{T}'(E,P)]$$

Here $\mathbf{M}$ and $\mathbf{M}'$ are suitable set-theoretic predicates, defined by strings of *observational* (phenomenological) axioms and applicable to various, intended qualitative measurement structures (E,ρ) of a fixed similarity type, consisting of a domain E and some relational structure ρ thereon. In contrast, $\mathbf{T}$ and $\mathbf{T}'$ are *theoretically* motivated set-theoretic predicates, expressed by theoretical axioms and satisfiable by appropriate, real-valued quantitative structures (E,P), closely linked to the presumed qualitative structures (E,ρ). This linkage is captured by a correspondence relation $\mathbf{C}(E,\rho,P)$.

As a simple illustration, take the popular qualitative measurement structure $(E,\precsim)$, given by a finite boolean algebra E of events over some sample space and impressed with a de Finetti-style qualitative probability $\precsim$ (at most as likely as). Then under the correspondence relation

$$\forall x,y \in E \ [x \precsim y \Leftrightarrow P(x) \le P(y)] \tag{1}$$

linking concepts E, $\precsim$ and P, the foregoing Ramsey representation formula is true of $(E,\precsim)$, just in case the predicate $\mathbf{M}$ is presented by the familiar Scott–

Adams axioms of qualitative probabilities, referred to in Adams (chapter 4 in this volume), and **T** is the predicate defined by the classical Kolmogorov axioms for finitely additive probability spaces (E,P). Here we use the symbolism $\mathbf{T}(E,P)$ as short for the sentence "The set-theoretic structure (E,P) *is* a finitely additive Kolmogorovian probability space," and similarly the notation $\mathbf{M}(E,\precsim)$ abbreviates the subject–predicate nexus "The set-theoretic object $(E,\precsim)$ *is* a qualitative probability structure in the sense of Scott and Adams."

Under the preceding instantiation, the Ramsey formula for *representation* says that, granted a qualitative measurement structure $(E,\precsim)$ of de Finetti's probabilistic data, a necessary and sufficient condition for the existence of a Kolmogorovian probability measure on E *agreeing* with $\precsim$ is the truth of Scott–Adams axioms in the measurement structure $(E,\precsim)$.

Regarding *uniqueness,* take $\mathbf{M}'$ to be the set-theoretic predicate determined by de Finetti's axioms for subjective probability, and let $\mathbf{T}'$ be a predicate generated by axioms for convex mixing. It is easy to check that, in our context, a convex mixture of agreeing probabilities is again an agreeing probability. We will see later that the uniqueness predicate $\mathbf{T}'$ is fully characterized by the barycentric subdivision of the simplex of all probabilities defined on the boolean algebra E.

As pointed out before, given theoretical frameworks $\mathbf{T}$ and $\mathbf{T}'$ together with a version of the correspondence relation (1), the main job of a representational measurement theorist is to identify the bodies of empirically adequate axiomatic systems for $\mathbf{M}$ and $\mathbf{M}'$ in such a way that both Ramsey formulas hold. A plentiful and varied supply of representation results arises in this way; some are trivial, and some are rather difficult.

The Ramsey sentence conception remains valid even in the context of fuzzy or probabilistic relations, where the atomic observations $x \precsim y$ are viewed as members of a more general lattice than a boolean algebra, or are replaced by probabilistic data $p[x \precsim y]$ requiring an equational correspondence

$$p[x \precsim y] = P[U_x \leq U_y],$$

involving a joint probability distribution of a family of real-valued random variables $U_x, \ldots, U_y$. Here the idea is that the observational probability p of ranking object y higher than object x must coincide with the value of a theoretically given probability distribution P of an agreeing ranking of a corresponding pair of random variables.

If we read the Ramsey formulas from right to left, they in effect tell us how to do science without numbers. Under a related interpretation, they tell us how to define real numbers in terms of their uses. The converse reading is of course what representational measurement is all about: a carefully controlled introduction of quantities into the context of qualities.

Generalizations of Ramsey formulas, involving empirical operations and several types of observational structure, should not detain us here. In any case, they do not lead to qualitatively different situations. Let me just add that the classical extensive measurement structure of von Helmholtz (1887) and Hölder (1901), represented by additive quantities, have won indisputable permanence in the corpus of representation results. Here I want to inject that, in the process of searching the measurement literature, I failed to find references to an equally important early work by Hahn (1907), pertaining to *infinitesimal* quantities. With due respect to Krantz et al. (1971), a well-known, ex-colleague of mine characterized representational measurement theory as the enterprise of proliferating boring corollaries to Hölder's theorem. The theorem in question is the foundation-stone of extensive measurement theory, and it concerns the order-preserving embeddability of Archimedean ordered groups into the additive group of reals. Hahn showed a similar embeddability of ordered Abelian groups into lexicographically ordered Cartesian powers of the field of reals. To complete the comment about Hölder, my ex-colleague's point is not to allow a tool become a straightjacket. Although today simple variations on the theme of Hölder's theorem will no longer do, for a while, nothing was suggested to take its place, except perhaps some separation theorems borrowed from linear programming and the mathematical background for solving functional equations. Be that as it may, in my view, whereas the correct mathematical language in which to speak "measurementese" is not yet available, there are several mathematically and foundationally interesting results that make the business of measurement attractive to both philosophers and applied mathematicians. The reasons why a flexible mathematical theory is demanded by measurement is easy to provide. Consider the measurement of subjective probability in the context of de Finetti's qualitative data structures $(E, \lesssim)$. Suppose we perturb the data by replacing the boolean algebra E with a quantum lattice of events, represented, say, by subspaces of a Hilbert space. In seeking an agreeing representation of $\lesssim$ in terms of a Gleason probability measure on the quantum lattice E, we find that not only we need some new necessary axioms, including $x \lesssim y \Leftrightarrow y^\perp \lesssim x^\perp$, to supplement the classical list of de Finetti's axioms, but more importantly we need a new method, because none of the old-known construction techniques work in this context.

Having completed the preliminary remarks on the Ramsey picture of measurement, let me now turn to the major task of this section, namely the discussion of certain methodological obstacles to the development of empiricist measurement theory. To set the tone of my remarks, I will start with some technical questions first.

TROUBLING PROFUSION OF REPRESENTATION RESULTS

One embarrassing problem the empiricist-oriented representational program suffers from is its endless proliferation of measurement representation results. From a logical standpoint, this problem stems from the fact that generally two existential Ramsey-style quantifiers cannot be melted down into one. The following example illustrates my point.

Suppose we have a representation of the qualitative probability relation $\precsim$ on some algebra of events E in terms of a quantitative probability P_1 on E under the correspondence rule

$$x \precsim y \Leftrightarrow P_1(x) \le P_1(y),$$

and a representation of the qualitative probabilistic independence relation $\perp\!\!\!\perp$ on the same algebra in terms of a probability measure P_2 on E under the correspondence

$$x \perp\!\!\!\perp y \Leftrightarrow P_2(x \cap y) = P_2(x) \cdot P_2(y),$$

resulting in an appropriate pair of observational axiomatic characterizations $\mathbf{M}_1(E, \precsim)$ and $\mathbf{M}_2(E, \perp\!\!\!\perp)$. Recall that, for a pair of events x and y, $x \precsim y$ means "event y is at least as likely as event x," and $x \perp\!\!\!\perp y$ stands for "events x and y are probabilistically independent." Now, because $\precsim$ is usually representable with more than one agreeing probability measure, there is no reason to suppose that P_1 and P_2 coincide, even if $\precsim$ and $\perp\!\!\!\perp$ are in some sense compatible. To grant $P_1 = P_2$, a joint representation result $\mathbf{M}_{12}(E, \precsim, \perp\!\!\!\perp)$ must be found ab ovo! However, usually this is not just the mere conjunction of the earlier established marginal representations. Simply the equivalence

$$\mathbf{M}_{12}(E, \precsim, \perp\!\!\!\perp) \text{ iff } \mathbf{M}_1(E, \precsim) \And \mathbf{M}_2(E, \perp\!\!\!\perp),$$

fails in general! What is needed of course is a brand-new set of empirical axioms (encapsulated in $\mathbf{M}_{12}$) together with another representation result, which may neither be easy to find nor simple to test.

Next time around we may run into yet another species of qualitative data, say, $\Diamond x$ (symbolizing "event x is more likely than not"), leading to a third marginal correspondence

$$\Diamond x \Rightarrow P_3(x) > 1/2.$$

So we need a new axiomatic system $\mathbf{M}_{123}(E, \precsim, \perp\!\!\!\perp, \Diamond)$, which covers all three species of data with one quantitative representation.

To finish the point, the representation result will have to be reworked from scratch every time a measurer runs into or comes up with a new type of data, closely related to but not definable in terms of the old data. Thus, measurement theories, unlike some nature scientific theories, are not rejected by measurers here and there piecemeal but as a matter of course holistically. We already know, from Ramsey, why this sort of conceptual game with representation results is empiricistically inevitable. For an empiricist, the interpretation of theoretical concepts (such as the probability measures introduced above) is thought to be *open* in the sense that their empirical meanings are not fully determined by measurements in which they occur. Now since new measurement techniques may be adjoined at any moment of time to the current stock of such techniques, the class of data structures is actually never closed, and thus the need for new representation results never ends.

To remedy this defect, some realists insist on interpreting the quantitative concepts P *literally* in the sense that the observational structures $(E, \precsim)$, $(E, \perp)$ and $(E, \Diamond)$ are presumed to be *identical* with or plain substructures of the respective $(E, \precsim_P)$, $(E, \perp_P)$ and $(E, \Diamond_P)$. Here the P-indexed qualitative concepts are those defined by means of biconditional correspondence rules, involving a single theoretical quantity P. Since under this view correspondence rules are perceived as definitions, the problem of representation disappears.

I do not accept this extreme position in measurement, because it leaves no room for explaining how *fundamental* quantities are measured, and it leaves out the important fact that measurement theories are *projected* onto their possible observational consequences, crucial in testing.

What the empiricists seem to need is a kinematics of measurement representation—a theory that characterizes the possible *revisions* of old representation results in response to new types of qualitative data. In the final subsection, I shall consider what is to be done about the proliferation of representation.

Obstacles to Common Extensions of Qualitative Measurement Structures

Here I want to urge a different point that so far as I know has not been noticed before: Two or more data structures of the same similarity type need not admit aggregation.

It is clear that a single measurement structure, comprehensive as it may be, but isolated from the rest of the universe, is not an appropriate object of study. Measurement specialists measure length, temperature, vacuum, probability, or what have you, in many smaller, possibly overlapping domains and in several compatible ways. The question is how to aggregate the measurement results of these domains and techniques. To understand the problem in question, it will help to compare the qualitative approach with a quantitative treatment. Although what I have to say here applies to many species of extensive measurement structures, I will confine my attention only to the case of measuring subjective probability.

Suppose we are given two qualitative probability structures $(E, \precsim)$ and $(F, \precsim)$, defined over the same sample space, but generally with different algebras of events, both satisfying, say, the Scott–Adams axioms for qualitative probabilities. What are the conditions for the existence of a *common extension* $(E \bigvee F, \precsim \bigvee \precsim)$? Here $E \bigvee F$ denotes the smallest boolean algebra of events containing both E and F as subalgebras, and $\precsim \bigvee \precsim$ designates a new qualitative probability, namely the common extension of qualitative probabilities $\precsim$ and $\precsim$ to the joint algebra.

Marczewski (1951) showed, among other things, that, for any pair of finitely additive probability spaces (E,P) and (F,Q), conceived over the same sample space, a necessary and sufficient condition for the existence of a common extension $(E \bigvee F, P \bigvee Q)$, which is again a finitely additive probability structure, is their *compatibility:*

$$x \subseteq y \Rightarrow P(x) \leq Q(y),$$

for all events x in E and y in F. (Along standard lines $\subseteq$ denotes boolean inclusion.)

This sort of pairwise compatibility of probability spaces enjoys the familiar properties of commutativity of observables arising in quantum mechanics. Unfortunately nobody had previously had the ambition to apply these techniques to the study of aggregating extensive measurement structures.

Observe that, although there are qualitative crossmodality comparisons, as in "Peter is a better Catholic than Paul is a Jew," nothing nearly that complicated is needed in the quantitative case.

Marczewski showed even a stronger result, stating that a common extension $(E \bigvee F, P \bigvee Q)$ always exists with the *mixed-independence* property

$$P \bigvee Q(x \cap y) = P(x) \cdot Q(y)$$

for all x in E and y in F, whenever the constituent subalgebras E and F are *algebraically independent:*

$$x \cap y = 0 \Rightarrow (x = 0 \bigvee y = 0),$$

for all $x \in E$ and $y \in F$. (Here as well as elsewhere 0 denotes the impossible event and 1 refers to the sure event.)

To see some of the details, let $E(x)$ be the smallest boolean algebra containing the algebraically independent E and $\{0, x, \bar{x}, 1\}$. The elements of $E(x)$ have the form of disjoint sums $x \cap y + \bar{x} \cap z$ with $y, z \in E$; thus, we can define the common extension $P \bigvee Q$ on $E(x)$ of probabilities P and Q on the constituent algebras by setting

$$P \bigvee Q(x \cap y + \bar{x} \cap z) = P(x) \cdot Q(y) + P(\bar{x}) \cdot Q(z).$$

Using convex mixing, this definition is quickly extendible to cases where F is generated by a finite partition. Common extension in the context of arbitrary boolean algebras is obtained by passing to limits over directed sets of finitary partitions.

There are serious obstructions to extending these extremely useful modes of aggregation to the qualitative case. We assume as a matter of course that, when two agents measure, say, length in the realm of overlapping domains of rods, there is exactly one attribute measured, namely length, and the magnitudes of this attribute are the same—modulo units and errors—for all rods in the shared part of the domains, irrespective of the agents' measurement methods.

Unfortunately this is only a small part of a more systematic difficulty besetting the empiricist conception of measurement.

There are no Worthy Categories in Measurement Theory

Most representational measurement theorists readily enlist the help of modern mathematics in general and that of ordered algebraic structures in particular. In the spirit of Klein's Erlanger Program, and following Maclane (1971), most mathematicians accept the dictum that, whenever new mathematical structures are constructed in a specified way out of given ones, one should regard the construction of the corresponding structure-preserving maps on these new structures as an integral part of their definition. In this manner, one would arrive, quite naturally, at various *categories*, for example, of qualitative measurement structures and their structure-preserving maps. In particular, the category of qualitative probability structures satisfying the Scott–Adams axioms is defined by the class of structures $(E, \lesssim)$ of the familiar sort together with the class of maps $h:(E, \lesssim) \to (F, \lesssim)$, where h is a boolean homomorphism from E to F such that

$$x \lesssim y \Leftrightarrow h(x) \lesssim h(y),$$

for all $x, y \in E$. It is immediately evident that these maps are composable in the usual associative way and that each structure has its unique identity map serving as a unit of composition. Likewise the category of Kolmogorovian probability spaces is given by the class of these spaces and the class of their maps $h:(E, P) \to (F, Q)$, where h is a boolean homomorphism from E to F such that $Q(h(x)) = P(x)$. These maps compose in the usual associative way, and the identity maps of probability spaces act as units of the composition operation.

What is particularly upsetting about measurement categories is their lamentably feeble structure. When compared with the category of Kolmogorovian probability spaces, which enjoys several kinds of products, sums, and a host of other extremely important structural constructions, the category of qualitative probability structures lacks these constructs in the worst way. This would not matter, except that their existence is absolutely fundamental in developing a full-fledged probability theory capable of serving as a foundation for statistics and statistical physics. True, in general, qualitative measurement structures do possess lexicographic products, various completions and extensions, but none of these is of much help in attempts at developing the qualitative foundations some empiricists presume to be possible. The traditional view is that, because qualitative measurement structures resist the usual modes of *functorial* combination, it is better to think of them as being embedded into richer theoretical frameworks and work with the constructions available at a higher conceptual level. Nobody questions this move, except when the higher level theoretical frameworks appeal to concepts completely devoid of empirical meaning.

To illustrate these ideas, let us examine in some detail the case of quantitative versus qualitative probabilities. We begin by noting that the space $\mathbb{P}(E)$ of all probabilities on a boolean algebra E is not just any old amorphous set living in Plato's heaven. It is blessed with an excess of algebraic, topological, geometric, and order-theoretic structure. For example, in addition to Bayesian conditioning everybody uses, $\mathbb{P}(E)$ is closed under arithmetic mixing $P \underset{a}{+} Q$, defined by $P \underset{a}{+} Q(x) = a \cdot P(x) + (1 - a) \cdot Q(x)$, where $0 \leq a \leq 1$. This operation enables us to show that the space of probabilities is actually a simplex, a notion generalizing an important geometric aspect of line segments, equilateral triangles, perfect tetrahedrons, and so on. The space of probabilities is closed under geometric mixing and several species of lattice operations, and it admits strong and weak topologies, and many interesting and important metrics. Last but not least, the simplex $\mathbb{P}(E)$ carries the familiar relations of *dominance*,

$$P \ll Q \text{ iff } Q(y) = 1 \Rightarrow P(y) = 1$$

for all $y \in E$; and *orthogonality*,

$$P \perp Q \text{ iff } P(y) = 1 \ \& \ Q(y) = 0$$

for some $y \in E$.

In sharp contrast, observe that the space $\mathbb{Q}(E)$ of all qualitative probability relations on E satisfying the Scott–Adams axioms is much harder to handle conceptually, due to an almost total lack of structure, readily available in $\mathbb{P}(E)$. Although we still have dominance and orthogonality even in the qualitative case, the algebraic and metric structures have all but disappeared. Space $\mathbb{Q}(E)$ is too coarse-grained relative to $\mathbb{P}(E)$ to be of foundational use. How is $\mathbb{Q}(E)$ obtained? Formally it is a collection of abstraction classes of probabilities, obtained by the equivalence

$$P \equiv Q \text{ iff } P(x) \leq P(y) \Leftrightarrow Q(x) \leq Q(y)$$

for all $x,y \in E$. To be more exact, space $\mathbb{Q}(E)$ is isomorphic to the quotient structure $\mathbb{P}(E)_{/\equiv}$ of probability measures, modulo their *order indiscernibility* $\equiv$.

This sort of abstraction explains the importance of the *projection* map

$$\sqsubset: \mathbb{P}(E) \to \mathbb{Q}(E)$$

that sends every probability P onto its qualitative probability ordering $\sqsubset_P$, defined by

$$x \sqsubset_P y \text{ iff } P(x) < P(y).$$

Thanks to Scott–Adams axioms, there is also a *Ramsey embedding* or *injection*

$$\mathbb{R} : \mathbb{Q}(E) \to \mathbb{P}(E),$$

going in the reversed direction and picking a probability $\mathbb{R}(\precsim)$ for every prescribed qualitative probability relation $\precsim$. These fundamental maps are brought together by the following identities:

$$\sqsubset \circ \mathsf{R} = id_{\mathbb{Q}(E)} \text{ and } \mathsf{R} \circ \sqsubset \equiv id_{\mathbb{P}(E)},$$

where id_D denotes the identity function with domain and codomain being equal to D.

Formally the first identity says that R is a *section* of the projection $\sqsubset$. There may be several of these; therefore, let *Ram* $\mathbb{Q}(E)$ be the set of all Ramsey embeddings (injections, sections) of $\mathbb{Q}(E)$ into $\mathbb{P}(E)$. It is clear that, for any pair of Ramsey embeddings R^1 and R^2, their arithmetic mixture $\mathsf{R}^1 {}_a^+ \mathsf{R}^2$, defined coordinatewise, is again a Ramsey embedding. The convex space *Ram* $\mathbb{Q}(E)$ provides a neat algebraic characterization of the problem of uniqueness of probabilistic representation.

Geometrically $\mathbb{P}(E)_{/\equiv}$ represents the barycentric subdivision of the simplex $\mathbb{P}(E)$; thus, we have a lemma that characterizes the problem of uniqueness geometrically.

LEMMA 1. *The space $\mathbb{Q}(E)$ of qualitative probability relations on a finite algebra E satisfying the* Scott–Adams *axioms is in* one-to-one *correspondence with the set of components of the barycentric subdivision of $\mathbb{P}(E)$.*

Proof. Ignoring the trivial case with one atom, it is easy to check that algebras generated by two atoms admit exactly five qualitative probability relations, precisely the number of components in a barycentric subdivision of the unit interval.

Now, as the picture (below) of the barycentric subdivision of a 3–simplex (equilateral triangle) indicates, algebras generated by three atoms, x, y, and z admit $10 + 21 + 12 = 33$ qualitative probability relations.

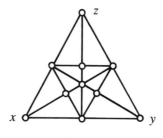

FIG. 11.1

Indeed direct inspection reveals that 10 such relations are defined by families of equivalences among events, and they correspond to the vertices (0–dimensional components) of the barycentric subdivision of $\mathbb{P}(E)$. In particular, upon setting $x \sim y$, iff $x \precsim y$ & $y \precsim x$, we get the following list of possible probability relations: (a) $x \sim y$ & $z \sim 0$, (b) $x \sim z$ & $y \sim 0$, (c) $y \sim z$ & $x \sim 0$, (d) $x \sim 1$ & y

$\sim z \sim 0$, (e) $y \sim 1$ & $x \sim y \sim 0$, (f) $z \sim 1$ & $x \sim y \sim 0$, (g) $x \sim y$ & $x \cup y \sim z$, (h) $x \sim z$ & $x \cup z \sim y$, (i) $y \sim z$ & $y \cup z \sim x$, and (j) $x \sim y \sim z$. Another 21 probability relations are determined by mixtures of equivalences and strict comparisons of events, corresponding to open segments (1–dimensional components) of the barycentric partition. Finally the remaining 12 probability relations are specified by possible strict comparisons, corresponding to open faces (2–dimensional components) of the barycentric subdivision.

Straightforward but tedious mathematical induction on the number of atoms in E, coupled with the classification of possible equivalences and strict comparisons of events, proves the validity of the lemma in general.

We see that qualitative probability relations provide a triangulation of the quantitative probability space $\mathbb{P}(E)$, which may be refined further by other species of qualitative data. Although qualitative probability relations may determine unique probability measures in some special cases, in no way do they determine their quantitative structure! For example, although every Ramsey embedding satisfies

$$\precsim \; \ll \; \precsim \quad \text{iff} \quad \mathbb{R}(\precsim) \ll \mathbb{R}(\precsim),$$

and similarly

$$\precsim \; \perp \; \precsim \quad \text{iff} \quad \mathbb{R}(\precsim) \perp \mathbb{R}(\precsim),$$

it does not define mixing and other important structure in $\mathbb{P}(E)$.

The appropriate moral to draw from these brief remarks is that representing quality in terms of quantity is one thing, and matching their structures is yet another.

In conventional treatments of subjective probability, it is customary to study one particular (generic) qualitative probability ordering and one instance of a representing probability measure. With overtones of realism, I am choosing the study of the *spaces* of these notions, together with their pairs of projective/injective maps.

Some Unexplained Jumps from Qualitative Reality to Quantitative Mathematics

Objects, events, and actions possess myriad properties and stand in countless relations. Of course most of these features are measurement theoretically uninteresting. Measurement focuses primarily on *qualities* (i.e., empirically detectable aspects in virtue of which things may be identified), qualified or compared. We have seen, for example, that, in considering subjective probabilities of events, the main relations or properties of interest were belief comparison $\precsim$, probabilistic independence $\perp\!\!\!\perp$, and epistemic possibility $\diamond$.

It is common to grant axiomatically or as a fait accompli that every quality ϕ

comes with its custom-made comparative $>_\phi$ (is ϕ–er than or is more ϕ than) assumed to be typically transitive and connected. Associated with every (strict) comparative relation $>_\phi$, there are what one might call the *indifference* relation $\sim_\phi$ (is as ϕ as) and the *weak comparative* relation $\gtrsim_\phi$ (is at least as ϕ as). The indifference $\sim_\phi$ generates (by virtue of being an equivalence relation) its abstraction classes that define extensionally the notion of ϕ–*ness* of things. Thus, thing x has the ϕ–ness of y just in case $x \sim_\phi y$.

In some cases, *rational* comparisons of the sort "is twice as ϕ as" or "is half as ϕ as" are introduced. In this context, it is particularly common to stipulate a closed empirical operation $\oplus_\phi$ on things with properties analogous to those of numerical addition. However, often it is not fully realized that, in order to avoid oddities of the sort $x \oplus_\phi x$ (e.g., placing a straight rod end-to-end in a straight line with *itself*), one must consider mereological part–whole relations, which will tell us when the combined objects are separated and, hence, composable, and when they share a common part and, thus, are not composable.

What exactly is the logic of passing from qualities ϕ to their comparatives $>_\phi$ and combinations $\oplus_\phi$? To my best knowledge, the empiricists do not have a good answer.

Suppose the quality ϕ we are interested in is television violence. Grammar enables us to form a comparative $>_\phi$ (movie x is more violent than movie y). This is hardly worth much, but measurement theory will tell us something about the order-theoretic properties of $>_\phi$. However, how will this knowledge alone help the measurer in *measuring* television violence without knowing beforehand a great deal about television violence per se?

It is important to note that empirically it is far clearer whether one movie is more violent than another, than whether a given movie is violent. In view of this, some philosophers tend to analyze qualities in terms of their comparatives rather than the other way around. For example, a violent television movie is on this view a movie more violent than most movies of its kind. If this view were correct, then it should explain how different species of comparative relations (including interval ordering, semiordering, and weak ordering—one of these for each measurement method) manages to pick out always the same quality, in our case television violence. However, as we have seen in the case of measuring subjective probability, it is far from trivial to show that two comparatives of a given species must refer to the same quality.

Transformation grammarians tell us that "x is more violent than y" is actually derived by a suitable transformation from "x is violent" and "y is violent." The problem with this suggestion is that there are no interesting comparatives that are definable classically in terms of properties. The following lemma explains why this must be so.

LEMMA 2. *Given a binary relational structure (E, ρ), the merging condition*

$$(x \rho y \,\&\, z \rho w) \Rightarrow x \rho w$$

is both necessary and sufficient *for the existence of unary relations U and V on E such that the decomposition*

$$x \; \rho \; y \; \text{iff} \; Ux \; \& \; Vy,$$

holds for all x,y $\in$ E.

Proof. Given U and V as wanted, evidently we have

$$(Ux \; \& \; Vy) \; \& \; (Uz \; \& \; Vw) \Rightarrow (Ux \; \& \; Vw).$$

Now, granted a binary relation ρ with the merging property, take the direct $U = \rho(E)$ and inverse $V = \rho^{-1}(E)$ images of the domain E under the relation ρ, and you will see at once that the decomposition holds.

Furthermore, it is not hard to see that the boolean dual of the margining condition in Lemma 2 (reverse the implication, and replace conjunction with disjunction) is necessary and sufficient for the existence of a disjunctive decomposition $x \; \rho \; y$ iff $Ux \lor Vy$. Indeed upon selecting U and V in such a way that their complements satisfy $\bar{U} = \bar{\rho}(E)$ and $\bar{V} = \bar{\rho}^{-1}(E)$, we find that the dual result also holds.

It is natural to ask whether there are similar results for some other logical decompositions. A truth table for binary logical operations shows that the only remaining meaningful decomposition we have not considered so far is the following: $x \; \rho \; y$ iff $Ux \Leftrightarrow Vy$. This decomposition works precisely when $(x \; \rho \; y \Leftrightarrow z \; \rho \; w)$ iff $(z \; \rho \; y \Leftrightarrow x \; \rho \; w)$. In verifying this result, we can set $U = \bar{\rho}(a)$ and $V = \bar{\rho}^{-1}(b)$ for some fixed $a,b \in E$. Here as well as previously $\bar{\rho}$ denotes the complement of ρ, and $\rho(a)$ is the image of element a.

Getting back to our problem, we see that there cannot be any logically interesting transformations that will take us from qualities to comparatives.

An equally objectionable move is to derive comparatives by quantifying over degrees or extents, as Seuren (1973) suggested. Seuren proposed analyzing "*x* is longer than *y*" in terms of "*x* is long to an extent to which *y* is not." Here "*x* is long to extent *e*" means *not* that *x* is exactly that long but that *x* is at least that long. Although the truth conditions for the sentences of the form

$$\exists e[x \text{ is long to extent } e \; \& \; y \text{ is not long to extent } e]$$

come out correctly under this interpretation, note that Seuren quantified into an intensional context. A far more troubling point is that the ontology of extents and degrees is quite unclear. Extents and degrees fall prey to objections raised against abstract objects: What is the nature of their domains, and what are the rules that generate them? We need to know what is meant by claiming that a given quality is present in each object to some extent or another.

There are a variety of other ways that extents or degrees might be built into comparative relations, but none of them is satisfactory as far as I can tell. For example, "x is brighter than y" may be analyzed in terms of a quantified conjunction

$$\exists d_1 \exists d_2[x \text{ is bright to degree } d_1 \ \& \ y \text{ is bright to degree } d_2 \ \& \ d_1 \text{ is higher than } d_2].$$

The inherent circularity is obvious: The relation "is higher than" is one of the comparatives we are trying to define!

Often differences of degree can themselves be compared, and the comparative constructions may be iterated. For example, we can pass from "x is longer than y" to "x is more longer than y than z is longer than w," and in turn to "x is *more* (more longer than y than z is longer than w) *than* (u is more longer than v than v is longer than t)." Never mind whether anybody can take in by ear this comparative. The question follows: How do we know that it makes sense for some given qualities and not for others? Comparatives of this sort are important in measuring the rate of change of a rate of change (e.g., in accelerated motion). Clearly these comparatives thrive in the riches of a given scientific theory.

The production of *double* comparatives is even more mysterious. Think about the relationship between the following comparatives and the underlying pairs of qualities:

1. Agent x has read more books in more languages than agent y.
2. Policy x makes more people happier than policy y.
3. Agent x types more words per minute with less number of mistakes than agent y.

In the last example, the description "the greatest number of words per minute with fewest mistakes" does not pick out a unique agent in general. It is not clear to me how these comparatives ought to be numerically represented.

Nozick (1981, pp. 490–494) proposed to measure moral weight by considering a simultaneous comparison of wrong-making features and right-making features of pairs of human actions. With considerable hand waving, Nozick assumed that the underlying measurement structures will lead to feasible numerical representations. Unless he meant the usual variety of conjoint measurement that ignores the crucial factor of interaction between right and wrong, which, therefore, is rather uninteresting empirically, one must remain skeptical about the merit of Nozick's measurement-theoretic proposal.

Finally we have the *intensional* comparatives of the sort "Jones is heavier than he was." It seems that this type of comparative might be reduced to the usual treatment of "heavier than" by stipulating the relation on the set of temporal slices of Jones. Unfortunately no such treatment will avail for "Jones looks heavier than he is" or "Jones is heavier than he looks." Some philosophers seek to refer to possible worlds or situations in which Jones might live or in which there is a counterpart of Jones. Evidently the domain of possible worlds in this case is quite arbitrary, and any relational or topological structure one wishes to impute to it is beyond proper justification.

It is unclear to me how measurement theory ought to reckon with more complex intensional comparatives, such as "Object x is heavier than S thinks y is" or "Agent S thinks x is heavier than x in fact is."

So how big a leap do we in fact make when we pass from real-world qualities to mathematical quantities? We are aware that a mathematical structure is somehow associated with a stereotype domain of objects and that this structure is then studied by purely mathematical means in order to obtain empirically important and theoretically interesting theorems. The knowledge of these structures is presumed to constitute a form of understanding of the nature of measurement.

The gap between qualitative reality and quantitative mathematics is measured by the extent to which measurement results developed internally within measurement theory reflect our external practice. The search for a smooth passage from the qualitative to a quantitative is in my view misguided, because every step in conceptualization is in effect a form of abstraction that denies or imputes degrees of freedom to reality and thereby creates a gap between what really is and what our concepts say there is.

A Plea for More Realism in Measurement

Often order relations are introduced not because there are some operational procedures to instantiate them, but because there is a need for characterizing approximation, one wants to solve extremal problems, and so on. For example, depending on the choice of a meet-closed subset S of E, the simplex of probability measures $\mathbb{P}(E)$ may be ordered in a number of ways for purposes of approximation by setting

$$P \lesssim Q \text{ iff } P(x) \leq Q(x),$$

for all $x \in S$. This sort of *stochastic order* relation may be refined further by defining a series of conditional stochastic orderings

$$P \lesssim_w Q \text{ iff } P_y \lesssim Q_y,$$

for all $y \in W$, where P_y denotes the classical Bayesian conditional "P given y," and W is a suitable subset of events in E.

For example, if the underlying sample space of E is partially ordered, we can take S to be the set of monotonic events in E (i.e., events containing with every sample all the other samples ranked higher).

These order relations are introduced primarily on theoretical grounds with no particular regards to possible operationalization; thus, there is neither a need nor a hope for a testable representation result. Additional examples of order relations on $\mathbb{P}(E)$ that are introduced in this measurement-like manner may be found in

Stoyan (1983). Some might suggest that this sort of methodology ought not to be part of measurement theory.

As I see it, representation of qualitative measurement structures is only half of the measurement-theoretic program, the embedding or injective part. The other half of the program—the projective part—concerns the development of qualitative structures, which serve as forgetful images of quantitative structures.

The nonexistence of a common extension of qualitative probabilities is seen in a different light when we realize that these probability orderings are coarse-grained projections of powerful quantitative concepts. In the passage to the qualitative, these structures have lost their capability to aggregate. Representation results proliferate because of the representationalists' perception that every qualitative structure must somehow be quantitatively represented. We have seen that, although joint representations cause serious problems, projections are free. In answer to the question raised at the end of the section about proliferating representation results, I suggest to project first and represent later.

REASONING ABOUT MEASUREMENT THEORIES

Whoever browses the recent theoretical books on measurement is struck by the type of reasoning used in their texts. Besides the extensive use of set-theoretic predicates (such as "is an extensive measurement structure" or "is a concatenation measurement structure"), there are repeated references to and justifications of various representation results.

The variety of measurement representation results is best seen as a repeated instantiation of a small number of simple Ramsey sentences of the following form:

$$\exists P[\mathbf{T}(P) \ \& \ \mathbf{C}(\rho,P)],$$

whereas uniqueness results may be viewed as realizations of the dual Ramsey sentence

$$\forall P[\mathbf{C}(\rho,P) \Rightarrow \mathbf{T'}(P)].$$

Here $\mathbf{T}$ and $\mathbf{T'}$ are suitable set-theoretic predicates, representing quantitative theories, and $\mathbf{C}$ is a set-theoretic correspondence between qualitative relations and numerical functions or quantities P. From now on, we shall adopt the habit of dropping explicit references to domains E, serving as parameters in Ramsey sentences, on which the relations and quantities P are presumed to be defined.

Let us now see what more can be said about the relationships between Ramsey sentences and measurement theories, as understood by the empiricists. We begin by associating with every correspondence $\mathbf{C}$ a conjugate pair of modal (closure) operators $[\mathbf{C}]$ and $\langle \mathbf{C} \rangle$. In particular, for every set-theoretic predicate $\mathbf{M}(\rho)$, we define a new set-theoretic predicate $[\mathbf{C}]\mathbf{M}(\rho)$ by putting

$$[\mathbf{C}]\mathbf{M}(\rho) \text{ iff } \exists P\{\forall\sigma[\mathbf{C}(\sigma,P) \Rightarrow \mathbf{M}(\sigma)] \ \& \ \mathbf{C}(\rho,P)\},$$

and, in a dual fashion, we define $\langle C \rangle M(\rho)$ by setting

$$\langle C \rangle M(\rho), \text{ iff } \forall P\{\forall \sigma[M(\sigma) \Rightarrow C^*(\sigma,P)] \Rightarrow C^*(\rho,P)\},$$

where C^* denotes the logical dual of C.

Therefore, in the case of $C(\rho,P)$ being interpreted as "P is a Kolmogorovian probability satisfying $x \, \rho \, y \Leftrightarrow P(x) \leq P(y)$, the predicate formula $[C]M(\rho)$ captures the existence of a probability measure together with the necessity of the qualitative axioms, characterizing the predicate $M(\rho)$. The meaning of $\langle C \rangle M(\rho)$ is related to uniqueness statements in the same manner. It would require a longer detour to give a full discussion of these modal ideas here. I confine myself to a simple lemma, which justifies the importance of previously given definitions.

LEMMA 3. *For any correspondence* C *the necessity operator* $[C]$ *satisfies the following axioms of modal logic:*

1. $[C]M(\rho) \Rightarrow M(\rho)$.
2. $[C][C]M(\rho) \Leftrightarrow [C]M(\rho)$.
3. $[C]M_1(\rho) \Rightarrow [C]M_2(\rho)$, if $M_1(\rho) \Rightarrow M_2(\rho)$.
4. $[C_1]M(\rho) \Rightarrow [C_2]M(\rho)$, if $C_1(\rho,P) \Rightarrow C_2(\rho,P)$.
5. $[C]C(\rho,P) \Leftrightarrow C(\rho,P)$.
6. *Solutions of the fixed-point equation*

   $$[C]M(\rho) \Leftrightarrow M(\rho)$$

   with predicate unknown M *(ρ) have precisely the form of a* Ramsey *sentence:* $M(\rho) \Leftrightarrow \exists P[T(P) \, \& \, C(\rho,P)]$ *for some predicate* T.
7. *Solutions of the fixed-point equation*

   $$\langle C \rangle M(\rho) \Leftrightarrow M(\rho)$$

   with predicate unknown $M(\rho)$ *have precisely the form of a dual* Ramsey *sentence:* $M(\rho) \Leftrightarrow \forall P[C(\rho,P) \Rightarrow T(P)]$ *for some predicate* T.

Proof. The clauses of this lemma are entirely trivial, except perhaps clauses (6) and (7), and these we proceed to prove.

Let $M(\rho)$ iff $\exists P[T(P) \, \& \, C(\rho,P)]$, and suppose $M(\rho)$ is true. Then $T(P_0)$ and $C(\rho,P_0)$ must hold for some P_0. Now $C(\sigma,P_0) \Rightarrow [T(P_0) \, \& \, C(\sigma,P_0)]$ gives $C(\sigma,P_0) \Rightarrow \exists Q[T(Q) \, \& \, C(\sigma,Q)]$ for all σ, and, hence, after substitution, $\forall_0[C(\sigma,P_0) \Rightarrow M(\sigma)] \, \& \, C(\rho,P_0)$. Consequently we have the truth of $\exists P\{\forall \sigma[C(\sigma,P) \Rightarrow M(\sigma)] \, \& \, C(\rho,P)\}$ and, hence, that of $[C]M(\rho)$. Thus, Ramsey sentences of the foregoing type are indeed solutions of the fixed-point equation in clause (6).

Now suppose $S(\rho)$ is a solution of the fixed-point equation in (6). Then by definition the modal closure $[C]S(\rho)$ is automatically a special case of a Ramsey sentence, and, therefore, so is $S(\rho)$, in view of (2). The proof of clause (7) is a formal dual of that of (6).

Therefore, every qualitative measurement predicate $M(\rho)$ is logically approximated from below by its associated Ramsey sentence $[C]M(\rho)$ in the sense of clause (1), where the degree of approximation is contingent upon the choice of the correspondence relation **C**. Empiricists tend to select **C** parsimoniously with special regards to the truth of **M**(ρ), whereas some realists grant **C** a priori with special emphasis on its explanatory power.

The obvious failure of the equivalence

$$[C \cap D](M(\rho) \ \& \ N(\sigma)) \text{ iff } [C]M(\rho) \ \& \ [D]N(\sigma),$$

explains the phenomenon of proliferation of representation results. The kinematics of representation is captured by iterating the correspondence-driven modalities, as in **[C][D]M**(ρ). Note, however, that iteration collapses to joint representation in the sense of **[C][D]M**(ρ) = **[C** $\cap$ **D]M**(ρ) precisely when the correspondence relations are independent.

The preceding modal reasoning is a special case of a more general approach, involving categories. In what follows, I will present a convenient category **Meas** of measurement predicates and relations between them. In this setting, the modal operators will act as abstract maps. Specifically an object of this category is an equivalence class of set-theoretic predicate formulas, modulo equivalence relation $\sim$, where

$$M(\rho) \sim N(\sigma) \text{ iff } N \text{ is obtained from } M \text{ by a type-preserving renaming}$$
of the variables of **M.**

To make things as simple as possible, we shall write formulas (playing the role of objects in **Meas**) with disjoint sets of variables. As our next step, we turn correspondence relations into abstractly conceived maps. To define a map **C**(ρ,σ) : **M**(ρ) → **N**(σ) in **Meas,** we first grant that the domain **M** and codomain **N** have no variables in common and then proceed to define **C**(ρ,σ) as an equivalence class, modulo $\sim$, of formulas satisfying the following.

$$C(\rho,\sigma) \Rightarrow M(\rho) \ \& \ N(\sigma).$$

For example, the identity map of $M(\rho)$ has the form [$\rho = \sigma$] & **M**(ρ) : **M**(ρ) → **M**(σ). The composition of maps

$$M(\rho) \xrightarrow{\ \ C(\rho,\sigma)\ \ } N(\sigma) \xrightarrow{\ \ D(\sigma,P)\ \ } T(P)$$

is given by existential quantification

$$D \circ C(\rho,P) \text{ iff } \exists[C(\rho,\sigma) \ \& \ D(\sigma,p)],$$

modulo equivalence $\sim$. It is simple to check that these definitions make **Meas** into a category.

What is **Meas** good for? It enables us to formulate many of the representation problems in terms of simple categorical constructions. For example, the pullback diagram in the following

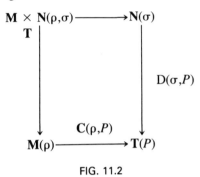

FIG. 11.2

captures the idea of joint representation. Indeed a joint axiomatization defines a predicate

$$\mathbf{M} \underset{\mathbf{T}}{\times} \mathbf{N}(\rho,\sigma) \text{ iff } \exists P[\mathbf{C}(\rho,P) \ \& \ \mathbf{D}(\sigma,P)],$$

which is precisely the pullback of the marginal representations $\mathbf{M}(\rho)$ and $\mathbf{N}(\sigma)$. Needless to add, none of this says anything about *how to* find such joint representations! Along similar lines, Ramsey sentences come out as maps $\mathbf{C} \circ \mathbf{T}(\rho) : \mathbf{1} \rightarrow \mathbf{M}(\rho)$ obtained from composing a correspondence rule with the theoretical predicate determining $\mathbf{M}(\rho)$. Here $\mathbf{1}$ denotes the terminal object of **Meas**, corresponding to a universally true, set-theoretic predicate formula, such as $[\rho = \rho]$.

Looking at measurement theories this way gives us a nice, global picture of how representation results are put together. The price paid, however, is a total lack of computational power in **Meas**. To provide a more realistic framework, we need a category that captures the full import of the domains of measurement structures. For example, in the case of measuring subjective probability, we can remain entirely within the category of measurable spaces and measurable maps. Indeed, if we let sets of the form

$$[x \geq a] = \{P \in \mathbb{P}(E) \mid P(x) \geq a\}$$

with $x \in E$ band together so as to form a new boolean algebra, the simplex $\mathbb{P}(E)$ becomes an important measurable space that carries probabilities of probabilities μ together with their averages $\sqcup\mu$—special probabilities on E—defined by the integral

$$\sqcup\mu(x) = \int_{\mathbb{P}(E)} P(x)\mu(dP) \cdot$$

Likewise the space of qualitative probability relations $\mathbb{Q}(E)$ is converted into a measurable space by taking the boolean algebra of its subsets generated by collections of the form $\{\rho \in \mathbb{Q}(E) \mid x\ \rho\ y\}$ for all $x,y \in E$. Under this arrangement, the projection/injection pairs of maps become measurable, and the problem of measurement can be developed entirely within the category of measurable spaces.

Our basic observation in this context concerns $\mathbb{P}$ and $\mathbb{Q}$. These are functors on measurable spaces, and the projection $\sqsubset$ is a natural transformation between them. What this means is that it does not matter whether we apply a boolean homomorphism first to the probability measure and then to the corresponding qualitative probability ordering or the other way around:

$$x \sqsubset_{Ph} y \text{ iff } h(x) \sqsubset_P h(y),$$

for all $x,y \in E$, where h is a boolean homomorphism from E to F. In contrast, the Ramsey embeddings $\mathbb{R}$ are *not* natural transformations in general. Furthermore, whereas $\mathbb{P}$ is actually a monad (triple), the measurement functor $\mathbb{Q}$ is most assuredly not! What this means in a less technical language is that, whereas $\mathbb{P}$ has the fundamental averaging operation $\sqcup$ defined previously, there is no similar operation in the qualitative case. Although it is possible to define a higher-order comparison of lower-level beliefs, it is impossible to define an average of higher-order comparisons. The reasons for this are simple to state: Averaging in $\mathbb{P}(E)$ does not commute with the order indiscernibility $\equiv$ defined by the barycentric partition of $\mathbb{P}(E)$. For this reason, there are no *composable* transition qualitative probabilities, corresponding to Markovian kernels, and there are no product qualitative probabilities either.

The overall situation in the context of measuring subjective probability is as follows. The category of measurable spaces is furnished with a powerful functor $\mathbb{P}$ that carries the structural information of probability calculus. Next we have a longer list of measurement functors (e.g., one for comparative probabilities, one for probabilistic independence relations, and so on) that interact with one another in rather weak ways. In general each of them carries only a fragment of the total structure available in $\mathbb{P}$. We already know what this structure is in the case of comparative probabilities. Upon introducing the equivalence

$$P \equiv Q \text{ iff } P(x \cap y) = P(x){\cdot}P(y) \Leftrightarrow Q(x \cap y) = Q(x){\cdot}Q(y),$$

for all $x,y \in E$ on probabilities, we get a new quotient set $\mathbb{P}(E)_{/\equiv}$, which is isomorphic to the set $\mathbb{Q}^*(E)$ of all qualitative probabilistic independence relations. It is easy to see that, in this case, the partitioning lumps together the Dirac probabilities (0–dimensional faces), the open faces of dimension 1, 2. . . . , and so on. The functor $\mathbb{Q}^*$ carries only the dominance structure, while $\mathbb{Q}$ has in addition the orthogonality structure as well. Now the joint measurement of comparatives and independence amounts to having a pullback $\mathbb{Q} \vee \mathbb{Q}^*$ in the diagram below:

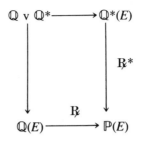

The pullback object is obtained by factoring $\mathbb{P}(E)$ with the common refinement of the respective indiscernibility relations for $\mathbb{Q}$ and $\mathbb{Q}^*$. What I am advocating here is of course that the theoretical functor $\mathbb{P}$ is always primary, and all the other functors are derived from it by a quotienting process. As we emphasized before, a good deal of important theoretical structure present in $\mathbb{P}$ is destroyed in this process of abstraction.

This type of reasoning about measurement theories is still in a preliminary state, but when more is known about the measurement functors involved, non-trivial applications in extensive measurement may be expected. This optimism is nourished by the success of this framework in clarifying the problem of uniqueness of (probabilistic) representations.

One virtue of categorical reasoning is that it helps get rid of ad hoc structures and reasoning about them, and retains only the natural ones. It seems to me that some ad hoccery is often present in various representation results in which suitable technical assumptions are added solely for the purposes of being able to obtain their proofs. The apparent lack of harmony in these accidental structures shows up at once at a functorial level, where certain, desirable natural transformations are simply not available.

I believe that the inherent unifying power and accompanying realist ontology sufficiently justify this general approach.

REVISING KNOWLEDGE IN RESPONSE TO MEASUREMENT RESULTS

Although we all recognize that measurement is a fundamental means by which we come to know the values of quantities, traditional measurement theories do not bring this fact out in the open.

The purpose of this section is to show how an observer's extant state of knowledge or belief may be revised in response to new measurement results.

Observational statements regarding a qualitative measurement structure $(E, \lesssim)$ may be viewed as propositions

$$[x \lesssim y] = \{\omega \mid x \lesssim_\omega y\}$$

given by the amount of samples ω in a sample space Ω. In a subjective self-parametrizing situation, we can put $[x \lesssim y] = \{\rho \in \mathbb{Q}(E) \mid x \rho y\}$. In either case, we get a boolean algebra $\mathbb{B}(E, \lesssim)$ of observational propositions generated by those mentioned previously. This opens up the road to defining probabilities on $\mathbb{B}(E, \lesssim)$. For example, if μ_0 is such a probability, then $\mu_0[x \lesssim y]$ may be thought of as the probability that x is not ranked higher than y in some experiment.

On the quantitative side, let (E, P) be a corresponding quantitative structure satisfying a set-theoretic predicate $\mathbf{T}$. Along similar lines as above, we have a boolean algebra $\mathbb{B}(E, P)$ of propositions of the form $[P(x) \geq a]$.

Now let us assume that the observer's beliefs are representable by suitable probability measures on $\mathbb{B}(E, P)$. Let μ be the probability representing the observer's current state of belief about the values of quantity P. Thus, $\mu [P(x) \geq a]$ denotes the observer's degree of belief that the quantity P exceeds or is equal to a on object x.

As is well known, a change of belief from the current state μ to a new state μ^* regarding the values of quantity P, brought about by observing $\mu_0[x \lesssim y]$, is given by the mixture of the following Bayesian conditionals:

$$\mu^*[P(x) \geq a] = \mu_0[x \lesssim y] \cdot \mu_{\mathbf{C}(x \lesssim y)}[P(x) \geq a] + \mu_0[x > y] \cdot \mu_{\mathbf{C}(x > y)}[P(x) \geq a],$$

where $\mathbf{C}(x \lesssim y) = [P(x) \leq P(y)]$ denotes the translation of observation $[x \lesssim y]$ into the theoretical algebra by a given correspondence rule $\mathbf{C}$.

In the case of knowledge, we may assume with the empiricists that the states of knowledge are representable by deductively closed bodies (filters) of propositions. In analogy with Bayesian conditionals, we can associate with every deductive system K its *conditional* $K_{\mathbf{C}(x \lesssim y)}$. It represents the body of knowledge, enriched by additional information $\mathbf{C}(x \lesssim y)$, and it is defined by the smallest deductive system containing K and $\mathbf{C}(x \lesssim y)$.

Let K_0 be a body of observational propositions, obtained during observing the structure $(E, \lesssim)$. Then the passage from the current state of knowledge K to a revised state of knowledge K^* regarding quantity P, brought about by receiving proposition $[x \lesssim y]$, is given by the following boolean conditional:

$$[P(x) \geq a] \in K^* \text{ iff } \left\{ [x \lesssim y] \in K_0 \Rightarrow [P(x) \geq a] \in K_{\mathbf{C}(x \lesssim y)} \right\} \ \& $$
$$\left\{ [x > y] \in K_0 \Rightarrow [P(x) \geq a] \in K_{\mathbf{C}(x > y)} \right\} \ .$$

In these rather simple examples, we showed how knowledge and belief states are affected by qualitative measurement results. It should be quite clear after a little thought that these revision rules can be generalized to more complicated species of data in a routine fashion. What is much more interesting, however, is the fact that this formalism is a special case of interactionist measurement theory in which the instrument is identified with the observer.

REFERENCES

Domotor, Z. (1981). Review of Roberts's *measurement theory. Journal of Mathematical Psychology, 24,* 88–92.

Friedman, M. (1983). *Foundations of space time theories.* Princeton: Princeton University Press.

Hahn, H. (1907). Über die nichtarchimedischen Grössensysteme. *Sitzungsberichte der Acad. Wiss., Wien, mathem. phys. Klasse, 116,* 601–655.

von Helmholtz, H. (1887). Zählen und Messen, erkenntnistheoretisch betrachtet. *Philosophische Aufsätze, Fues Verlag, Leipzig,* 17–52.

Hölder, O. (1901). Die axiome der quantität und die lehre vom mass. *Berichte der Sächsischen Gesellschaft der Wissenschaften, mathem. phys. Klasse, 53,* 1–64.

Krantz, D. H., Luce, R. D., Suppes, P., & Tversky, A. (1971). *Foundations of Measurement* (Vol. I). New York: Academic Press.

Maclane, S. (1971). *Categories for the working mathematician.* New York: Springer.

Marczewski, E. (1957). Measures in almost independent fields. *Fundamenta Mathematicae, 38,* 217–229.

Narens, L. (1985). *Abstract measurement theory.* Cambridge, MA: MIT Press.

Nozick, R. (1981). *Philosophical explanations.* Cambridge, MA: Harvard University Press.

Pfanzagl, J. (1958). *Theory of measurement.* New York: Wiley.

Ramsey, P. F. (1950). *The foundations of mathematics.* London: Routledge & Kegan Paul. Original work published 1929

Roberts, F. S. (1979). *Measurement theory.* Reading, MA: Addison-Wesley.

Seuren, P. (1973). The comparative. In F. Kiefer & N. Ruwet (Eds.), *Generative grammar in europe* (pp. 528–564). Dordrecht: Reidel.

Stoyan, D. (1983). *Comparison methods for queues and other stochastic models.* New York: Wiley.

Author Index

Subject Index